She Made a Way

She Made a Way

Mother and Me in a Deep South World

NIBS STROUPE
Foreword by John Blake

RESOURCE *Publications* · Eugene, Oregon

SHE MADE A WAY
Mother and Me in a Deep South World

Copyright © 2024 Nibs Stroupe. All rights reserved. Except for brief quotations in critical publications or reviews, no part of this book may be reproduced in any manner without prior written permission from the publisher. Write: Permissions, Wipf and Stock Publishers, 199 W. 8th Ave., Suite 3, Eugene, OR 97401.

Resource Publications
An Imprint of Wipf and Stock Publishers
199 W. 8th Ave., Suite 3
Eugene, OR 97401

www.wipfandstock.com

PAPERBACK ISBN: 979-8-3852-0854-8
HARDCOVER ISBN: 979-8-3852-0855-5
EBOOK ISBN: 979-8-3852-0856-2

VERSION NUMBER 05/30/24

Contents

Foreword by John Blake | vii
Acknowledgements | xi
Introduction | xiii

1 A Life in Four Challenges | 1
2 Trying to Find Home | 13
3 She Would Be There for Me When I Got Up in the Morning | 22
4 Lessons in Life | 33
5 All Shook Up | 43
6 A Change Is Coming | 57
7 You Can't Go Home Again | 72
8 Brave New World | 83
9 A Hard Rain's Gonna Fall | 92
10 Where Do We Go From Here? | 103
11 Finding New Paths | 115
12 New Horizons | 127
13 The Rutted Roads of Life | 138
14 Hard Times | 148
15 On To Writing | 157
16 Highway 61 Revisited | 165
17 Going Home | 176
18 Final Days | 185

Epilogue | 191
Bibliography | 193

Foreword

AT FIRST GLANCE, THE brick church that stands on the corner of an Atlanta intown community does not look like anything out of the ordinary. It is a modest building sitting on the corner of an intersection in a rapidly gentrifying neighborhood. The church is flanked by large, handsome Craftsman houses, a playground and magnolia trees that line the sidewalk out front.

But for a patch of time, this nondescript church became a magnet for the national media. Correspondents from Time magazine, National Public Radio and other assorted national media outlets once descended upon Oakhurst Presbyterian Church in Decatur, Georgia. They wanted to tell the story about this unusual church and its senior pastor, the Rev. Gibson "Nibs" Stroupe. This was the first time that many people across America heard of Stroupe.

They told a story about a church that had almost died but had been born again. Stroupe, along with his wife and co-pastor the Rev. Caroline Leach, had taken the helm after it had been decimated by an exodus of White members. The membership had dwindled to about 40 members and there was talk of closing the church's doors. Stroupe, along with others in the congregation, had kept the church doors open. And gradually they transformed Oakhurst into a vibrant multicultural church where a rainbow mixture of Black, white, straight, gay, affluent, and working-class members not only shared pews, but power.

It was hard not to be inspired. It was as if the first-century church in the Book of Acts had been transported to a contemporary American setting. The "dividing wall of hostility" between groups with a history of mutual hostility had been broken down at Oakhurst. This was the way church was supposed to be. One smitten Time magazine correspondent discovered the atmosphere at Oakhurst as one of "equanimity" and "heavenly" music—a refuge from the endless racial and political divisions that have only grown worse since that story was written over two decades ago. The correspondent, like others, touched on Nibs' personal story: Here was a White man who had grown up in the Jim Crow South, drinking deeply of the racism that pervaded his segregated world, but he had somehow changed.

I know this story so well because I was one of those journalists who stopped by Oakhurst to write about Nibs and the church. But unlike the other journalists, I stayed and joined Oakhurst. And what I discovered was that the story behind Nibs' conversion on race was no racial kumbaya story. It was much richer, confounding, and ultimately more inspiring than any brief news report could capture. And today I would make another argument: At a time when the United States is more divided than arguably anytime since the Civil War, Nibs' story is more urgent than ever.

Nibs is one of the most insightful and thought-provoking commentators on race and religion in contemporary America. His range of experience is virtually unmatched by any of the leaders that the media traditionally go to for commentary on race and faith. He has a visceral understanding of how racism warps the souls of White America, and the psychological games many play to deny their complicity because he's played those games himself. As Nibs once told me, he grew up in the "belly of the beast"—the segregated world of Helena, Arkansas where White supremacy was widely considered to be normal and ordained by God. "I know this stuff; it's in my veins," he once told me.

I would learn later, though, that I couldn't understand how Nibs escaped this world without understanding his relationship with one remarkable person: his mother, Mary. She was a single mom and a hairdresser who raised Nibs after his father abandoned the family. She raised Nibs virtually alone, guiding him to a church community where he found surrogate fathers. She also taught him respect. She insisted that he address Black men and women as "Mr." and "Mrs." though it was customary at the time for even White children to call Black adults by their first name.

And yet she unwittingly taught him something else: racism. Not the virulent N-word slinging kind, but the passive racism that accepted racial segregation as the norm. She opposed the civil rights movement when it swept through the South in the 1950s and 60s, telling Nibs to put aside the questions about race that he began to have as a teenager.

"Don't mess with this, Nibs, and don't fret about it," she once told him. "It is not our business." Nibs heard the same message from the White church leaders who talked about God's love in his boyhood church: ignore questions about racial segregation. The segregated status quo is what God intended. And this led to one of his most profound insights. Most White people don't learn racism from overtly bad people like frothing Ku Klux Klan members who burn torches.

"I had been taught racism by my family, my church, and my teachers—by really decent white people in my hometown on the Arkansas side of the Mississippi River Delta," Stroupe said in a 2018 interview for *The Atlantic*.[1] But Nibs changed, and so did his mother. And in the pages that follow you'll find out how. Mary Stroupe would turn out to be one of a succession of powerful women that Nibs would meet that would change the trajectory of his life.

I've heard Nibs preach countless sermons by now. And I've heard snippets of the story about his mom, but I always hungered for more. There's a moral authority that Nibs brings to his stories that comes from the choices he's made—a lifelong pattern of entering into relationships and building community with people who at first seemed so different from him.

I now know something that I didn't know when I first came to Oakhurst over two decades ago to hear Nibs preach. Journalists raved about his eloquence. Yet his greatest sermon has nothing to do with what he's said from the pulpit. It's how he's lived. And that story starts with the woman who gave him his first lessons on faith and courage: Mary Stroupe.

John Blake is an online columnist for CNN, and author of *More Than I Imagined: What a Black Man Discovered about the White Mother He Never Knew*.

---

1. Conor Friedersdorf, "Doubting MLK During a Strike in Memphis."

Acknowledgements

I WANT TO THANK all who contributed to the writing of this book. Thanks to John Blake and the Reverend Reggie Avant who urged me to write it. A special thanks to Dr. Collin Cornell who did the critical review and copy-editing of the manuscript. Thanks to all who read the initial manuscript and to those who offered insightful suggestions: Reggie Avant, Dee Cole Vodicka, John Vodicka, David Billings, Patty Bonner, Mary Gould, Lorri Mills, and Ed Loring.

I counted on many people's memories in order to put this memoir together, and I am grateful to those who took the time to share with me some memories of Mother, in both her glory and in her struggles: Bonnie Armour Adams, Debbie Reece, Margery Freeman, Ed Loring, David Billings, Christine Callier, Inez Giles, Maud Cain Howe, Lyda Kitchens, and Mary Wetzel.

And, of course, the main sharers of the story of Mother in my adult years: my partner and spouse the Reverend Caroline Leach, and our children David and Susan. They all read the manuscript and gave me very helpful feedback. Caroline helped me to shape the narrative from her perspective as a strong woman like my mother, whose very strength was often seen as a negative by Mother. David and Susan gave me their insights from experiencing Mother as "Grandma," who welcomed them at Christmas with long stockings filled with gifts and goodies, but who also felt tension with her when we shared her small space in Helena. I am grateful that in all these there was a sense of a shared humanity and family.

I don't know what Mother would think of this story of her raising me as a single white working mom in the patriarchal 1940's and 1950's, but I do hope that I have done her justice in her strong and valiant efforts not only to raise me as a man, but also her willingness to change and grow, as we both discovered new dimensions in the world, both the world outside ourselves and also inside ourselves. As we shifted roles in the last ten years of her life, it was my honor and privilege to care for her as she had cared so deeply for me.

Introduction

It is one of my earliest memories. I am trapped in our room in our home on Porter Street in Helena, Arkansas. I say that I was "trapped" because it felt like that to me at a young age of four. It was in a hot, sticky room on a Sunday afternoon, with both doors shut. Summer in the Mississippi River delta in 1951—hot and muggy, no air conditioning, only a small rotating fan whirring on the dresser, trying to draw me some cool air. I had been ordered by my mother to take a nap, and failing that, ordered to lie there quietly until she opened the door to tell me that I could get up and play. At least I had open windows on three sides of the room—to the east Fannie and Mack Thompson's house, facing the Mississippi River a mile away. To the south was our backyard, where I longed to go and play in the fifty yards or so of ground before the steep climb began to Crowley's Ridge; to the north was a window to the screen porch, where we would often go sit in the evenings to seek to cool off and get relief from the stifling heat.

On this particular afternoon, though, these windows were not welcome entries into relief but rather reminders that I was trapped by my tyrannical mother, who refused to allow me to get up and play until she gave me permission. I fumed and tossed and turned, waiting for the excruciating time to be ended. In my fuming on that hot Sunday afternoon in 1951, I had no idea of the depth of the story that underlay my confinement. It would take me decades to learn the depths and nuances of that story, but for now I will say that my mother worked six days a week as a beautician in someone else's shop. The only time that she had to take a nap and rest during those grinding days was on Sunday afternoons, after attending church and Sunday school and eating Sunday dinner.

I grew up fatherless in a patriarchal world. My father, for whom I was named, had abandoned me (and my mother) for another woman before I was a year old. I was born in Memphis, and after my father left, we lived in Memphis for a time, living with an Irish woman, who she kept me while my mother worked as a beauty operator. This Irish woman nicknamed me "Nibs," using an Irish word for the British aristocracy, who consider themselves to be the center of the world—"his Nibs" and "her Nibs." That appellation is even heard on occasion now to refer to the Queen of England in an affectionate way. I have come to use "Nibs" as my primary name—one of the great ironies of that development is that I don't know the name of the Irish woman who named me. My mother told me during my childhood, but I have simply forgotten it.

I may be projecting onto to my mother a sense of shock and loss in my father's departure—for reasons that will become clearer, we never talked much about him or his departure. Undoubtedly, she felt loss, and undoubtedly, we were poor, and she was looking for shelter. She would find shelter with her grandmother's sister, Bernice Brown Higgins, who had recently been widowed. Because of this, Mrs. Higgins needed fiscal and physical companionship in her small home on Porter Street in Helena.

It is not surprising that these two women, my mother and Mrs. Higgins (whom I called "Gran") pooled their resources in Helena to create a new household. We moved from Memphis sometime in my second year to live with Gran on Porter Street in a green clapboard house facing the north. That small home—two bedrooms, one small bath, a combined living and dining room, an average sized kitchen and a wonderful back porch and spacious side porch—would become my constant and stable home until I left for college in 1964. It was in the east bedroom of that house where I would find myself confined on that hot, sticky afternoon in 1951, fidgeting while my mother sought some rest from the grind of her life, on the couch in the living/dining area. I would come back often to this home until my mother's death in 2004.

I was raised by these two women, who taught me perseverance, humor, and compassion. I am writing this book as the story of that journey. It is a story of women's agency in a man's world. It is the story of the power of race and gender, and it is a story of finding some release from such captivity. And most of all, it is the story of my powerful and determined mother, Mary Elizabeth Armour Stroupe, who dedicated her life to me so that I might find life. She stood no taller than five feet at her tallest, but she was a giant in my life, and as I later found out, in the lives of others.

It is the journey of my mother and me, a journey that was unusual for a white, Southern single mother and her son in the 1940s/50s. It was unusual in that over the course of time, we made each other better people for the changing world that was coming. It was a journey fraught with peril but also promise. The peril of being poor and manless in a patriarchal, white supremacist Southern world. My inner peril and deep anxiety about being abandoned by my father, all the while giving thanks for my mother who stayed and raised me and saved me. My mother's peril at choosing to stay a single mom, focusing her energies on raising me as an economically fragile mom, yet fortified by strong birth family ties. The promise of two women, Bernice Higgins and Mary Stroupe, joining together to form a family and a stronghold in the midst of male domination, even though they had been abandoned by their men through death and divorce. Though I never mistook my mother and Gran for Ruth and Naomi, like those two powerful biblical characters, they engaged the male world together and prevailed. Like women everywhere, but especially Southern women (both black and white), they had learned to seek to find a way to define their humanity in the midst of male domination.

I will be telling the story of my mother and I negotiating our individual selves, our selves together, and our relationship in a world that changed. The external world changed dramatically from our 1947 move to Helena to the early decades of the 1970's, when I permanently left home. Yet our internal world also changed as my mother and I discovered a deeper and larger world out there. This larger world envisioned Black people as siblings rather than enemies, envisioned women as equal partners with men, celebrated people who loved others of the same gender, and began to see that money was not the key to life. I grew up being immersed in racism and sexism and homophobia and militarism and materialism by my mother and by other people who loved me, people whom I loved and trusted. Most of them taught these things to me not because they were mean, but rather because they too were caught up in their cultural environment by these repressive and oppressive powers. This book will be about seeking liberation from those powers, while knowing that captivity to them came to me from people who loved me and whom I loved.

My mother and I had a powerful connection because she dedicated herself to raising me as a "real" man, becoming both father and mother to me. "Manless" herself, she nevertheless taught me what a real man is: protective, loving, nurturing, challenging. Trapped by and influenced by these very forces, she taught me to begin to think about liberation from them, a liberation that would take me out into a whole new world, while bringing her along also towards her own liberation. These will be stories of that journey towards liberation, fashioned by a woman who was a captive herself but who gave me the foundation to work against those oppressive values.

David Billings—author of a profound book on white supremacy called *Deep Denial*—and I became good friends in high school, and we continue that friendship. He provides a fine introduction to my mother:

> I picture Mrs. Stroupe at the ironing board with an ever-present cigarette in her mouth and throughout baseball season the Cardinals would be on the radio. Nibs' house was a retreat for me. Mrs. Stroupe was part of our discussions—she was direct with us, often chuckling at us when we were too full of ourselves. As Nibs and I grew into our teens, she would discuss events with us, people we all knew in Helena and church dynamics. She didn't allow rudeness or unkind remarks and certainly she didn't allow cussing. She didn't allow the N-word or the word "Neegra," which was like saying the N-word with a southern drawl, a way of speaking that was thought at the time not to be as hateful but nonetheless was condescending as hell anyway. She made room for me in a world larger than the one I lived in, when I walked through her door for the first time, with her at the ironing board, smoking a cigarette and listening to the Cardinals on the radio.

Because Mother had raised me in this manner, she was also positioned to be changed by my journey when I inevitably took the paths to which she had been pointing me. These were paths which she had not directly explored, but they were paths which began to lead me out of the narrow world of Southern white supremacy. She had enabled me to imagine a world beyond our immediate context, and over the course of moving into those worlds, we were both able to change each other—quite an unusual partnership for Southern white people at this time, or in any time! And, now to begin the story. Although I grew up in the Arkansas side of the Mississippi River delta, my mother's family roots were in the hill country of north Mississippi. As Nina Simone once put it: "Everybody knows 'bout Mississippi."

1

A Life in Four Challenges

IN THE LATE AFTERNOON on an early summer day, one year before I would enter first grade, I remember sitting on our front porch stoop in the late afternoon. I was looking east down Porter Street, which runs quickly down a hill and heads on a flat level towards downtown Helena and the Mississippi River. I was looking that way because I anticipated seeing my mother walking the mile home from work, after a long day of being on her feet all day, fixing women's hair and listening to their stories—narratives that were a combination of gossip, trouble, advice and survival in a man's world. My mother would be dressed in a white uniform with stout white shoes.

As I saw her start pulling the hill on the last leg of her walk, I ran inside the house to get my ball and glove, because I wanted her to play catch with me. As she got closer, she saw me and smiled and waved, and I waved and smiled back, and I ran to her to hug her. I also asked her: "Momma, do you have time to play catch with me?" She laughed and said, "Of course I do, Nibs, just let me go inside and change my clothes, and we'll play a little catch." She went inside, changed clothes, brought out her glove, and we played catch. She had learned how to throw a baseball somewhere. She threw not like a "girl" but like a boy—her arm motion was just right.

This scene was repeated many times in my life. I'm sure that on some occasions she would say "No," but I don't ever remember her saying

"No." For a long time, I thought that she enjoyed playing ball with me after a long day at work. It was only after Caroline and I had children of our own that I realized the depth of what I had asked my mother, as a single working parent, to do on these occasions. When our kids were little, I would come home from my work as a minister at the church, and sometimes I was really tired. Like the days of my youth, however, our kids too would run up to me to welcome me home and to ask me to play with them. I would do it most of the time, but it was only then that I realized what my mother had done for me. After long days of working on other women's hair, she would come home to me, and I would want her to play with me. I was oblivious to this process as a boy—for some reason, I thought that she would want to play ball with me. It is testimony to her character (and perhaps to my ego as an only child) that I never knew any of this, until I had children of my own. When I asked her about it at that point, she replied: "Of course I was tired, and it was hard, but I wanted you to be happy. And, I sometimes said 'no' because I was just too tired."

I am intrigued that I do not remember her saying "No" on those occasions, and I will address that issue later. I will endeavor not to idealize my mother in this journey, so at this point I will say that we were both invested in making this new, "single family mom" configuration work—her for her own agency and self-understanding. It was a combination of her own self-understanding, her continuing development of her own sense of agency, and her focus on raising me as a single mother. It was almost as if she had said: 'I can do this.' I had great investment in not being abandoned by the one parent who chose to stay with me.

After my spouse Caroline and I had children, I asked myself: "How did Mother do it?" Caroline and I were dual parents, not a single parent like my mother, and we were often worn out. How did my mother do it? Who was this woman?

Gran told me stories of our maternal family history, of the Browns and the Armours. I was not interested in my father's family stories, although as I later came to find out, those stories were much closer than I ever thought they were. Even with my growing knowledge of my father and his history, I am still not interested in his family history—that will be a book for another time. In this way, I am heeding Barack Obama's words from the Preface to his book *Dreams from My Father*. In it he expressed regrets that he had not celebrated more the person who stayed (his mother), rather than focusing on his absent father. That's my plan—to celebrate the person who stayed—and I am sticking to it!

Gran, born in 1880, remembered stories of her great-grandfather William Brown, born in 1827 in west Tennessee. He was a staunch Presbyterian, who used to work the fields in the religiously prescribed white clothes. The women in the family had to wash these clothes and make them white again despite the dirt and mud from the fields. While she didn't care for that religious belief of working in white clothes, Gran did inherit his conservative Presbyterianism and joined First Presbyterian Church in Helena. It was in this church that I was baptized and raised as a child of God, and where funerals for both Gran and Mother were held.

This church was an important part of my life as a child and a youth. We swam in the sea of white supremacy and segregation, and no Black people were allowed to worship or be members there, although they cooked and cleaned and kept the nursery. We were mostly a working-class Presbyterian church—a church of a few planters and lawyers and doctors but mostly clerks and teachers and farmers. Whether they did it consciously or not, this church, as racist and sexist and homophobic as it was, made a huge difference in my life. I was a bright, compassionate, scared little boy, loved and sustained by the powerful women in my life, but also dominated by anxiety at my father's absence. Part of my self-definition became "boy abandoned by his father," with the implication being that something must be wrong with me, else he would write me or come to see me. The church stepped in, however, to help me hear something else, joining with Mother and Gran in their work to raise me. My primary definition would be child claimed by my Father (and Mother), the God we know in Jesus of Nazareth.

Two women—my mother Mary Stroupe and my Gran Bernice Higgins—joined with my church to shape me into who I am. They loved me and nurtured me and challenged me. They gave me a sense that I was somebody, even as I told myself that I was nobody because my father had left me. Black people were not on my radar at this point—I had accepted the white supremacist view that they were not human beings like me. Compared to their lives, I had it easy, but in those days in the early 1950's, I was feeling lost without a father around. But these women—and the church—they gave me love, they taught me love!

They also taught me what the Bible calls "demonic powers," especially the original American sin of white supremacy and racism. I learned these structures like race and gender and sexual orientation from loving white people—Mother, Gran, my neighbors, my segregated school, my segregated church. Whenever I write about these powers, I always recall that I learned them and came to believe them because people I loved taught them to me. This knowledge does not make me innocent, but it does clarify why racism and these other powers are so complex, and why they are so difficult to eradicate in ourselves and in society as a whole. In saying that "loving white people" taught me these things, I do not intend to diminish the horrors perpetrated on Black and other people of color by these same people classified as "white." In this sense, it is like the coronavirus, in that it seems to be transmitted seamlessly between people and between generations, and it can be just as harmful and deadly.

At the same time that Mother taught me white supremacy and racism, she also undercut it a bit. I could never say the N-word in her presence. Of course, she knew that I used it at other times, but I could never use it in her presence. She also would not allow me to refer to Black adults by their first names without adding a "Mr." or "Miss." She indicated that all adults are entitled to that respect, no matter their skin color or classification. When I protested that all my friends were doing it, she shook her finger at me and replied that she was the boss, and I would obey. And, I did.

She was still captured by the power of race, and it was only after I had gone off to college and had begun to change my mind and my heart on race, that she admitted to one of my college friends that because of my change, she had changed. After my mother died, one of her longtime neighbors told me that she was shocked that I had put my mother in the "racist" category in my first book about race.[1] She told me that every white person in the neighborhood thought that Mother was a radical on race because she had Black colleagues at work and because she would allow them to come in to her house through the front door rather than through the back door. These controversial "front door" visits came not in the 1940's but rather in the 1990's.

Mary Elizabeth Armour was born at her paternal grandmother's house in Byhalia, Mississippi, in May, 1919 on what is now known as Highway 78, then known as Pigeon Roost Road. Her father was one of six Armour siblings—four brothers, two sisters—and like the people of that generation, they were a close-knit family and stayed close, even after marriages. My mother was the first child born to that generation. She never got taller than five feet, but she weighed over ten pounds at birth!

---

1. Nibs Stroupe, *While We Run This Race*.

Her family nickname was "Sugar," later shortened to "Sug," and it is the name that everybody in our family used for her, except for me.

It is an oddity to me that these six siblings had only eight children between them, with my mother being the first. One of these six siblings, Bernice, was only eight years older than my mother, and while they were technically "aunt" and "niece," they were more like sisters and were good friends all of their lives. Whatever the dynamics behind the low birth rate, this was a tight family, supportive of one another and of spouses and children. When our son David was in elementary school, he wrote to my mother inquiring about her family history, and she wrote these words back about her family life in Byhalia, Mississippi: "I spent most of my life in Byhalia. Four people lived in the two-bedroom house: my parents, my brother and I. My mother developed cancer, and when she became ill and bedridden, we moved to my grandparents' home. This was my father's parents. Then there was a houseful of people: my grandparents, the members of our family, my father's two sisters and a brother. The other two brothers lived close by."

Even though it is now developing as a bedroom community for Memphis, Byhalia has always been a rural small town with the kind of mentality that goes with it. Its population when my mother was born was 514, and the Census of 2010 showed a population of 1302. Byhalia is in the hill country of north Mississippi, located some forty miles from the Mississippi River, which forms the western boundary of the state of Mississippi. It is thus not in the Delta, but the white families of Byhalia, including my ancestors, harbored many of the same attitudes of the Delta. Byhalia was founded in the 1830's and named for a Chickasaw word (*bihalee*) meaning "great white oaks." Pigeon Roost Road, on which my mother was born, was improved in 1835 in order to "accommodate the removal of the Chickasaw Nation to Oklahoma," as a local historian put it. Quite an accommodation it was! In 1832, the Chickasaw Nation had been defeated in battle and had signed the Treaty of Pontotoc which ceded the lands that would become Byhalia and its county, Marshall County. With the Chickasaw people removed, Byhalia was officially founded in 1838, on the stagecoach trail that ran from Memphis to Oxford to Pontotoc.

When I was growing up and visiting there, I was told that Byhalia's main claim to fame was that William Faulkner had died in the Byhalia Sanitorium in 1962. But, as with all of us in the Deep South, the Civil War and its history dominated the story of Byhalia and Marshall County in my childhood. Eleven Confederate generals came from Marshall County, but they must have been out somewhere else in 1862, because Union troops under the command of General Ulysses S. Grant occupied the county in that year and stayed there until the end of the Civil War. Byhalia and much of Marshall County was used as a staging ground by Grant for raids further south, most importantly on Vicksburg. On April 9, 1865, the telegraph brought difficult news to the white people of Byhalia and Marshall County: "Hell's to pay. Lee's surrendered."

The end of the Civil War brought in the era of Reconstruction, and Marshall County was an important part of that shift and that struggle. The victorious Union wanted to establish rights for the Black people who had been freed from slavery, and Mississippi was a central part of that attempt. In a previous book, I note that the famous journalist and antilynching voice Ida Wells was born into slavery in Holly Springs in 1862, which is the county seat of Marshall County.[2] I first discovered Wells and her story in research for preaching on Black History Month in 1985, and I was instantly taken with her and her story. When I did my initial research, she was not very well known, especially in the South, and I was astonished by her. First, she accomplished so much, and though I thought that I knew something about Black history, I had never heard of her. Part of that was my white, male arrogance that I should know everything, but a larger part was that she had been forgotten in history. I am so grateful to her daughter Alfreda Duster, who collected Ida B. Wells's unfinished autobiography and finally got John Hope Franklin to publish it as *Crusade for Justice* in 1970 in the University of Chicago series on Black history.[3] Without that, we might have missed much of her story.

Wells's proximity to my family history in Marshall County also attracted me to her. She was born about a decade before my great-grandmother Wille Brown Armour ("Big Mama") was born in Cayce in Marshall County. It was Big Mama's house that my mother mentioned earlier, when she and her family moved after her mother was stricken down with cancer. Though Big Mama and Ida B. Wells likely never knew one another in Marshall County, the geographic proximity immediately struck me. And, finally, my attraction to Ida Wells came from her similarity to my mother, Mary Armour Stroupe. Both were diminutive—five feet tall at best—and both were strong-willed women of agency in their

---

2. Catherine Meeks and Nibs Stroupe, *Passionate for Justice*.
3. Duster, ed., *Crusade for Justice*.

own lives and in the life of the world. Whenever I think of one of these women, I also think of the other.

The white South would use violence and laws to disenfranchise Black people and to force them back as close as possible to slavery. While they were doing this, they would revive the idea of the "Lost Cause" and thoroughly discredit the democratic period known as Reconstruction. The white South rose again and re-established what Doug Blackmon called "neo-slavery," a system that would prevail until the Voting Rights Act of 1965 was passed by Congress. It was in the era of neo-slavery that my mother grew up in Byhalia. She not only grew up in it—she breathed it in and believed it, that white supremacy was God's will. She later immersed me in it.

I don't know where my mother lived as a child, but I do know that she lived in Helena for a while because her younger brother "Bud" (Maurice K. Armour, Jr.) was born in their house on Arkansas Street in Helena in 1925. Her parents were Maurice K. Armour, Sr. and Vila Sanderson Armour, and they were back in Byhalia by the time my mother entered second grade there in 1926. According to her report cards, she was an excellent student. In her early teens, one of the four major obstacles in her life appeared: her mother was diagnosed with cervical cancer in the early 1930's and began treatment. As she wrote to our son David in his family history, when her mother got too weak to take care of the family any more, and needed to be taken care of herself, they moved in with Mother's paternal grandparents, John Armour ("Big Daddy") and Willie B. Armour ("Big Mama"). Both of them were quite the characters and were remembered fondly in the family stories. John Armour was a blacksmith in Byhalia and was a staunch Presbyterian. He would get blackened and dirty during the day, and in the warmer weather would ask the women in the family to draw him a tub of water in the outside. They would draw it out of the well in the morning and let the sun warm it during the day. When he would come home late in the day, he would get in that warmed, clean water to wash himself off and to relax a bit. He would often say to himself and to the family: "Ah, there's nothing like taking a bath in a tub of clean water that has been warmed by the sun all day!" Unbeknownst to him, my mother and her aunt Bernice ("BB")—who, as I mentioned were more like sisters—would often slip into that tub of water and take a bath before he got home. He was none the wiser—they never told him, knowing that there would be serious consequences if they did.

Willie Brown Armour ("Big Mama") who had been born in nearby Cayce, was the dominant family figure. The family story is that her own mother died when she was but eight years old, and she was the oldest daughter. So, it fell to her to do the cooking for the men farmers in the family, and she began her cooking career at age eight, standing on a soapbox in order to reach the stove. She would be cooking for her family and extended family for the rest of her life. She and her younger sister, Bernice Higgins ("Gran"), became the matriarchs of the family, and they would alternate hosting Christmas dinners, one year in Byhalia and one year in Helena. These would be huge affairs, feeding some 35 people twice on Christmas day, with elaborate meats, vegetables, and desserts prepared far in advance of the occasion. My mother told me that Big Mama grew weary of the many years of cooking, and that she said that when she died, she did hope that St. Peter would not ask her to cook a meal prior to entering heaven, because if he did make such a request, she was not sure what her answer would be.

The Armour house into which my mother and her family moved, when my grandmother was weakened by cancer, was on Highway 78 in Byhalia. It had been built by the men in the family, but Big Mama was deathly afraid of tornadoes. Byhalia is located in what is known as part of "Tornado Alley" in the South because so many tornadoes have struck there over the years. Before her house was built, she made the men build a "storm cellar," away from the house. The storm cellar was a wood or concrete reinforced pit in the ground, where people could take refuge in case of a tornado. The men scoffed at her fears but did as they were told and built the storm cellar first. Answering Big Mama's fears, the house was later blown down by a tornado in 1952, but the storm cellar survived. The house was located near the railroad track, and Big Mama was known to have a generous heart. During the Depression, many homeless people riding the rails stopped at her house asking for food. She never refused them, but she did wonder why so many people stopped at her house, when there were other houses around. On one occasion, she got her answer from one of the many hobos: "Mrs. Armour, your house has been marked by us for a long time. You are known to have a good heart and to have such good food!"

Vila S. Armour, my grandmother, mother of my mother, died in 1934 of cancer, when my mother was fourteen years old, and her younger brother Bud was only eight years old. It was a huge blow to them all, the first major obstacle that my mother had faced. After my own mother's death in 2004, I found some of her dream journals, in which she was looking into the psychic realm. As she began to develop in that area, she wrote in her journal that it was her own mother who was guiding her and loving her. She wrote in 1988 that she believed that the progress that she was making was because "Mama was guiding me from the other side"—words written over fifty years after her mother's death. Big Mama began signing my mother's report cards until Big Mama's death in 1937, when my mother was a senior in high school. It was yet another blow to her and to her family.

My mother was an excellent and well liked student at segregated Byhalia High School. In her "yearbook" of 1934–37, which was actually a small notebook, were comments and poems like these. "Dear Ole Sug—I wish you much luck and happiness throughout your life. May you always have the sweet smile and disposition that you have now. Always, Mary Jo Ingram."

"Dear Mary Elizabeth: My ideal school would be to be principal of about 500 students as good, as smart, as intelligent, as pleasant, as agreeable, as promising as you are. Your friend, E.S. Samuels."

Lest I get carried away with my mother's "sweetness," here's one more note that is especially intriguing, a note that shows the feistiness that would get her through the rest of her life: "I hope that you never have to slap me as you did that Olive Branch boy. I was glad that you let him have it, but would be mad if it had been me. A Senior Classmate, Leroy Johns." Throughout her high school years, she got B's and C's in Deportment, meaning that she was not a passive, quiet person but was rather energetic and talkative and mischievous. She also was tenacious—she played girls' basketball in high school, and those were the days when the women's basketball court was divided into two halves. On one half, a team would have its offensive team against the other team's defensive team, and on the other half of the court, the roles would be reversed. No players could cross the half court line, so there were no fast breaks, which are at the heart of basketball today, whether men's or women's basketball. My mother was short (under five feet), but she was a stout defender in basketball. Since she was short, she found it necessary to use physical force to guard her opponent—elbowing sharply, stepping on toes, grabbing jerseys. She had a special enmity for a girl from the Potts Camp, Mississippi team, and she remembered that she and this opponent often fouled out in the first quarter of their games because their physical play with one another was so filled with animosity and poking and trash talk—Mother claimed that this one girl's arsenal also included biting.

My mother was sweet and loyal and smart, but she was no pushover—she stood up for herself and held her own. She also worked at a high intelligence level—she was valedictorian of her high school class and had hoped to go college. She graduated in 1937 and faced the second big obstacle of her life. That year found the debilitating power of the Depression still strong, and her family had no money to pay for college for her. Her family had been through traumatic times in her high school years—no money, the death of her mother in 1934, and the death of the matriarch Big Mama, Willie B. Armour, in 1937, the year of her graduation. For the short term, she stayed home after her graduation, seeking to fill in some of the holes left by the deaths of the two powerful women in her life.

At some point in that graduation year, she decided to go to what was then called "beauty school," now called "cosmetology school." It would require many hundred hours of training in order for her to be officially certified and sanctioned by the state to be a beautician, to be someone licensed to work on women's hair. She never shared with me her thinking on this decision, but I do know that she was ready to get out of small town life, so she moved to Memphis, Tennessee, about forty miles north. There she entered a beauty school in the Moler System of Colleges, and in 1942 received her certification of merit to be licensed as competent for "Beauty Culture." She would continue in this profession until her retirement in 1986. Though she never went to an academic college as an official student, she would spend the last ten years of her career as a teacher and the director of the School of Cosmetology at Phillips County Community College in Helena. She had already been working as a beautician, starting in 1941 in Memphis. As a working woman as World War II began, she was in the middle of a huge transition in the city, and while she went back to visit Byhalia often, she never returned to live there. She had become a "city" girl, as she described it.

Until late in her life, I never knew much about my mother's dating life or romantic interests. I don't know where she and my father met, although I assume that it was in Byhalia, because my father's family lived there also. Indeed, my father's brother, Phil Stroupe, signed my mother's high school notebook on December 20, 1935: "Dear Beth: Absence makes the heart grow fonder. Try to keep near." Phil and Mother remained friends for the rest of their lives, even after the divorce between my mother and my father. As I would find out later, the two families were much closer than I had ever imagined.

When I was a young boy, perhaps the age I was in the story that began this book, I "woke up" into a family of women, and I didn't think much about the absence of men in our lives, except for the huge one: the absence of my father. When I asked my mother why she was no longer married to my father, her answer was: "He left me for another woman, and we got divorced." In my younger years, that settled it. I did not reflect on my mother's dating life (before her marriage or after her divorce), and it was only when the hormones hit me in early adolescence that I gave it any thought at all. Like all kids growing up in patriarchy, I did not have consciousness about the sexual life or sexual desire of women. I was taught in church that sex was not a good thing, that it was not a pleasurable engagement. By the time that I reached adolescence, I began to have an idea that there might be more to sexuality than I had been taught. By then, I also had the universal reaction that all children have when they think of their parents having sex—ugh to the nth degree! Until I became a teenager, I believed that it was better to be asexual and just use sex for procreation. Even though we were staunch Protestants, we shared the Roman Catholic view of sex—not recreational or pleasurable, but only for reproduction.

In the latter part of her life, Mother did tell me that she had dated someone seriously prior to marrying my father. He was a Byhalia resident, and his name was Bob Buford. I cannot recall how we got into that conversation, but I remember her telling me: "We probably would have gotten married, but he was killed in World War II, and it broke my heart." Here I found the third big obstacle that my mother had to face in her life: her fiancé was killed in World War II. She did not mention it again, and neither did I. It was only after her death, as we were looking through the things that she kept, that we found letters to her from Bob Buford, letters written to her after he had left Byhalia for World War II. I don't know if he was drafted, or if he volunteered, but here is an excerpt from one of those letters, written from the Army Air Base in New Orleans eight days after the Japanese had bombed Pearl Harbor. It was written to her at her Garland Street address in Memphis:

> Mary Dearest: I received your letter today and I am answering it now. The last letter I wrote you was in peace times, and now for this one, we are in war with Japan. . . . .I have taken the physical exam for overseas service but don't know when I'll go. I don't

know whether I told you in my last letter about my passing the physical exam for enlisted pilots. Well I passed it the last of November and went before the flying cadet board yesterday and got by it okay. Mary, I had planned on seeing you at Christmas but it looks like that's out, as all leaves for that period have been cancelled. . .If you don't know what you are going to do with all those pictures, I'll bet I know a lad that would dearly like to have one. I'll give you three guesses, and you can guess the same name all three times, and it'll be Bob all three of them. . .If you think that Memphis is beautiful and busy, just check out Canal Street in New Orleans. I believe it's the prettiest street I have ever seen. Another thing I can tell you about N.O., which isn't good, but I like it, and that is everybody drinks and goes in for a good time. I've been to several dances for servicemen given by different churches, and did we have fun.

Well, Darling, I'd better sign off as it is time for "Taps." If anything should happen to me, I want you to know that you are the sweetest of them all. There goes the damn lights blinking, so adios until another time. Love, Bob.

I don't know if they ever saw one another again. Then came one of the saddest letters that I have ever read, from LC Buford, who was either Bob's father or brother. It was sent from Texas on January 30, 1944:

My Dear Miss Mary Elizabeth: I know you will be interested in knowing the following: Robert has been "missing in action" somewhere over Greece since January 11th. It is possible, of course, that he is safe. I received the message last night from War Dept. Yours, LC Buford

Apparently, Bob Buford did make it overseas, and it brought him to his death. I can only imagine her heartbreak when she received this letter in Memphis. I don't know when Mother learned that he was definitely killed in action, if she ever did. By the time we talked about it in the late 1990's, it had been over fifty years, and it still was tender to her. I had never heard about Bob Buford before this time, and even stranger to me, I had never even thought about anything like it. My view was straightforward and narrow—my mother married my father; my father got involved with another woman and divorced my mother; my mother stayed with me and raised me. That was enough narrative for me at the time.

2

Trying to Find Home

I don't know how my mother and father got together to get married. As I would find out many years later, there was a much closer connection between the families. I would not learn this until I was a young adult. Mother's brother "Bud" was married to Flossie Stroupe, my father's sister, but I would not learn this until Flossie's funeral in Byhalia in 1974. Given that knowledge, it makes sense that Mother and my father might get together. Mother, mired in grief about the loss of Bob Buford, was likely feeling lost and wondering what the future was. My father, returning from fighting in the war, was part of the boom that happened after World War II.

I don't know much else. They were married on Christmas Day, 1945—and yep, I counted up the months until my birth. It was eleven months, so they weren't forced to get married by a surprise pregnancy. Christmas was always my mother's favorite holiday, but I did not know until after she died, that Christmas Day was her wedding anniversary. It was a pattern of secrecy and guardedness in regard to my father, a secrecy in which I participated. If he was not interested in me, if he was never contacting me or seeing me, then what did I want to do with him? The less said, the better, but I would later learn that this secrecy and silence was deep and wide.

I also know nothing about their life together. Mother wasn't volunteering the information, and I wasn't asking. Of course, now I wish that I had pursued this story more, but my perception was this story was wrapped in pain: my mother's pain at my father's infidelity and departure, and my pain at his continuing absence and lack of contact. I don't know where they lived after they got married. I don't know how long he stayed around. I don't know if he was still with us when I was born in November, 1946. I was born in Methodist Hospital in Memphis, so I am assuming that they were living in Memphis when I was born. I was named after him—my legal name is Gibson Preston Stroupe, Jr.

I don't know when they separated. Her story was always that he had gotten involved with another woman and had left her. This would be the fourth big obstacle that Mother faced—the death of her mother from cancer when she was a teenager; the lack of money to send her to college; the death of her fiancé in World War II, and now the divorce from my father. I don't know when that happened, but there is one clue that I have found. There is a letter to Mother from her father in the summer of 1947, indicating that Mother and I are living with Gran in Helena. So, he was gone before I was a year old.

To my knowledge, my mother never dated anyone else. There were no eligible men around our house. I am assuming that she was approached by various men after my father left her, but if so, I didn't know anything about it. I would like to think that she did date someone, but I don't believe that she did. Why not date someone else? I don't know the answer to that question either, because we never talked about it. Having a man around would mean that I would not be the center of my mother's life, so I understand why I did not push her on it. She may have perceived that and decided to give up that part of her life. She had already lost two men—her fiancé through death and another through divorce—and that may have been enough pain. She was a strong woman, like my spouse Caroline Leach. In 2010, one of the male saints of the church died, and I remember that in the eulogy at his funeral I used the Jewish idea that God allows the world to continue to exist because across the globe there are forty saints who are seeking to live godly lives. Buddy was one of those, I asserted. Later on, Caroline and I were talking about his wife's situation, and we wondered whether she would get married again, and she indicated that likely she would not. I then asked Caroline: "If I died, would you get married again?" She replied: "No, one is enough." I wasn't quite sure how to take that comment, and she added in a sweet voice that made me suspicious: "Oh, you're just so wonderful that no one else could ever match up to you." That conversation did help me in my thinking about my mother's lack of romantic relationships after her divorce—one was enough.

Our daughter Susan also had a powerful insight into my mother, into "Grandma," as she called her. Susan wrote to me: "So that led me to thinking about Grandma, as the Hamilton lyric goes, 'never being satisfied,' and when your father left, or as Mom speculates, when she kicked him out, she seemed determined to make her own way, including in how she raised you. I was thinking about how you said that you have no memories of her even dating, and so I started considering: 'why would she?' What man in Helena in the 1950's would have satisfied her? Of course, her imagination was probably still limited by only considering white men, and certainly I imagine that NONE of the white men in Helena or the surrounding areas would have made good life companions for her, with the amount of independence and agency that she had. But I imagine that lack of satisfaction in the men around her—perhaps her seeing their lack of imagination about the world—also really influenced how she raised you, to be a man that imagined the world differently than the men who raised her, or the men who courted her. Of course, she probably grieved deeply for the man who was her sweetheart who died in the war, but the fact that she so rarely talked about either of her beaus (that we knew of!) also tells me that she really centered herself, and you, in her own narrative."

If Susan is correct, and I believe that she is, Mother's next steps, after my father left her, would be back to work—back to work in the harsh world as a beautician, but now as a single mother, in a patriarchal world. And, she was looking for shelter. My mother was caught in a difficult position—single mom, very few dollars, but able to work. For a short while, we lived in Memphis with the Irish woman who re-named me, but it was not feasible economically or socially. I don't know if she considered moving back to Byhalia to live with her father, or whether it was even possible. He had re-married by then and had two step-daughters from his second wife. Even if there were an invitation to return to Byhalia, how could she earn enough money to survive in a town of 600 people? Memphis had enough women for a beautician, but there were no family support structures to assist in raising me. Returning to Byhalia would also threaten that sense of agency, that sense of her creating her own narrative.

There were two main reasons that Mother did not return to Byhalia to live and work. First, the family of her ex-husband lived there, and in a very small town, that would have been difficult for her internally and externally. Second, I think that this idea of her living out of her own agency, her own definition, is one of the main reasons that my mother did not return to Byhalia to live with her father or other close relatives. She was determined to forge her own path as much as possible. Divorced woman with no children—Memphis it would be! Divorced with an infant son to raise—Helena and Bernice Brown Higgins, her grandmother's sister became the answer. It would be the main route to survival and even to re-defining and re-locating the idea of "home," more on the terms acceptable to the agency of Mary Elizabeth Stroupe.

I do not mean to imply that Mother was "superwoman," or to minimize her struggle or situation. In a 1991 journal entry, she writes a prayer to God about the long loneliness of her journey: "Father, do I think that I am unworthy of love? Why have I been so lonely and hungry for love all these years? I have never known a man who loved me for what I am! Have I been in my unconscious mind telling myself I am unlovely and therefore no one can love me? All my life I have been teased about being a little girl who snores and a big girl who snores. Am I using this for an excuse?" So, yes, Mary Elizabeth Stroupe, my mother, took all her insecurities and struggles and got ready to move into life as single, working mom—move into a white, patriarchal world. Helena and Gran were looming before her. Could she do it? Could she survive economically? Could she survive emotionally? Would she try out another man? Would she need another man to support her and to help give her stability?

In those days, Helena, Arkansas, was deemed a small town, but to a Byhalia, Mississippi, native it looked huge—11,000+, with West Helena right next to it, having another 7,000+, thus approaching 20,000 people. Helena is a town about fifty miles south of Memphis, on the Arkansas side of the delta of the Mississippi River, which ran about a mile wide at Helena. It was a river town and not unknown to my mother. Mrs. Higgins and my mother's grandmother, Willie Brown Armour, were sisters and were the matriarchs of the family when my mother was growing up. Mrs. Higgins (known as "Gran" to me and others) and my great-grandmother Willie Brown (known as "Big Mama" to all family members) would host Christmas celebrations on alternate years, one in Helena and then the next year in Byhalia. There was no bridge over the Mississippi River at Helena until 1961, and I heard many harrowing tales of Model T trips to Helena from Byhalia, where Big Mama and her six grown children lived. Tales like the car being tied to a team of mules to be let down the levee to catch the ferry across the River on rare snowy or icy trips; tales like tractors replacing the mules to do the same later on.

I don't know who initiated the negotiations for us to live with Gran. I just know that I woke up on that hot summer day in the small bedroom on Porter Street, which was then our home. My mother would remain in that home until her death in 2004. Mother and I shared one of the bedrooms, and Gran had the other. Gran became my "de facto" grandmother, even though technically she was my great-grandmother's sister on my mother's side. When we moved into her home, she was 67 years old and recently widowed. She had two grown sons, Jack and Brown Higgins, who lived in Helena. She had several grandchildren, including Brown's son who was also named Brown. Gran's "Brown" birth name persevered! The young Brown Higgins, who was called "Brownie" by adults to distinguish from his father, was my age, and we would run and play together. He was the youngest of Gran's grandchildren, and I was an only child. He was impish and creative and outgoing, while I was quieter and more reserved, but we made it work, sharing this grandmother.

My memories of Gran are vivid. She was a tall and stout woman with a twinkle in her eye. She wore lace-up, high top "granny" shoes, and she usually had a pinch of snuff in her mouth. Though she was conservative and unfriendly to the modern world, I remember her delight in getting a television set in 1955. Her sons and families came up to the house every Sunday night to eat her cooking and to watch TV, especially the Ed Sullivan Show. She was a great cook, and I looked forward to her summertime meals, when she would put a plate before me, piled high with black-eyed peas and "hot water" cornbread. That cornbread was cooked on a flat iron skillet, using corn meal, salt, bacon grease and water. We would eat together on the small back porch, which was screened in to keep the flies and mosquitoes off of us.

Having been raised in a religious family, she was conservative and strict. If Brown or I smarted off to her, she would respond: "You better be quiet, boy, before I pop your jaws." She never hit me, though —it was just a warning. She did spank me one time with a switch, but that story will come later. There was no cussing or drinking of alcohol in her house, although she did keep a small amount of whiskey for medicinal purposes and for use in the eggnog at Christmas. Despite the elaborate family gatherings at Christmas at her house, she retained her puritanical, religious ways and would not let my mother or anyone else decorate the house for Christmas. To do so was a pagan act in her eyes. Mother was a huge Christmas fan, so those two ideologies clashed. The initial compromise was that Gran allowed Mother to put a small Christmas tree in our small bedroom, but Mother gradually wore down Gran's resistance. After a couple of years of being jammed in the small bedroom with two twin beds, two dressers and a table, the Christmas tree was finally liberated to be in the living room/dining room open area of the house.

Mother eventually wore Gran down in other ways. The hand-cranked wringer washer that lived on the back porch, and was brought in to the kitchen to be hooked up to the kitchen sink at washing time—it was replaced by an electric washer, purchased by my mother on credit, with many monthly payments. Gran would not allow a clothes dryer, however. Everything had to be hung up outside on the clothes line which ran from the house to the garage in back of the house. As soon as I was tall enough, one of my jobs was to hang out the clothes on the line, whether it was 90 degrees or 30 degrees. I remember hanging out clothes on that line in the morning, coming home from school to find them frozen on the line.

I don't know when Gran joined First Presbyterian Church in Helena as a member, but she was a loyal participant. The church celebrated the sacrament of communion only four times a year, on the first Sunday of the beginning of every quarter of the year. In order to receive the sacrament, one had to be a confirmed member of the church. Since that wouldn't happen for me until I was twelve years old, I was fascinated by the sacrament and wondered if the recipient of the elements received some magical power.

Gran saw it in another way. She remembered her mother telling her stories as a little girl about the elders who came to visit families prior to the sacrament of the Lord's Supper. The elders (all male of course) would examine the adults in the family to see if they had lived lives worthy of communion for that past quarter. If so, the elder would give the adults tokens which they presented to the ushers on the Sunday morning of the sacrament, and they would be permitted to receive the elements. If their lives did not measure up for that quarter, they would receive no tokens and thus no communion in worship. Though we were far beyond the token stage by my childhood, that approach stayed with Gran. I remember her choosing not to take the elements of the Lord's Supper on several occasions, and because I wanted to receive them so badly, I asked her why she refused to take communion, especially since it came around so seldom. She replied: "Nibs, I don't believe that I have lived a life worthy of communion this quarter, so I will have to decline to take communion until I can do better." That direct connection to God seemed powerful to me, and I was impressed that Gran felt so close to God—and so judged by God. I have since decided that she was wrong on that religious issue—none of us are worthy of the Eucharist, of the grace of God. The whole point of communion is that we are indeed unworthy and in need of the grace of God. Yet, I remain impressed that Gran felt so close to God, and I wish at times that I felt that closeness.

Despite her religious gravitas, Gran had a great laugh and a great sense of humor. She was especially open to the irony of life and to her ability to laugh at herself. When she had her first son Jack, she was fortunate in that he was quiet and well-behaved. She told the story about herself about Jack's days as a toddler. When she would take Jack as a young boy to visit other women with young children, she would be struck by how undisciplined the other boys were. She wondered what was wrong with those mothers, that they could not better control their sons. She shared that she even prayed for one of the mothers, whose son seemed out of control, hoping that God would send that young mother some better ways of disciplining her son. Then Gran had her second son Brown, and he was a handful, always on the move, always into something. Gran declared that Brown was God's answer to her prayer about the other mothers. The issue was not their method of parenting but rather her good fortune in having a quiet son first. Brown was a reminder to her of her judgmental attitude, and I am grateful to her for wanting to share that story with me.

She loved watching pro wrestling on television, and although she knew that it was all choreographed, on occasion she laughed so hard at the antics of the entertainment, that she laughed her false teeth right out of her mouth! She would be there every day for me when I walked home from school and on Saturdays, when my mother worked part of the day, and of course, she was there for me all day during the summers when school was out. It was a convenient and workable arrangement between her and my mother. Mother provided physical and fiscal relief for Gran in her widowhood and in her poverty, allowing her to stay in her home. She had never worked outside the home and got only a small pension from her husband's pension and Social Security. She provided for us a home, a great care-giver for me, and a mitigation for Mother's loneliness. Though I did not realize it at the time, she would be a rock for me until her death in 1959. She formed with Mother a powerful family unit of women who would take over and raise me in a patriarchal world, without apologies. They knew that they could do it, and they did.

Gran genuinely loved me, and I related to her as my grandmother. I made good grades in school, and I was more like her first son Jack, with my quiet ways and reserved manner. She was always bragging on me to other people—her earlier lesson from God notwithstanding. As I looked through my mother's papers after Mother's death, I found a letter from Mother's first cousin Jean, whose father Dell was one of my grandfather's brothers. Jean always used a formal title for Gran that conveyed Gran's authority in the family: "Mrs." In this letter of May, 2001, Jean was sending to Mother an article from a local Baptist paper in Atlanta, describing the fact that Oakhurst Presbyterian Church, where Caroline and I co-pastored, had been named one of 300 outstanding churches in the country. It had a picture of me in the article. This is what she wrote to Mother: "I figured Nibs had not sent this article to you just as he did not before. Real good picture of him, and I know that I see 'Mrs.' with a smug face, saying 'I told you so.'"

My mother was working her way through major losses in her life—the death of her beloved mother in 1934, the power of the Depression that stripped so many families of money and sustenance (leaving no money for her to go to college), the death of her fiancé Bob Buford in World War II, and then the flight of my father from their marriage soon after I was born. When I came to consciousness in Helena on that hot summer day, we were living on Porter Street with Gran, and Mother was working as a beautician at Ted's Beauty Shop, which was located in the Cleburne Hotel on the other end of Porter Street near the Mississippi River. She would continue in the cosmetology world until she retired in 1986.

After her death in 2004, I received a letter from my college friend and long-time colleague Harmon Wray—he was president of the Honor Council at Rhodes College when he and were both on it in our senior year. His words have stuck with me as an apt description of my mother: "I know that you had a very close bond with her. I think this is often true with us only children, but I suspect it's especially true when one's mother is one's only parent as well. I know that it's been a hard road for you, with the frequent trips back and forth and often not a lot of happiness to show for it. It makes me think of your homily, or eulogy, at Theon's funeral, where you said something to the effect that we're not meant necessarily to be happy. That has stuck with me. Maybe we're not, but it seemed to me that in some ways your mother was a joyous person, or at least I thought that she was at those few times long ago that I was with her."

I'm grateful to Harmon for pointing out the joyous nature of my mother—she had grit and determination in these early days, and she did weave it together with joy. She tried to instill these things in me, as she stayed with me and raised me and loved me. All of this was lived in the larger world of white supremacy, patriarchy, homophobia, and the centrality of the Confederacy. The story of my mother's life is something that Black women have lived for generations because their men have been forced out of the home by white supremacy. Yet for white women, my mother's story was unusual at this time of the 1940's and 1950's. There were Black people all around me as a child, but I did not see them as people like me. I saw them as a sub-species, not because I chose to do it, but because people who loved me—including Mother and Gran—taught these ideas to me.

Gran told me a story of pride from her heritage. She indicated that her mother told her a story about her mother being a girl during the Civil War. When the Union soldiers (she called them "Yankees") came in to occupy the territory, her mother's family sent the people they held as slaves to take the horses and other family possessions into the woods so that the Union soldiers would not confiscate them. I still have a book in my office that Gran used as a justification for the history of slavery and our participation in it. It is entitled *Is Slavery a Sin in Itself?* by James M. Sloan. Of course, Dr. Sloan's answer is that slavery was not a sin. It was published in 1857, the same year that the United States Supreme Court ruled that African-Americans Dred and Harriet Scott were not human beings like people classified as "white" and thus not entitled to rights under the Constitution.

Mother also taught me contravening forces on the issue of race, which I will explore later, but for now, I want to note that as I lay in that east bedroom on Porter Street in 1951, feeling hot and oppressed and trapped, high school students like Barbara Johns in Virginia were organizing school boycotts in order to seek racial justice. Lawyers like Thurgood Marshall and his mentor Charles Hamilton Houston were traveling through the South as they sought to break down the infrastructure of white supremacy. These were powerful forces flowing through all of us in the complex and diverse South, but it would be years before the work of these pioneers and others would overflow the confines of racism in the South.

3

She Would Be There for Me When I Got Up in the Morning

>"An' they chased him 'n' never could catch him 'cause they didn't know what he looked like, an' Atticus, when they finally saw him, why he hadn't done any of those things. . .Atticus, he was real nice. . . . ."
>
>His hands were under my chin, pulling up the cover, tucking it around me. "Most people are, Scout, when you finally see them."
>
>He turned out the light and went into Jem's room. He would be there all night, and he would be there when Jem waked up in the morning."[1]

THESE ARE WORDS THAT close the great novel *To Kill a Mockingbird* by Harper Lee. In this part, the narrator Scout is an adult reflecting back on her childhood in Alabama. In this story, she and her brother Jem have just been saved from death by Boo Radley, whom many townspeople, and Scout herself, considered weird—on the margins and scary. I had not read the book when the movie was released on Christmas Day, 1962. It came to Helena in May, 1963, as I was finishing up my junior year in high school. The movie made a powerful impression on me, and indeed I saw it three nights in a row. I also cajoled Mother into coming to see

---

1. Harper Lee, *To Kill A Mockingbird*, 322.

it with me on one of those nights. I was, of course, impressed by the power of racism in the book and by Atticus Finch's attempts to overcome that power in his representation of wrongly-accused, African-American Tom Robinson, in a rape trial. What impressed me by far, however—what brought me back for three nights in a row, what motivated me to get Mother to attend with me—was the presence and commitment of Atticus Finch to his children, Jem and Scout, as a single parent. I've thought of Harper Lee's approach to this best-selling and award-winning novel. In it she uses the adult Scout ("Mary Louise") to reflect back on her childhood and on being raised by a single parent in the white supremacist South of Alabama. I'm using the same approach in this book. It is a book of memories and dynamics, based on actual happenings and memories of childhood.

When I first saw the movie, I immediately thought of my lost and absent father. Where was he? Why wasn't he there for me? It didn't take me long, however, to recognize that the Atticus Finch of my life was my mother. She was the single parent who had stayed with me, who was there for me, who would be there when I woke up in the morning. I remember telling her after we had seen the movie together: "You know, Mother, you remind me a lot of Atticus Finch. You stayed with me, and I want to thank you." She sort of brushed it off with her response: "Oh, Nibs, you know that I love you, and yes, you will always be my little boy, no matter how old you get." Then she gave me a hug.

She did reveal that she didn't think that the movie was as good as I did. She never revealed why, but I'm guessing that it was because the movie brought up racial justice themes, and these were taboo in the deep South where we lived. She might also have been wondering if I would move in that direction and thus jeopardize myself both physically and emotionally by shifting on race. She might also have had misgivings about the extremely positive portrait of the single father Atticus Finch in the movie (and in the book). Her ex-husband, who had fled and was never there for her or me in the mornings, no doubt crossed her mind in the movie.

I was born in Methodist hospital in Memphis in November, 1946, on the day before Thanksgiving. Obviously, I don't remember any of that, and the only story that I remember Mother telling about the birth was that it was standard for women to stay in the hospital for a few days after giving birth. She had to stay over Thanksgiving Day, and she did not want to miss the great food of that holiday, so she talked her "aunt" Bernice into sneaking the goodies of Thanksgiving into the hospital for her. When BB (my name for "Bernice") protested that they would kick her out for seeking to do that, Mother told her to put the food in small jars and bring it all in a big bag. Mother cajoled, and it worked. BB complied—Mother got Thanksgiving dinner the day after giving birth to me! I do not remember any stories of my father being around at my birth. I am intrigued that Mother prevailed upon BB rather than my father to sneak the food in. I don't know if that means that he had already left my mother by that time. I want to infer that, but I simply don't know, and I never asked. BB turned out to the be one of my best advocates in our family, and perhaps that it why I remember this story.

It is a powerful theme that the earliest parts of our lives, especially our births, where we come into existence, are not available to our memory. We have to depend on others, on our family, on our community to tell us about these fundamental events in our early lives. I've always been struck by that fact—being born, eating, walking, talking,—we have very little, if any, memory of these. If we are fortunate, we have photographs, but that is really the community sharing knowledge with us. I don't remember my father; I don't remember the Irish woman who renamed me; I don't even remember her name. She named me "Nibs" as a nickname, taking it from the Irish poking fun at the lords and ladies.

My earliest memories are like the ones in that hot, sticky Sunday afternoon in our bedroom in the Porter Street house in Helena. I just "discovered" myself and my consciousness in that stuffy room in Helena, Arkansas. Helena was founded in 1833 as a river town, after the Choctaw Indian peoples had been "removed" to the west. It was named after the daughter of Sylvanus Phillips, an early European explorer, and for whom the county is named. There is a statue near my home in Helena that commemorates the crossing of the Mississippi River by the more famous European explorer, Hernando DeSoto, in 1541. Helena was dependent on the River for its economy, mostly farming, and a bit later, lumber and its by-products. It billed itself early on as "Arkansas's only seaport," and indeed, its semi-pro baseball team was known as The Seaporters. Located on the Arkansas side of the Mississippi River Delta, it was rooted in the "most Southern place on earth," as author James Cobb named the Delta.[2] Helena was a place of strict segregation, and in 1919 one of the largest massacres of African-Americans in American history occurred in

---

2. James C. Cobb, *The Most Southern Place on Earth*.

Phillips County, where over 230 Black people were slaughtered in several days of white rioting. This mass lynching was in response to Black tenant farmers seeking to band together to get higher prices for their cotton. It became known as the "Elaine Race Riot," but has been recently been renamed more accurately as the "Elaine Massacre." It started near Elaine, but advanced into Helena, the county seat of Phillips County.

Race has been at the center of Helena since its European beginnings. Indigenous people were removed in order for white settlers to come in. One of white Helena's bragging points is that it contributed seven generals to the Confederacy in the Civil War, the most famous of whom was Irish-born Patrick Cleburne, who came to call Helena his home, and who was killed at the Battle of Franklin in 1864. I grew up in Helena, believing that history began and ended with the Civil War years of 1861–1865—I had fully digested and appropriated the Lost Cause.

It was only after Caroline and I moved to Norfolk, Virginia, for our first ministry, that I learned there was significant American history before and after the Civil War. Despite its deep loyalty to the Confederacy, Helena had Union troops in it, beginning in the summer of 1862, and it finally fell to the Union in July, 1863, on the same day as Vicksburg fell, thus depriving Helena forever of its pride of falling to the Union—because of the importance of Vicksburg's defeat, no one remembers Helena's defeat.

Despite the fact that the Helena of my childhood centered on the Civil War, Helena did not have a traditional courthouse square centered on a monument to the Confederacy. There were no Confederate monuments in the downtown area—they were rather in the Confederate Cemetery, where they should be, with one large caveat—that cemetery is located in the middle of a Black neighborhood. Instead of the Civil War, it is World War I that dominated downtown Helena. Near the county courthouse, at one end of the Cherry Street drag, is a monument called "The Doughboy" commemorating American soldiers from Phillips County who died in the war to end all wars. A few blocks west of there is "The Hut," a log building erected in 1921 in honor of Americans in World War I—its design was based on the mountain huts in Europe in World War I. I went to many high school dances there, and indeed, my 50th high school reunion in 2014 was held in The Hut.

In spite of the white identification with European culture, Helena had a rich mixture of people—African-Americans, Chinese and Lebanese, Italians, and a strong Jewish community, who even built a synagogue there, which we Anglo-Protestants called "The Temple." It remained a river town, though, known for its rough life and its proneness to flooding from the mighty Mississippi River—one of its main downtown streets was lost to the Flood of 1927. The Union soldiers who took it over in the Civil War described it as a low-lying, flood prone, mosquito-infested place, and they often called it "Hell-In-Town." That name stuck around—a native Black Rapper called it "Helltown."[3] Music was vibrant and varied in Helena—white country music was strong, and Helena was the birthplace of Harold Jenkins, who became "Conway Twitty." It was also home to some of the greatest Delta blues players, such as Robert Johnson, Sonny Boy Williamson, Robert Jr. Lockwood, and Howlin' Wolf. The oldest continuous blues radio broadcast in America is a show called "King Biscuit Time," broadcast on KFFA in Helena since 1941. In order to capitalize on this blues heritage, the town started the Helena/Delta Blues Festival in 1986, which at one time drew almost 50,000 people there for the four-day festival.

Beginning in northeast Arkansas there is a strange geological formation, a set of hills that cuts onto the edge of the Delta. It is known as Crowley's Ridge, and it ends at Helena-West Helena (the towns consolidated in 2006). The Ridge runs behind our Porter Street house and ends about a mile later. Fifty yards or so from the back of our house began the steep climb onto the Ridge, and I spent many afternoons climbing that Ridge and roaming around its wooded areas, including an old military road used during the Civil War. The house into which my mother and I moved was Gran's house, and Mother paid her a small amount in rent each month. It was a small house—1150 square feet or so, with a small back porch and a spacious side porch on the east side of the house. The house was made with green clapboard shingles on the sides. Entering the house through the front door, you would enter an open area which served as a combination living room/dining room. Our bedroom was straight through the living room to the south. Leaving our bedroom, shared by Mother and me for the first twelve years of my life, you would come to the small bathroom, then continue straight through the other door which served as an entry to Gran's bedroom. From her bedroom, there were doors to the living room area and to the kitchen. In the living room near the north wall, there was a huge gas space heater that was used to heat the whole house. Needless to say, when the cold of winter hit, we

---

3. See Stephanie Smittle, "Helltown, born and raised."

would all three gather close to that space heater. It had replaced a coal-burning stove, which backed up to the coal shoot in the wall.

To the east lived Fannie and Mack Thompson, who would later turn their home into a florist shop, and my first real job was delivering flowers for them during the summers. To the west lived two unmarried sisters, though one, Mrs. Sullivan, was a widow. The other sister was an eccentric woman whom we all called "Miss Mattie." Gran was good friends with Mrs. Sullivan, but she always warned us children to take care around Miss Mattie. Across the street to the north were the McCarty family—they had a daughter, Ellen, who was my age, and we played a lot together, because they had a big open lot adjacent to their house. Ellen was a fast runner and was assertive for a girl in those days—she could outrun most of us boys. She would also later be one of the first girls whom I kissed—in the fifth grade. Our neighbor to the south was Crowley's Ridge—no one lived on it until many years later.

Going out of our house and turning left to the west, in a block or so you would come to a poorer Black neighborhood, where the houses were ramshackle—it was called "the Alley" when I was younger, and later became Administration Avenue. Every day we would see the Black adults and children walking down Porter Street past our house, on the way to downtown Helena, which was a mile away. Despite the proximity of these Black children, we never played together—it was strictly forbidden by the code of neo-slavery. As they walked by our house, I found myself thinking about them. Of course I had accepted the white supremacist idea that they were the dreaded "other," to be feared and controlled. Yet, on some occasions, I found myself wondering if they might be people like us—they looked like us, and they seemed to act like us as human beings. I was not going anywhere with these thoughts at this time, however—it was simply too dangerous out there, and I was feeling vulnerable as a boy being raised by women in a patriarchal world.

Though we lived in a patriarchal world, my mother escaped much of it because she worked as a beautician at Ted's Beauty Shop in downtown Helena at the other end of Porter Street, about a mile from our house. I don't know how or when Mother started that job at Ted's—she was there when my memories began. In my younger days, I thought that it was owned by a man named "Ted," but Mother let me know that it was named after the woman who owned it—Ted Bostick. I can remember nothing else about Ted, but as I write this, I am just realizing that such female ownership reinforced the sense that beauty shops in the 1950's were a woman's domain, whether one was classified as white or Black. No males, except salesman, were to be found in those beauty shops.

Ted's was located in the Cleburne Hotel, which had been opened in 1905 and named after General Patrick Cleburne. It had a colonial revival style with huge columns in the front, facing Cherry Street, the main downtown street. In its youth, it was quite a grand place, near the railroad depot for travelers to stay, housing barber and beauty shops and other stores. I would often stop by Ted's Beauty Shop on my way home from school. It was a fascinating place to me—a woman's world! All women beauty operators, and all kinds of white women there, getting their hair done, getting pampered, getting listened to, getting a chance to share their stories and local gossip, getting a chance to exhale and be accepted without the censoring or lustful eyes of men to put them in their places. It was a refuge from patriarchy, even though they were often getting their hair done and having themselves made up for their men (and other women). When I would enter Ted's, there was an intriguing set of smells wafting through the air, a strange mixture of perfume, shampoo, dyes, chemicals, hair spray, and cigarette smoke. As a young boy, the women there—both operators and customers—would fawn over me, and I loved the attention. Part of it was my relationship to Mother, and part of it was that in my childhood, I was still in my innocent youth, a young male fascinated by being allowed to enter this women's world, not yet so tainted by the crushing patriarchy that awaited them outside the confines of the beauty shop.

By the time we had arrived in Helena, the Cleburne Hotel had begun to decline, and whenever I would visit Mother at Ted's, she would warn me of the unsavory characters who lived in the hotel. There were no bathrooms in Ted's, so I would need to use the Men's Room in the hotel, and Mother always warned me to wipe the toilet seat and to put toilet paper on the seat before I sat on it. The lobby was paneled with dark wood, and it always seemed dark and foreboding in there to me. It had a great attraction, though—pinball machines! No gambling allowed (that I as a child was aware of), but my cousin Brown and I would often go there to play the machines. We both had good hand-eye coordination, so it was a source of pride for us to hone our skills on those machines. Mother, however, did not approve because she thought playing such machines in such an atmosphere would soil my character, or at least lead me into some unpleasant situations.

Brown's father (Gran's son) worked across Porter Street from Ted's at the post office, and Brown and I would often meet at the lobby of the Cleburne Hotel to play the pinball machines. On those trips, I would not visit Mother at Ted's because she would not allow me to play the pinballs if she knew I was there. There were obviously many eyes in the hotel lobby, though, because she would always find out that I was there, and she would admonish me when she got home. She also expressed hurt that I had chosen pinball over her, but she perceived that I had not come in to see her because I knew that she would forbid me from playing the machines. I did not like sneaking around in her territory, but I did not want to miss playing pinball. We finally compromised that I would check in with her before playing pinball and would check in with her when I left. She needn't have feared for my safety in the lobby of the Cleburne—she had put the fear of God in me about the people there, and I was always watchful—but the pinball machines were something else!

When I left Ted's Beauty Shop on my way home, I re-entered the patriarchal world. I don't know when I became aware, deep in my heart, that my father had abandoned us. It just seemed that the fact of his absence was always with me. He did provide child support (not always regularly), but I never heard from him—no letters, no visits. I don't remember ever asking my mother why he didn't contact me, because it was such a painful subject, for both of us.

My mother and I rarely ever talked about my father. Having counseled many families on these issues of divorce and separation as a pastor, I know how painful these conversations can be between the child and the parent who stays. The parent who stays tries not to demean the absent parent, but they cannot easily answer the question of why the absent parent does not visit the child. In my childhood, I stopped asking my mother about it because I perceived how painful it was for her, or so I thought. The story had always been that he had left her for another woman, but as I grew to be a young adult and got into therapy myself, I began to see what a strong woman she was. I began to think that she might have been glad for him to go. In terms of our daily lives as a single mom family, it was almost as if my father had merely been a sperm donor. I never had any photos of him. I didn't really notice this until last year when I was looking for a photo of me and our kids to post on Facebook on Father's Day. I had a brief thought that I ought to post a photo of my father, but I didn't have one. I have never had one; I don't ever remember seeing one of him in our Porter Street house, and I don't know that I want one now.

We never had talks about him, and Mother never lamented his absence to me, though I certainly felt that absence but didn't say it. It was rather that we must push on and act like we could do well without him, as natural as could be.

This began a pattern for me of pushing intimate and important things deeper inside me rather than expressing them to Mother or Gran or anyone else. I had no siblings with whom to discuss these kinds of things. I had this simmering tension inside me. On the one hand, there was my mother's hard work to keep us "normal," proving to people, and perhaps to herself, that single moms could do it—who needs a man anyway? On the other hand, I had this feeling of lostness and abandonment inside me, which I felt that I could not share with her. To do so would tarnish her efforts to proclaim that not only would we survive without a man, but we would thrive also. This "inwardness" made it difficult to trust the outside world, because I did not want to let anyone in to see what I assumed was the truth: I was abandoned by my father because I was unworthy as a son.

In the midst of these struggles, however, the truth was that I was bright and energetic, and people noticed me, especially adults. Getting this warm response began a paradoxical pattern of feeling a need to please others—family, church, school—but also feeling on the margins of those communities, because I internally felt so outwardly branded as boy abandoned by his father. The church community of First Presbyterian Church in Helena was one of those communities. As I noted in the Introduction, they began to teach me that my primary definition was not boy abandoned by my father, but rather son claimed by my Father (and Mother) God in Jesus Christ. It was a powerful teaching to me, and they did it in both word and deed.

I experienced this love many times, but one story leaps out now. Ted's Beauty Shop where my mother worked was about a mile from our house. Sometimes after school I would walk to the shop to see my mother and then walk home. We had no car; indeed, Mother never owned a car by herself until I was a young adult. On this particular day, when I was in the second or third grade, it started pouring down rain while I was in the beauty shop. I needed to go on home, so Mother told me to bundle up and get on home. I started out in the cold rain—it hurt my heart, and I am sure that it hurt my mother's heart too. I was cold and beginning to get soaked. About two blocks into the walk, I heard someone call my name: "Nibs, do you need a ride home?" It was Lyda Kitchens, a wealthy member of our church, driving in her car. Her family's history included involvement in the Elaine Massacre, but I was light years away from that knowledge on that day. On that day in the cold, pouring rain, her voice was angelic! I leaped into her car, and I remember sitting in the back seat, feeling warm and dry and loved.

Other communities were central to me also. Mother's extended family was so important. As I have noted, Gran was essential, but my grandfather Maurice Armour, and the Armour family in Byhalia were also important to me. I have a note written by Gran to my mother in June, 1953 from Byhalia. Apparently, Gran and I had gone there for a visit in the summer, and I am certain that Mother appreciated the solitude and rest, while missing us at the same time, too! I had written some words to Mother: "Going with Twinkie to Bible school. How are you doing at the shop?" Gran had added her own commentary about my going fishing with Grandaddy: "The fish weighed 40 pds, almost as big as Nibs. We are about to die with the heat. Will try to take care of your son."

We also had a family move in across Porter Street where the McCarty's had previously lived. It was Dr. Troy Paine and his wife Jimmie, with son Johnny, and daughters Sheila and Denise. Dr. Paine was a family physician, and his son Johnny was one year younger than me. We would become good friends and run together a lot. They later built a swimming pool in their back yard, where I learned to swim. I am grateful to them and to other neighbors for their many kindnesses to our family. Replacing Mrs. Sullivan and Miss Mattie was a new family—LP and Sue Sellers, with children Debbie, Lisa and Paul. Though their children were much younger than me, Sue and Mother became good friends and counselors to one another. Daughter Debbie, who became a nurse, would become the primary care-giver to my mother in Mother's last year, some 45 years later.

This tension inside me—this need to appear normal and capable, while feeling abnormal and incapable—would lead me to seek to please my sets of communities who gave me meaning and stability. It meant that I also would soak up the prevailing ideologies of my white, Southern atmosphere in the late 1940's and 1950's: white supremacy, patriarchy, homophobia, belief in redemptive violence, and materialism. I don't remember deciding to believe in any of these. I just absorbed them. To use St. Paul's evocative phrase in his New Testament Letter to the Ephesians 2:2, I came under the "power of the prince of the air," meaning that as I breathed in the love and support of the communities which sustained me, I also breathed in the pollutants that accompanied that love: the ideologies that I mentioned. I didn't choose to receive and believe in the superiority of people classified as "white" and in the inferiority of people classified as "Black," but I definitely believed those ideas.

I didn't decide that women were inferior and were property of men, especially with two strong women as my primary family! Yet, I definitely believed it, that women belonged to men, that women were incomplete without a man to guide them. This ideology was an especially powerful and paradoxical ebbing and flowing of the tides of my life—dependent on these "inferior" women who were so powerful in my life. I didn't know the word "homosexual" until late in my childhood. People attracted to others of the same gender classification were invisible to me in my childhood. There was no "winking and nodding" for me about same-gender attraction, just oblivion. When the hormones hit in adolescence, things changed considerably, as I wondered about my own sexuality, but the powerful attraction to girls and women helped to settle that anxiety down.

In the midst of this turmoil and these contradictions, I headed out into the world and its communities, which I so desperately needed for approval but which I also deeply feared and somewhat resented because I feared them so much. I had deep angers in me as well as deep anxieties. I had gotten a tricycle at about age six, and my friend Ellen McCarty from across the street sometimes came to ride it. On one occasion, Ellen took over the tricycle and would not get off. I went in to tell Mother and get her to come out and order Ellen to get off the tricycle. She told me: "Nibs, it is your job to get her off your tricycle. You go handle it—you cannot hit her, but you will get her off. If you don't, I will punish you, not her." So, I went out to Ellen to tell her to get off my tricycle, and when she refused, I grabbed the tricycle and shook it so hard that Ellen finally fell off and ran across the street to tell her mother. Her mother did not come out, and I remember being astonished and somewhat disturbed at the level of anger in me, an anger that would seem to shake the world and me. It would be the beginning of many lessons for me in learning to navigate my way in the tension of being raised by women in a racial and patriarchal world. My mother would be my guide in these lessons—she didn't shoot a crazed, mad dog as Atticus Finch did, but she did begin to teach me to how to survive and even to thrive in this kind of world and in our kind of situation.

4

Lessons in Life

I BECAME AWARE THAT I had a lot of anger in me, but I also felt strong pressure from Mother to be a "good boy" and to present myself to the world as a nice boy who was obedient, courteous, and kind. I experienced that anger in another way soon after the tricycle incident. Two doors east of us on Porter Street lived another widow named Mrs. Landers. She and Gran were good friends and would often visit in one another's homes. I never knew much about Mrs. Landers except that her home was all brick, that she was a wonderful flower gardener, and that she was always nice to me. She had many kinds of flowers in her garden, but what I remember are lots of daffodils, purple irises and many kinds of tulips. I passed her garden as I was walking home from school and loved looking at the flowers and enjoying their wonderful smells. For some reason that I still do not understand, I also deeply resented those flowers and their beauty. Perhaps in my inner turmoil, I did not like the bold and outright beauty of those flowers. They seemed to proclaim that the world was fine and functioning, and they seemed to glorify the God who created them. So, I acted out against them. I started picking off the blossoms of the flowers and just dropping them on the ground. It would be one thing if I had picked them and given them to Mother or Gran and asked for Mrs. Landers' forgiveness later—an innocent little boy's mistake. I don't remember having animosity towards Mrs. Landers—it was the beauty of the flowers that I resented—it was purely destructive.

I did this several times, and after one of those occasions, Gran asked me if I knew anything about the destruction of the flowers. I felt then that perhaps Mrs. Landers had seen me destroy the flowers, and that I was definitely in trouble. Yet, I had learned my lessons in racism well, so I bluffed and lied and said that I had seen an N-word boy picking those flowers, but I did not know who he was. My bluff worked—Gran seem satisfied and told me to let her know if I saw that little N-word boy again. I recognized that I was on the edge of being caught, and I told myself to stop, but I did not. I did wait for a few days to let things calm down. Then, on my way home from school, I did it again, and I looked up to see Mrs. Landers standing on her front porch, looking at me. She had seen me, and it really scared me! The only consolation that I had was that I knew that I could outrun her to our house, so I took off, making up a story as I ran home to tell Gran, before Mrs. Landers got there. I do not remember the story that I created because when I arrived home, Mrs. Landers was already standing there with Gran. I was astonished—how had she beaten me home? How could an old lady like that beat me home?

Gran said: "Nibs, I am so ashamed of you. I never thought that you could do something like this. Go out and get you a switch because you are going to get what is coming to you." I had to go out and get a branch off one of the small bushes outside our house, and for the only time in my life, Gran gave me a "switching," hitting my legs over and over again in her anger and embarrassment. It hurt my legs, but I took it without crying or hollering out. My thoughts during the switching were not on the agony but in trying to figure out how Mrs. Landers got to my house faster than I did. Gran never gave me spankings or switchings in response to my misbehavior—she would wait for Mother to come home from work and do it. But, on this occasion, she could not wait—I got it from her, and I got it again from Mother when she got home from work. It was only after I reached adulthood and had engaged my captivity to racism that I recognized how much danger that I had added to little Black boys' lives in the neighborhood when I lied and said that a little Black boy had harmed Mrs. Landers's flowers. Black people have beaten and even killed for much less than that.

My anger would find its expression in another neighborhood story. As I stated earlier, Gran and Mother would on occasion share leftover food with a Black family who lived down the street from us on Administration Avenue. They also shared clothes that I had outgrown or clothes that Gran and Mother no longer needed or wanted. It was wintertime, and Mother had bought me a new warm, woolen cap for my head. I called my old one my "Dooda cap" (I have no idea of the origin of that name.). I wanted to keep the old one, too, but Mother indicated that since I had a new one, she would share the old one with the family who came to our back porch door.

On one occasion not long after that, I looked out our window and saw a group of Black people walking past our house on the way to town. On the head of one of the Black boys was my Dooda cap, and when I saw that, I ran out the front door, jerked the cap off his head and said "What are you doing with my Dooda cap on? It's my hat!" The boy said nothing, but even if he had been thinking about an answer, my mother had followed me out and said to me: "Nibs, get away from him and give the cap back to him. I gave it to his family. You've got a new cap, and he needs one." "No, Momma, I want this cap—it's mine." "Suit yourself," she said, "but if you keep this one, I'm giving him your new one." I responded, "That's okay with me—I want this cap." She went and got the new cap and gave it to his mother and said: "I'm sorry for my son's behavior—please take this one," and she did. I was satisfied, but later I would marvel at the level of anger that I had, an anger that led me to make such a mess of things, believing that the power of race gave me the privilege to attack this boy and his family in such a way. I did not think of it in those terms then, but I do so now.

In my turmoil, I also was filled with many fears, mostly centered on abandonment. I often imagined monsters appearing out of nowhere to snatch me and take me away from home. In my childhood years, I had a recurring dream. I was on a freight train, speeding through the flat Delta landscape—in the Delta, you can see for miles, and I could do so in the dream. As I was riding the rails, out in the fields, far away, the monster Frankenstein appeared. I don't know how I knew it, but I knew that he was after me. I was deeply frightened. He began to chase the train because he wanted to get me and take me away. He got closer and closer to the train, and I kept telling the engineer to go faster, to get me to my momma so that I would be safe. Frankenstein got closer and closer, and the dream always ended in this chase. Frankenstein never caught me, but I never got home, either. This caught-ness and this fear, never safe but never totally abandoned, would be a theme for me for much of my childhood, youth, and young adult years.

As I noted, Mother and I shared a small bedroom in Gran's house. We started out sleeping together in a big bed, but at some point my mother bought two twin beds for us to use. When bedtime came, my mother would tuck me in and then leave the bedroom so that I would go to sleep and so that she could exhale. Gran usually went to bed early, so Mother had some time to herself. My fears were so great, however, that for a long while, I could not go to sleep unless Mother was sitting on the end of the couch in the living room, nearest our bedroom. I can vividly remember the lamp light being on in the living room, with Mother under it, crocheting or doing needlepoint or some other sewing project. "Momma, are you still there?" "Yes, Nibs, I'm here—go on to sleep." I would ask that question several times before finally relaxing and going on to sleep. Part of it was fear, part of it may have been my genes—I still don't like to go to sleep. There seems to be that primordial fear that if I turn loose of control during sleep, Frankenstein or some other monster will get me. Over the months, Mother would move down the couch away from the bedroom, until I got the message that she was still there, and to use the Atticus Finch image, she would be there for me in the morning.

If I had a scary dream at night, I would climb into the small twin bed with Mother, and she never made me get out. We still have those twin beds in my house now, and as I think back on those nights, I can only be amazed at how scrunched up she was in that small bed, when I got into it. I know that she was exhausted and had to get up for a hard day's work the next day, but I do not remember her ever refusing me entry into her bed. This pattern continued until I was on the edge of adolescence, when at Gran's death, Mother moved out of our room and made Gran's former bedroom her own. As I got older, I was ashamed that I still needed to do this, but I still did it—it was so comforting to me. Indeed, there are times now when I hug up to Caroline at night, I am flashing back to the comfort and exhaling that I did when I got in bed with my mother. I'm sure that she had her own ambivalence about me getting into her bed, especially as I got older, but I do not remember any shaming from her for doing it. It may have mitigated her loneliness as well.

In the midst of these fears and angers, I began to step out on my own, to seek to find and to establish my identity. My first memory of taking such a step was in Sunday school at First Presbyterian Church, which felt like my second home. We were always in church, and there were no excuses for missing Sunday school and worship. From Mother's point of view, if you were not in worship on Sunday morning, you were in the bed sick. This came from a woman who worked five days a week and often most of the day on Saturday. In our segregated schools, we changed schools between third grade and fourth grade, and went from elementary school to junior high school, the latter encompassing grades four through eight. Our church marked this transition with a Sunday school assembly in the beginning of the fall. At this assembly, those students going into the fourth grade would receive Bibles with our names in them and the date of transition. In the fall of 1955, the church had the assembly for those of us entering the fourth grade. The Sunday school superintendent would call out our names, and we would walk up before the whole assembly to get our Bibles and receive applause from the adults. On this Sunday, the superintendent, Mr. Thea Epes, began calling our names in the assembly: Jennifer Fey, my cousin Brown (William Brown Higgins, Jr.), Frank Kitchens, Jr. (Lyda Kitchens' son), and they all came up to get their Bibles.

Then he called out "Gibson Preston Stroupe, Jr.," but I did not move. There was a little nervous shuffling. He went on to the next rising fourth grader, Katherine Virginia Wood, and she came up to get her Bible. Then he returned to me and said "Gibson Preston Stroupe, Jr." Still, I did not move. There was a little bit of nervous buzzing now. My mother was sitting several rows behind me, and I knew that her glare was burning a hole in me. I would not turn around to look at her, nor would I step forward to get my Bible. The superintendent was wise and caught on, and he then said: "Nibs Stroupe." I came forward to get my Bible. I was establishing a new official name for myself, and it was a defining moment for me. I would no longer be named for the person who had abandoned me—I would now start establishing a new identity. When we got home, my mother admonished me, but she did not really punish me—she seemed to understand what was going on. I still have that Bible on the bookshelf in my office, some 65 years later.

I loved playing sports of any kind—especially baseball, with football and basketball in close second. Any kind of sports and games were a great gift to me. I had good hand-eye coordination, so that was a bonus for me. I was chosen to be on the Coca-Cola Bottlers Little League team at age six, and I loved it. In the summer, the games would start in late afternoon in the unrelenting heat. I would often depend on others, especially on Brown's dad ("Big Brown," who was Gran's youngest son), whom I called Mr. Higgins, to give me a ride to the games. If my team were playing, Mother would walk to the games from work to see me play. On cloudy days when rain was threatening and when my team had a game scheduled to play, I would sit out on our front porch stoop, praying to God to hold off the rain and to allow us to pray. On one level, that seems silly, because God has many other things to take care of. And, in the punishing heat of the Delta, I can imagine that the farmers were sending up prayers in the opposite direction—we need the rain! Yet, being a church-goer, I believed in the power of prayer, and I prayed that prayer many times as afternoon thunderstorms rolled up out of the west.

I loved the game of baseball, and I still do. I'm not sure why I love it so much, but in my adult years, I have reflected that perhaps it is because it is a lot like life. There is no clock to the game—it is not clear what time the game will end. The best hitters in baseball have an average of 30%, meaning that they will fail 70% of the time. It is a game where one has to learn to deal with failure and frustration. My goal was to be a professional baseball player, and though I was short, I was a pretty good player. That changed, however, when the pitchers began to throw curve balls in the league next up from Little League. I could handle the fastball, but the curve balls looked like they were going to hit me, and I ended up flailing at the pitches, never adjusting to the curve ball. Thus endeth my baseball career.

I also liked football and basketball, but there were two major problems. In football, I discovered that I did not like to get hit. I was short and small, and I usually played defensive back, and I distinctly remember when my football career ended in junior high school. A huge running back broke through the line and came running toward me. I tried to tackle him, but he simply ran over me—I did not have the power to stop him. I got up and said to myself: "After this season, that's it for me. I can't do this very well, and I will get smashed by these guys again and again." Basketball was the same way—I was coordinated and could handle the ball as a guard. I was a good shooter and an excellent defender (having inherited my mother's basketball genes), but I suffered again from a great disability in basketball—I was only 5 feet, 5 inches tall. As we moved into junior high sports, it became clear that I would not be able to compete unless I just gave all of my passion and energy to basketball. I decided not to try out for the team any more.

One place I did excel, however, was in academics. My birthday is in November, so I was ineligible to enter the first grade in public schools because a child had to be six years old by October 1 to do so. I had learned to read early on, mainly from Mother reading to me so much and from my love of comic books like *Little Lulu*. Because I loved the comic books so much, I would nag my mother to read the same one over and over again. When she did that, especially at bedtime, she would often try to skip over some words, and I would catch her, saying: "No, Momma, you missed some of the words." After a few times of this, she would turn the comic over to me and tell me to read to myself, which I did.

I'm not sure where she got the money, but Mother decided to enroll me in a small, private home-based first grade program, taught by Mrs. Sisson in her house. There were about six of us kids in grade one through three, and I do not remember much about it, except that it happened. I was sad to be separated from my many friends who were born prior to October 1, but I was also glad to be in school. I still have some of the first grade readers from that class.

I entered segregated Jefferson Elementary School for second grade, and I was on my way. It was about a mile from our house, so I would walk there and back every day, rain or shine. I excelled there in academics—it seemed so easy to me that I could hardly believe it. I had thought that my time in Mrs. Sisson's first grade would have put me behind the other students, but the always-true emphasis on small class size proved out here again. I was ahead of my fellow students in the second grade. I was delighted in the ease at which I took on the school subjects.

As I mentioned earlier in the Sunday school story, we had a big transition from third to fourth grade, going into junior high. That school was about four blocks further away from my home, and it covered fourth through eighth grades. I have always been a small person in stature, and I remember arriving at the junior high school for fourth grade. I was astonished at the size of the eighth graders—they were huge! To paraphrase from the Israelites' awe of the people in the Promised Land in in Numbers, they looked like giants to me! Still I excelled in junior high school academically, and I began to get the socialization skills that I would need. In the violence of Southern white culture, and as we got closer to adolescence, fighting among the boys was common. I didn't like to fight because of my lack of size, but I did like the adrenalin that came from fighting. I had my share of fights, and though I did not win many, I did put up a good fight. That anger deep in me came out in a rush in such fights. One could not afford to get a reputation as an easy mark, and I was not an easy mark. I was short and cute in the fourth and fifth grades, and I had eighth-grade protectors in those years, so that reputation cut down on the number of fights also.

Though I never thought of our family as poor when I was a child, money was always an issue for us. My mother did not emphasize it, but she did remind me that we had to watch our pennies. I remember that she had some envelopes in her dresser drawer, one marked "gas" and one marked "electricity" and others marked similarly. She would put small amounts of cash in those envelopes each week when she got paid, so that by the time the monthly bill came due, she would have the money. On days when I needed money as a child, I would be tempted to steal a dollar or two from one of those envelopes. Mother must have perceived my lust for the cash, so she warned me on occasion: "Nibs, I know that you need some money, and I will try to get you some, but please don't take money out of my envelopes. We need it to pay the bills, and without it, we might not have any heat—you wouldn't want that, would you?" That was convincing enough in my early years.

On Saturday afternoons, the local Malco theater would have a double feature movie, and when I got old enough to go without Mother, I would go with friends. The movies were a raucous occasion, with many kids there without parents, and lots of noise and shenanigans. I was short and could get in on the children's ticket price long after I had passed the age to do so. Mother agreed to pay the ticket price for the movies—an easy childcare solution for her on Saturday afternoons. She usually worked on Saturdays at Ted's Beauty Shop until mid-afternoon, so having me in the movies then would give her and Gran a breather. I would go by Ted's on Saturday before the movie to get the money from her for admission to the movie. She could not afford to pay for popcorn and soda, and as I got older and started earning a bit of money myself, I started using that to buy treats at the movies. On weeks when Mother's money was especially tight, she would ask me if I had any money, so that I could pay for the movie tickets. I said that I did have some, but that I planned to use it for refreshments at the movies. She told me that I would need to use that money to get into the movie. This went on for a few weeks, and I started lying to her, telling her that I did not have any money. On one occasion, she told me to empty my pockets, and there was the money. She said: "Nibs, don't be lying to me. We need to stick together on this."

I was ashamed of my deception, but I was also mad that I had gotten caught. On future occasions when I would go to get money from Mother for the movies on Saturday, if I had money for refreshments, I would tape it on the inside of my socks, so that when I showed Mother my pockets, she would not detect my "extra" money. I did this several times, and though I felt guilty about it, I sure enjoyed the soda and popcorn. I never told Mother this story, so as far as I know, she never knew about it. As

I reflect back upon it, it shows me how tight things were financially for her (and thus for me). It also shows me why I still have my Calvinist Presbyterian heritage. Not quite total depravity on my part then, but not far from it.

All during these early years in Helena, I was not aware of Black life in Helena. I did not think that people with brown skin who were classified as "Black" were human beings like me. I was taught this by Mother and Gran, by my church, by the schools, and by neighbors and friends. I received this teaching it—and I accepted it—because it came from people whom I loved and trusted, and who loved and trusted me. It would take me several decades to realize that there was a whole dimension of Black life in Helena that I did not know existed, that I did not think was even capable of existing. I have much regret over that, both for my own consciousness and participation in white supremacy, but even more so for the innumerable injustices perpetrated against people classified as "Black," including the Elaine Massacre started in Elaine, about twenty miles from Helena, in 1919 and spread to Helena. At least 230 Black people were killed in a white race riot.

As I noted in the Introduction, my mother did try to balance this powerful force of race a wee bit, forbidding me to use the N-word in the house and forbidding me from calling any adults by their first names unless I put a "Mr." or "Ms." with it. She sometimes shared her wisdom on the general, repressive nature of white male supremacy. One day when she got home from work, I told her: "Momma, I hate Jews." She replied: "Nibs, why do you say that?" "Because they are Jews." She replied: "Do you hate Rayman?" I said, "No, I don't hate Rayman. He's one of my friends." "What about Ruth?" she asked. "Oh, well, she's a girl, but she's nice." Then Mother summed it up: "Nibs, both of them are Jewish. Do you hate them?" I was shocked. "No, Momma, I don't hate them." Then she drove it home: "Well, Nibs, I think that you should be careful about whom you think you hate." The world had just become more confusing, but I am grateful for my mother's push. I only considered later that Mother was the beautician for several of the Jewish women in town. While she suggested some limits on the power of prejudice in this example, she was not as forthcoming on race. That engagement between us would come much later. At some point in my elementary school career, my mother was diagnosed with breast cancer, but I did not know the extent of it at that time. She kept that hidden from me. All I knew was that Mother was going to the hospital in Memphis for a few days and that Gran would take care of me while she was gone. I missed her, but I never felt the danger of what she was dealing with in those years in the 1950's. Apparently the doctors were successful and got the cancer, because the breast cancer would never return. It would be another kind of cancer that would attack her many years later, a cancer common to our family.

In the early spring of 1959, Gran had a heart attack, but fortunately, the doctors were able to save her. It did mean that she would be confined to the bed for at least a month, and Mother and I and the rest of the family knew that this would be very difficult for her. Gran was an active person, always cooking, always doing chores, always cleaning up. It was a challenging month or so for her, but she began to get up and move around a little bit. On the morning of May 20, 1959, she got up to eat breakfast with me at the small kitchen table while Mother was getting dressed for work. As we were talking at the table, all of a sudden, she slumped and laid her head down on the table. I shook Gran but got no response. I hollered at Mother: "Momma, something's happened to Gran." Mother came running in, looked at Gran and touched her, then said to me: "Nibs, run across the street and get Dr. Paine—hurry!" I was in my pajamas and was embarrassed, but I did it. I ran across Porter Street and banged on the Paines' door. Dr. Paine came to the door, and I told him what had happened. He grabbed his bag and immediately came over, but it was too late. Gran had died of a thundering heart attack at that kitchen table at age 79. I was in the seventh grade. It would prove to be a huge transition for us, but there was also another one coming for me. The hormones were hitting, and adolescence with all its anxieties and terror and wonders was on its way.

5

All Shook Up

I WAS SITTING ON Gran's bed the night after Gran had died of the massive heart attack in our kitchen. The day that she died, May 20, was almost the end of the school year, and I had been working hard to maintain a perfect attendance record. A funeral service would be held for Gran at our church in Helena, and then her body would be buried in the cemetery in Byhalia, about two hours away by car. I was thinking about this when I joined Mother in Gran's bedroom that night. Mother was sorting through Gran's dresses to decide which one to use for her burial, and she asked my opinion. After a couple of dresses were rejected, I said to her: "Mother, I don't think that I can go to Byhalia with you for Gran's burial. I can go to the funeral with you, but I need to go on to school after that to keep up my perfect attendance record." My mother slumped to her knees and replied: "Nibs, don't you love me anymore? I need you to be with me in Byhalia." She then started crying, and it was the first time that I had ever seen her cry.

I was astonished. I had always seen my mother as a superwoman type of person, and here she was so vulnerable and hurting. It hurt my heart to have caused her so much pain. I replied, "Of course, Mother, I'll go with you. I'm so sorry to have done this." She said: "Thank you, Nibs, I need you in my corner on this." I was agreeing to go, but in my heart, I was gnashing my teeth: I so wanted that perfect attendance record. I tried to think of a scenario where I could go over to Byhalia and get back before school closed for the day, but it was not possible. In my hurtful declaration to my mother, I had not realized the dynamics of her (and our) situation. With Gran's sudden death, Mother's world had been thrown into chaos. Could we stay in the house? Would Gran's sons want to sell the house? If so, where would we go? Back to Memphis? Byhalia? I simply did not think of these implications—I was only thinking about my perfect attendance record.

I don't remember much about the day of Gran's funeral. I do remember the Reverend Harold Jackson coming to our house to say a prayer with us before we went to the church for the funeral. It was a powerful acknowledgment of our frailty and our mortality but also about God's promises to us about the power of love overcoming the power of death. I also remember a caravan of cars making the two-hour drive to Byhalia for the burial. We returned to Helena that day because Mother had to go back to work the next day—money was tight. Gran's eldest son Jack inherited the house, and he decided to allow us to stay in the house and to pay him rent for it. Even in my short-sightedness, I felt relief when Mother told me this.

Gran's death meant that we were now on our own in a way that neither of us had experienced together. There would be no Gran waiting for me when I got home from school. There would be no Gran cooking suppers for us every night. There would be big changes coming. I would be home by myself in the afternoons for the first time in my life. Mother reminded me of this a couple of days later at the supper table: "Nibs, this is a hard time for us. You'll be coming home to be by yourself now after school. I know that I can trust you, but I want to caution you. You're old enough to stay by yourself, but I want you to be careful. Your friends can come over, but only after you've got your homework done. If you have somebody over that I don't know, please call me to tell me. And, if there is somebody that you don't know who wants to come in, tell them that they cannot do it."

Another big transition was that soon Mother moved out of our joint bedroom into Gran's bedroom. In the midst of all the chaos and change, I can imagine that this was one of the only positive changes for her—a room of her own, privacy and space! I had mixed feelings about Mother's moving out of our room. Since adolescence was coming on, I was feeling the need for some privacy too, but I was also a little uneasy. What would happen when I had those night terrors? Could I go get in bed with her in her room? Though we never talked directly about it, I never got back in bed with her again—the matter was settled.

There was also another transition early in the summer. During that first summer without Gran, I would play outside all day and come in at supper time. On one occasion, when I came home for supper, Mother was sitting at the table eating a sandwich. I said to her: "When are you cooking supper? Where is it?" She said: "This is supper—fix yourself a sandwich." "But, Momma, you usually fix a big meal like Gran did." She looked at me and said, "Yes, I do, and I'll be glad to keep trying to do that, but you have not done your part." "What is that?" I asked. "You didn't wash the dishes last night or today, and that was our agreement. Do you remember that?" "Yes, Momma, I do," was my doleful reply. She laid out the new plan: "Well, here is the new agreement: I'll cook us supper unless I am really tired, and you will wash the dishes. No dishes, no supper. Got it?" She held out her hand for a "formal" handshake, and I shook her hand and said, "Yes, Momma, I'll do it." I kept washing the dishes, and she kept cooking great meals. This practice helped me out later on. Soon after Caroline and I got married, a friend asked Caroline why she decided to commit to our relationship. I thought that she would comment on my good looks, on my strong intellect, on my kind heart. Instead her answer was: "He washed the dishes."

This period was the culmination of a time of transition for Mother and me, a time that would shake things up in ways that I had not imagined. First, in 1955, her father (my grandfather) died at age 63 of lung cancer. He was in his bed in his home in Byhalia and was covered in a big oxygen tent, which was used at that time to help people with breathing difficulties. He was the first of the six siblings of that generation to go, and it was a difficult passing. A couple of years later Mother's only sibling, Maurice Junior (nicknamed "Bud"), and his family would move from Memphis to Chicago, a very long way from Helena. It was a second big loss for Mother. She had three males to whom she was close—her father, her brother, and me. Her father had died, and her brother had moved to Chicago. And now, as the decade closed, Gran suddenly died.

Mother began to make some changes, including setting the rules on washing dishes. Gran's sons had decided to take some of Gran's furniture out of Gran's house, so we found ourselves needing furniture. Since money was so tight, Mother decided to take up the necessity and the hobby of buying old, beat-up and sometimes broken-up furniture, then stripping the finish off of them and re-finishing them. The first piece that she did was an old bar table from the Cleburne Hotel. She had a friend, Bob Wetzel, cut the legs down, and she remade and refinished that into a long coffee table for the living room. That table was still in good shape and in her living room when she died in 2004.

About 1957, she and her aunt Ila Naylor, one of the six siblings, bought a car together and shared the use of it. Ila lived in neighboring West Helena, so it was relatively easy to do. They would continue in that buying and sharing pattern until Mother bought her first car by herself in 1966. In search of furniture to redo, Mother would take me around with her, driving around the county, looking for furniture at antique sales, estate sales, and even getting pieces from the side of road that others had thrown out. She enlisted my help in dragging these into the car, and I helped her on the next couple of pieces after the Cleburne Hotel table.

There was an old chifforobe in our bedroom that she decided to make into a full dresser for me. I helped her to cut down the long wardrobe part to make a flat top for the whole piece, and then we had to strip off the old paint and finish, then sand it, then re-finish it. It was a long, boring process to me, and after that one, I ended my career as a furniture re-finisher. This kind of work was not long and boring to Mother—it was therapy for her. She spent many hours and many years in doing this and basically re-did all of the furniture in our house. I can still picture her out in our back yard, stripping down some old hunk of wood, smoking her cigarette, listening to the Cardinals play baseball on the radio. I am still using that refinished dresser today in our bedroom to store my clothes. It is one of the pieces of furniture that I brought back home with me after Mother died.

In the middle of this transition period, the polio plague was raging, and many of us were deeply afraid of it. I never knew anyone who got polio, but Mother did. No one knew the cause of it, and in these Covid-19 days, I am often reminded of the sense of fear and dread about polio that was present in the 1950's. When the vaccine finally came out, I proclaimed that I would not get a polio shot, because I hated shots so much. Dr. Paine would sometimes make a house call to our home to give me a shot that I needed, but I would lock myself in the bathroom and not come out. On the occasion of the polio vaccine, however, there was no negotiating with Mother. She put it bluntly: "Nibs, you are going to get that shot. If not, and polio does not kill you, I will." I didn't know if she was joking or not, but I dutifully lined up in the school to get my shot from the school nurse. I did the same when the Covid vaccine became available.

After Aunt Ila (really my great-aunt) and Mother bought the car together, we began to take some trips together. The Armour family had its annual July 4th reunions in Byhalia on farm land owned by Dell Armour, another of the six siblings. We would drive over there for a day or so, and the highlight for me was the annual family baseball game, in which everyone was cajoled into taking a turn at bat or in the field. There was much laughter and cheering and cheating, and as an intense baseball boy, I would often complain that the adults were not taking the game seriously enough. My mother told me: "Nibs, lighten up, this is a family celebration, not a major league game. We're just so glad to be together. Who cares which side wins?" I did, but I learned to enjoy the game and the family. That family stream of humor started to flow into my system, and I began to learn that this laughter, this celebration of life, was one of the family's and Mother's main coping mechanisms for getting through the difficult times.

The only one of the six siblings to leave the area was Thurman Armour, and he and his wife Thelma and daughter Camille moved from Byhalia to the Tampa, Florida area. Thurman was already suffering from emphysema, and they decided to get someplace warmer, where they hoped that he could breathe more easily without the "cold" weather of north Mississippi.

The Armour family reaction was negative to this move, and in the usual, white Southern response, the family—including Mother—blamed his wife Thelma for the move. They knew that Thurman would never have left the family ties to go to Florida on his own. Even at a young age, I noticed this dynamic, that all the negative reaction to Thurman's departure was visited upon his wife, not him. I later learned that Thurman had been the one who decided to make the move.

Despite this negative energy to the break-up of the family cluster by one of the six siblings, there was an upside to the move—the beach! Mother and Ila and her daughter, Linda (who had Downs Syndrome) and me took the long drive down to Tampa in 1957. It was the first long trip for Mother and me, and I was fascinated by it. We stayed overnight at a motel in Troy, Alabama, my first time in a motel. Little did I realize that when we were in Troy, we were near the place where John Lewis was living as a teenager. He would later be rejected from attending Troy

University because he was Black, a process that led Martin Luther King, Jr., to nickname him "the Boy from Troy."

I had never seen the ocean in person, and I remember first seeing it and hearing it and smelling it in Tampa—I was hooked! I felt like I was in an alien world, but it was so intriguing. We visited the tourist sites at Silver Springs and rode in the glass-bottom boats there. We visited the Seminole Native American village nearby, and I noticed a great dissonance in my experience of the Seminoles. In the movies that I watched on Saturday afternoons, the Indians were portrayed as savages, and I remember wondering how white people ever survived going out West, because the Indians were so violent and vicious. Mother never talked about people classified as "Indians." I had no idea up to that point that people classified as Indians, now Native Americans or Indigenous People, had ever lived in our area. Of course, they had—Choctaw people had been forced out like many others in the Trail of Tears. Part of my ignorance was that for white, Southern life, there was only one focus: those classified as "white," and those classified as "Black."

As we walked through the Seminole village in Florida and experienced them and talked with them, I began to wonder about those perceptions from the Western movies. The Seminole people did not seem so savage—in fact, they seemed just like me. I would later learn that it was not the people classified as "white" who had a hard time surviving in the West—it was rather those classified as "Indians." It was a whole new world there in Tampa, and it opened my eyes to many new horizons, though I would not act on these new perceptions for years.

I'll mention one more trip because it was another eye-opener. Mother wanted us to go to Chicago to visit her brother Bud and his family. They were very close as siblings, and it was a blow to her when the family left the South to head for Chicago. She saved up her money (in those envelopes in the dresser drawer, I assume), and in the summer of 1958, we boarded the City of New Orleans train in Memphis for an all-day ride to Chicago. I had been on trains before, but never a trip like this one. We had coach seating, and Mother told me to sit by the window. In a similar vein to the trip to Tampa, a whole new world opened to me as we rode through the countryside and the towns of Missouri and Illinois on the way to Chicago, rolling past farms and trees and fields. Mother had brought food for us, but she also wanted to treat us to a meal in the dining car of the train.

When we entered the dining car, our waiter was a well-uniformed and courteous Black man, and he seated us at a table with an older white gentleman, dressed in a coat and a tie. It was a more formal setting than I had ever experienced, and my eyes were wide in wonder: fine linen tablecloths, pieces of silverware arranged in patterns that I did not recognize, gleaming glasses at the table. The waiter gave us menus and asked what we would like to drink. My mother ordered coffee, and I got a soft drink. Mother introduced herself and me to the man across the table, but I do not remember his name. As I began to look at the menus, the prices were so high! I exclaimed to Mother: "Momma, these prices are too high—we cannot afford to eat here!" The man across from us chuckled when he heard my lament. Mother told me: "Nibs, I've been saving up my money for this trip, and I included money for this, so order what you want. Don't worry about it." "Okay, Momma, but the prices seem too high to me." I don't know if I embarrassed her in front of the man or not, but she shushed me quickly and told me to go ahead and order. I ordered a hamburger and fries and enjoyed them immensely. The man across from us signaled to the waiter for his check, and after he had paid his bill, he told Mother: "Mrs. Stroupe, it has been such a pleasure to meet you and your son. I so enjoyed eating with you. And, I hope that I haven't overstepped the line, but I went ahead and paid for your meals also. It's on me—use your meal money for something else."

These trips were not the only transitions for us. There was also a powerful internal transition happening in my life—adolescence and the hormones were hitting. Previous to this, girls had been "the plague," something inferior that boys and males had to put up with. Now with the hormones kicking in, suddenly I experienced this strange and compelling fascination with girls. I thought about this transition many years later when I was converted on the legitimacy of people of the same gender being attracted to one another. I asked the woman who was the vessel of my conversion: "When did you decide to become attracted to girls?" Her answer was: "About the same time that you did." I was puzzled by her answer for a few seconds, but then it hit me. She didn't decide to be attracted to girls—she just was. It took me back to this time in my life. I did not decide to become attracted to girls—it just happened. The simple lines were fading, and a new, complex world was upon me.

I did not want to talk with Mother about it, but she obviously knew. For my eleventh birthday party in 1957, she suggested that we have a small, sock hop dance party at our house. I could not believe that she would suggest that, but she did! We had pushed back the furniture in the small living/dining room and put on some records. We took off our shoes and danced and danced away to the burgeoning rock and roll music. Mother discreetly stayed in her bedroom (with the door open) and then brought out cake and ice cream. In the meantime, I kissed Ellen McCarty behind our couch—a discreet and utterly innocent kiss, but a kiss nonetheless. I had crossed over from shaking her off of my tricycle to kissing her.

In that same year I went to another birthday party and was dancing with a girl named Mary. We were dancing to Elvis' "All Shook Up," and I remember thinking that this was a new and powerful feeling, that everything was indeed all shook up. I was hoping that Mary would be my girlfriend, but she moved away before I could work up the nerve in my sixth-grade self to ask her to be my girlfriend. This began a time when I did not share as much with Mother, especially on these subjects. I could not imagine my mother ever having sexual feelings or inclinations, so I knew that she had no insights on this. In addition, I was conflicted on these feelings. The church world taught all of us that these feelings were naughty and were to be repressed. Yet the feeling was so powerful and later felt so good. The only talks that Mother and I ever had on this was her warning me of the dangers of masturbation. That talk did not prevent the practice, but it did add a lot of guilt.

This time of being all shook up also led to many fears developing in my adolescent self. My mother had a strong sense of her agency, and she was a take-charge type of person. In my childhood years, some of that rubbed off on me—I was curious and inquisitive. As I have indicated, my fear of abandonment made me more tentative and hesitant, but when I transitioned into adolescence, my fears gained strength. Some of you may be old enough to remember the "Thriller" TV series—no, not the Michael Jackson song, but rather the series in the late 1950's with Boris Karloff. Movies and TV shows have gotten a lot scarier and a lot more violent since those days, but this series was scary enough for me. It was about ghosts and evil monsters, and I remember watching one of them and being really scared by it. The next morning, I woke up in the darkness by myself. Mother had already moved into Gran's old bedroom, and on this winter morning, she was already up and fixing breakfast in the kitchen. Our house was small, but on that winter morning when I was so scared, it seemed like a long way from my bedroom to the kitchen. I lay in the darkness, petrified, knowing that at any moment the monster from the TV show would pop out of the closet in the darkness and snatch me away. I felt vulnerable and defenseless and alone—I was terrified.

I called out to Mother, as I had in many previous years: "Momma, are you there?" "Yes, Nibs," she replied, "if you are scared, come lay down in front of the heater until breakfast is ready." It was a great suggestion. In the long living/dining room area was a large gas space heater that was on and was warming the house. I still had to find the courage to get up and make a run for it, which I did. I jumped out of bed and sprinted to the little rug that was in front of the heater. There I lay down, letting the heat and the light from the kitchen and my Mother's noises comfort me. I was able to go back to sleep in the darkness, soothed by the warmth and light of my mother's presence.

Fear began to take deeper root in my heart, as the rivers of adolescence began to flow into me and into others. I became cautious and hesitant, afraid of failing and proving that I was inadequate. In the smash musical *Hamilton*, so many people were thrilled and identified with the multiracial Alexander Hamilton, but I identified with Aaron Burr in the play. He was so anxious and so cautious and so afraid to get out there. He stood in stark contrast to Hamilton, who was "not giving up my shot." I knew Burr's character very well. My mother, while not being as assertive as Hamilton, nonetheless took on challenges and rose to the occasion—she would do what she had to do to survive and thrive. For my part, I always tried to avoid challenges, and it took me a long while to learn that there is never a moment when there won't be challenges.

I became afraid of trying new things. I did not want to try to learn to ride a bicycle, because I could see that such an endeavor involved trial and error, and I could not stand to make many errors. To do so would reveal that I was inadequate, and that revelation would show everyone that my father had left me because I was unworthy. I longed to be able to ride a bike, but I was so afraid to try. Mother could not understand my hesitancy and fear on the bicycle, especially since she knew that I had such good hand-eye coordination. She bought me a bicycle for my birthday, hoping that I would try it out. She gently cajoled me to try it, but I continued to say that I was not ready—the bicycle sat on the side porch for weeks. I suspected—but, I never knew for sure—that my mother had arranged a method to get me on the bike.

One of my friends came over and asked to look at the bike, and he asked me if he could take a ride. I said "Sure," and he took off on down Porter Street. He came back in a few minutes, and said "Man, this is a great bike—I know you like riding it." I replied: "I haven't ridden it yet—I don't know how." "Wow," he said, "It's easy—let me show you." I stepped up on the bike, and he showed me how to do it—"Get going!" he hollered out. When I was hesitant, he gave the bike a shove, and off I went down the slight incline in the opposite direction on Porter Street. It was a great feeling! But he had not told me how to use the brakes—this was a pre-modern bike where one braked by putting pressure on the petals. So, I rolled on into a small ditch and crashed, but I was not hurt. I jumped up, and the thrill of riding overcame my fear of having made the mistake. I walked the bike back up the slight hill to our house, and my friend said: "Oh, crap, I forgot to tell you how to stop!" I said, "Show me." He did, and I got back on and rode that bike everywhere. When I came into the house, my mother was grinning widely and said, "I see you got the hang of it."

I was missing having a man in my life, but I did not want to tell my mother about that for many reasons, the main one being that it would imply that something was wrong with her raising me as a single mom. But the manly things came around, and I felt lost at sea. I began to have to tie a necktie for events, and I could not figure it out to save my soul. This was long before the web where I could have gone in private to learn it. I messed up many ties—I even began cutting them to make them shorter. The power of patriarchy began to show in me. I did not want to ask my mother to help me with this, because I felt that it was a man's work. It became obvious though, and Mother finally said one day after a particularly maddening attempt to tie the necktie correctly: "Nibs, do you want me to show you how to tie a tie?" "Wait, do you know how to do it?" She replied: "Of course, I used to tie Grandaddy's ties all the time." She showed me a simple knot that I have continued using until this day. The same process applied to learning to shave. When the peach fuzz arrived, an electric shaver appeared on my dresser, and my Mother said: "I thought that you would like this—it's a simple way to shave that Grandaddy and Hart and many of the men in our family use." My mother had begun to get the dynamics: my entrapment by patriarchy, a sense that men must teach me "manly" things. We never talked about it, and I'm guessing that she did not see it in such ideological terms. She began to work around my captivity to patriarchy and taught me many "manly" things, helping me to glimpse a different vision.

There were men in my life—men from family, from church, from school, from sports.

Grandaddy was a primary and intimate man until his death in 1955. I used to love climbing up in his lap, smelling his cigar breath, and hearing his great belly laugh, rooted in the Armour family's powerful sense of humor. Gran's younger son Brown was always gracious to me—he would pick me up for baseball games and other events, and he used to include me, with his own son Brown and other boys, on an annual summer pilgrimage to St. Louis to see the Cardinals play some baseball games. One of the men from church, Joe Brady, took an interest in me. Mother fixed his wife's hair, and he always seemed drawn to me. On one occasion in Little League baseball, I made an error at second base, an error that allowed the opposing team to score the winning runs in an important game. I ran from the field crying and cursing, and I parked myself out on the street, between cars so that I could weep at my error and my loss. Mother came out to console me, but I told her to go away. In a few minutes, Joe Brady came out and put his arm around me and told me about his errors in sports, indicating that they were part of the game. His male presence did the trick for me—I stopped crying and came to sit in the stands, where others expressed the same sentiment. Later, when we walked home together, Mother said: "I'm so glad that Mr. Brady came out to talk with you." As I replied, "Me, too," I knew instantly that she had sent him.

The first adult male to whom I was really drawn was a teacher and football coach in junior high school, Coach John Coleman. He was rugged and tough and had a reputation as a "badass," but he had a soft spot for me. I remember him talking about me in a basketball practice for junior high team. My lack of height was already marginalizing me as a basketball player, but I stayed with it because I loved sports so much and could stay in touch with what I imagined to be my masculinity. In his motivational talk, he brought up the work ethic of us players, and he singled me out to say: "Now, look at Nibs. He wants to be a professional athlete. He works his rear end off to be a good player, but he has some limitations. More importantly, he has a brilliant mind, and he uses that too. So I want all of you to think about finding your passions and to work your butts off to achieve your goals, like Nibs does." I was embarrassed but proud! From my view at that time, he was "a real man's man," and he had given me his blessing.

I was a person with a compassionate heart and was known as a kind person. I obviously got this from Mother, but I also felt marginalized because we were poor and because my father had left me. I was manless in a patriarchal world, and I felt on the margins of life. Though I did not recognize it at the time, this sense of being on the margins helped me lean toward the pain of others and lean towards others on the margins. When the time came for me to see myself and the world in a different way, I had been prepared by my mother and by my life experience. In my white, patriarchal Southern world, a male who was compassionate was seen as weaker than others, with the only exception being that such a man might make a good minister. Many people told me that I would likely become a minister because of my compassionate heart, but I resisted that notion because ministry seemed too effeminate to me, too emasculating. It would be a long time before I considered that perhaps that initial impression of me was correct for different reasons.

My connection of the church to "womanly" concerns was strengthened early in junior high school when the pastor's wife at our church decided to form a children's choir. I liked to sing and was good at it, so I did not have to be encouraged to do it. There were fifteen girls in the choir, and I was one of four boys. A problem developed—the pastor's wife decided that we should wear choir robes. We all were required to wear what I called blouses and skirts, and we four boys rebelled at wearing what we deemed to be girls' clothes, especially those skirts! I went home to tell Mother that I would never wear such a "sissy" uniform. She replied: "Yes, you are, Nibs. You signed up for the choir, and you will stick with it. You wear a uniform to play baseball, and you'll wear these uniforms for church." I wore them, but I was not happy about it, until I discovered that I could sneak in comic books underneath my skirt to read during the service.

The other adult male who resonated with me was the next minister of First Presbyterian Church, Reverend Harold Jackson, a native of Louisiana. He was a vigorous man, a fine preacher, and he believed in engaging modern life. He had an infectious belly laugh and a deep voice, and he was outgoing and compassionate. He gave me an image that if I were to become a minister, I did not have to yield my masculinity to do it. Mother really liked Harold, and he often came up for visits. One of the reasons that he liked her was that he could call on her to provide financial assistance to families in need in the community. When he made the requests, she would not ask him to justify it, or to tell her why that particular family should get the money. It was simple: if she had the money, she would share it. Later on, in my ministry with people who were in financial difficulties, I so appreciated people like Mother who would not ask me to justify the request for money for others—if they had it, we would get it. Harold also encouraged us to think about a larger world. In 1963 he led our youth group in a reading of a play about Dietrich Bonhoeffer entitled *Cup of Trembling*. Bonhoeffer was a Lutheran minister in Germany, who made a difficult decision to participate in a plot to assassinate Adolph Hitler. He was later executed for that action. It would take me a decade to realize that Harold had us reading this play about resistance just as the civil rights struggle was taking off in the South. He also encouraged me to read Alan Paton's 1948 novel about apartheid *Cry, the Beloved Country*, in which I would meet a Black man for the first time.

Gender issues became huge to me in those years, as the hormones kicked in, and I became attracted to girls and women. My sexuality was not an area where I would ever let Mother in. Accompanying my hormones was a huge attack of acne, which mortified me and which would last for years. Our only conversation on sex came in the car on the way home from church one Sunday. I had begun to masturbate, and I would often cut out photos of attractive women from *Look Magazine* and others. I kept these photos in a shoebox under my bed and used them as needed. On this drive home from church, Mother said to me: "Nibs, I found your shoebox full of pictures of women. I want you to be careful with that—boys who do that sort of thing often have to go to psychiatrists." I was mortified that she had found the box, but I knew that she was wrong—my friends were already looking at *Playboy Magazine* and using it. I was using relatively innocent photos from popular magazines. I didn't argue with her, but it solidified my determination to keep her out of that part of my life. I simply said "Yes, Mother, I'll be careful." I got rid of that box and became much more careful. We never discussed sex again.

Mother was always interested in current affairs and in politics. The voting precinct was near our house, and I remember Mother coming home one day after work with steam coming out of her ears. She had been to vote on her walk home from work, and one of the male poll workers asked her for whom she was voting. She replied: "That's nobody's business but mine." He shot back: "Oh, we'll know later on today who you voted for." She gave a sharp answer: "Well, that may be true, but I better not ever hear about it, or else you will wish that you never took a look at my ballot." In light of the lies about the 2020 elections and the attempt to "identify" who voted for whom through signature matching, this early conversation that Mother had becomes so much more powerful and relevant.

In the 1950's the Civil Rights Movement began to be publicized in the South. I do not remember being aware of the lynching of Emmett Till in 1955 or of the Montgomery bus boycott that began that same year. My first awareness of the Movement was in 1957 when the Little Rock Nine integrated the white public schools there. Most of my friends began using the name of the primary organizer, Daisy Bates, as a curse word. I took it up too, and it would be a long time later that I would learn that the demonic powers were not in Daisy Bates but were rather in me and in my friends. I did feel some compassion for the Nine, and I was stunned at the screaming white crowds that surrounded those children. I was embarrassed and even a bit shocked when President Eisenhower sent in the Screaming Eagles paratroopers from Ft. Campbell in Tennessee to restore order. I mentioned this to my mother, and for one of the few times, she shut down the discussion: "Don't mess with this, Nibs, and don't fret about it. It is not our business." Her tone told me that this was not negotiable, so I dropped it. It did not last long, however, because she had raised me to think for myself and to have a compassionate heart. With that combination in the white supremacist South, a change was coming. It wasn't in the near future, but there were definitely markers on the road.

6

A Change Is Coming

HERE COME THE 1960'S! It did not feel exuberant like that when I entered the decade at my segregated Central High School as a ninth grader. By the time the decade ended, however, my mother's life and my life would be dramatically changed. I began the decade as a conservative, white male Southerner, with all the baggage that entails. Mother began it as a conservative but compassionate single mom, trying to get me through high school and on to college. Both Mother and I changed in this decade—no one who lived through the 60's would ever be the same. Indeed, we as a culture have been fighting over the 1960's for some sixty years now, as the 2020 presidential election demonstrated.

The decade began in a Presidential election year, not unlike the one of 2020. Our civics teacher's first project for us that fall was an assignment to write a paper on the two major candidates for President, Richard Nixon and John Kennedy. We were to give their background and indicate for whom we would vote and why. I was interested in politics but had not paid much attention to the presidential contest. I went home to ask Mother, and we had a conversation about it. She indicated that she was going to vote for Richard Nixon, that she did not like Kennedy because he was a Roman Catholic and might be bound to the Pope, and that she had liked President Eisenhower—Nixon had been Vice-President during those years. She then added: "I do not like the way Richard Nixon looks, but I will vote for him. He looks deceitful to me, but I guess that all politicians are." Little did either of us know that a little over a decade later, the nickname "Tricky Dick" would be appended to Richard Nixon. Mother often judged politicians by how they looked. She was a post-modern person in that sense: image is everything. She hated Lyndon Johnson because of the way he looked: "You know that he is lying, no matter what he says," was her way of describing it. For that year of 1960, she was a Richard Nixon woman.

I leaned heavily towards Nixon in my report, and in my concluding argument for whom I would vote, if I could vote at thirteen (voting age was still at twenty-one at that time), I indicated that I would choose Nixon. I gave several reasons, but these were the three main reasons:

- Kennedy does not have enough experience in governments or foreign affairs. Nixon accompanied President Eisenhower on many foreign tours.
- Kennedy wanted to give up Quemoy and Matsu to the Russians. [Raise your hand if you have ever heard of them!] The old saying goes: "if you give them an inch, they'll take a mile." These islands are important in the defense of Formosa [modern day Taiwan].
- Kennedy's ideas were too wild. His ideas about teachers, help for the aged, and schools had too much socialism in them. [Echoes of the 2020 election]

As I entered high school, I would ride the bus to school for the first time in my life. The bus stop was about a block down the hill from my house, so it wasn't a far walk, but it was incentive to get my driver's license. We still shared a car with Aunt Ila, but I could get it enough to mitigate riding to school on the bus. In Arkansas you can still get a driver's license at age fourteen because of all the farms, so I began to work on getting the license in the tenth grade. Because I had a strong incentive, I was not afraid of trying this new adventure. Mother gave me driving lessons, and she was a good, patient teacher. As in my younger days, she would come home from work and take time to take me out for driving lessons. We also would practice on Sunday afternoons, taking the long drive on Highway 44 to Elaine. I was given the driving test by an Arkansas state trooper, and I failed! When I asked him why I failed, he told me that I had forgotten to put on the emergency brake when he had me stop on a hill. Also, he noted, with his stern trooper face, that I had looked over my right shoulder when backing up rather than looking over my left shoulder and using the sideview mirror.

I was greatly saddened, and I told Mother: "I will never pass this test." Mother responded: "Nibs, you will pass the test. You are a good driver. Just get back out there and do it. Remember how you got back out there and got Ellen off your tricycle when you were little? Just do that. You can do it." My cousin Brown and other friends also encouraged me. So, I tried again and passed—yay! On the first day after getting my license, I walked down to the beauty shop to get the car from Mother. As I was pulling the car out from the parking space, I had a minor accident—wow! Indeed, I had not looked over my left shoulder to see a car coming nearby. Nobody hurt, no real damage. Mother was not scolding—she said: "This was actually an early warning—you now see how quickly this can happen. Nobody hurt—just be careful." She must have been raging inside, especially at the additional rise in car insurance costs, but she never demonstrated it to me.

Early in my high school years, Mother gave up managing Ted's Beauty Shop and became an operator at another shop in town. I thought that it was a demotion for her, but she told me that she was tired of trying to manage Ted's, trying to come up with salaries for the four operators and two part-time workers. "I'd rather just worry about my own salary," was the way that she put it. She had a strong following from Ted's and brought most of them with her, so the new shop was glad to get her, and she made more money there.

She was an avid reader and was always reading books on religion. She leaned towards the progressive side in her readings. She found women at church who would form a central core of friends and thinkers and investigators over the years, and they crossed class lines in doing so. She and Mary Wetzel, a native Ohioan who had gone to the University of Arkansas, became best friends for the rest of their lives. They encouraged one another in enlarging their minds and their points of view. Mary's husband Bob, a school teacher and woodworker, joined in the friendship, and he became a valuable ally for Mother in her own work of re-finishing furniture. Mother and Mary and two other women, Maud Cain Howe and Lyda Kitchens, became a core group of church women who were beginning to think of women's rights and to think of expanding their horizons. Maud Cain and Lyda were widows of wealthy planters, while Mother and Mary were middle class and lower middle class, so it was a fascinating crossing of many boundaries.

Mother also stayed in touch with her rural roots by becoming good friends with her next door neighbor, Sue Sellers. They would talk across the small fence almost every day in the summer evenings and visit one another in their homes when the weather turned cooler. Sue was an organizer and active person, and her husband L.P. was a part-time farmer and a worker at a power plant. Both of them were what could be described as "good, country folk." As I began to branch out in high school, these friendships would fill in the gap left in Mother's heart by my finding a larger world. Mother never complained to me about this—she simply went out and got what she needed in terms of friendship and mitigating the loneliness.

I continued to be an excellent student in high school. Though I made a few B's, I made almost all A's, and Mother expected that. Her main emphasis continued to be my behavior. She indicated that if I made an occasional B, she knew that I would bring it back up to an A the next semester, which I did. She tolerated that variation, but she made it plain, as she had all through my school years, that she never wanted to hear of me causing any trouble at school or anywhere else. And I never did. Only on one occasion did I get a spanking in junior high school. I grabbed my ankles and got four whacks on the butt, given by the principal for going up the wrong way on the one-way stairs. I thought that I would get another whipping when I got home and told Mother, but she let that one pass. She said that I been wrong, but it was not a "spankable" offense.

I was confident in the classroom, but outside the classroom, I was more anxious. Though I was attracted to girls, I never had a girlfriend in high school. I had dates for dances and movies, but my anxiety overcame any romantic impulses that I might have had. I was afraid to get serious with anyone because I was afraid that any girlfriend would see that I was not a real man. I had dropped out of school sports by high school, so that made me question myself and my manhood. I liked sports, with its discipline and adrenalin and teamwork, but I was simply not big enough or good enough to avoid being a benchwarmer. I decided that I would stick with what I could do well—academics. Mother never pushed me to date. She never asked me or teased me about girlfriends—her lack of pressure in this area helped me to sense that I could be normal without having a girlfriend. This orientation helped me move some energies toward finding a deeper and larger world. Her antennae were strong on this one.

That larger world would come calling in 1962, the year of the Cuban missile crisis and the Civil Rights Movement. There were increasing tensions between the USA and the Soviet Union, especially as the Soviets began to test the new and youngish President Kennedy. They had known that President Eisenhower was a warrior, and they wanted to find out about Kennedy. In the nuclear age, we began to think about the unthinkable: a nuclear war. Schools and homes began to make preparations. We would have nuclear war drills in school—in an exercise that seems ridiculous now, we would have school drills in which we would get under our desks to simulate a nuclear bomb attack. Oakhurst Presbyterian Church, where Caroline and I served so many years as pastors, had two concrete basements that still had "certified nuclear bomb shelter" signs on them. Our neighbors, the Paines, invited Mother and me to help them prepare a bomb shelter in their home, in exchange for allowing us to come into the shelter in case of attack. Johnny Paine and I had the duty of keeping the shelter area clean and well-stocked. My mother recalled the years of fear from "Big Momma" who always insisted on building a storm shelter in the tornado alley of north Mississippi. As Mother put it, "I think of Big Momma when we work on this—a big difference, though, now it involves millions of people, not just one family or one town."

This anxiety about nuclear war was discussed often, and we held our collective breath in September, 1962, as the negotiations and threats over the Soviet missiles in Cuba played out. There were many discussions in the culture and in the church over whether owners of bomb shelters should allow others to come in to the shelter if there were an attack. As a youth, I was asked to write an op-ed for the local paper on whether to allow others into one's bomb shelter. It was entitled "Teen Talks," and Mother helped me to develop some ideas about it, and to shorten it down to meet the word limit—already I was demonstrating the preacherly tendency to go on and on and on.

Here's an excerpt from that column, which appeared in late 1961 in the *Helena World*: "Everyone should have a fallout shelter. All who do not will be killed almost instantly in the event of nuclear war. . .How can we win the world for democracy if we are not prepared for war? We might as well give up places like Berlin and South Viet Nam if we can't fight for them. . .Of course problems will arise. If we are attacked and someone wants to come into your shelter, what will you do? Even though this is a hard decision to make, you must let him in. You are your brother's keeper." Here I see the combination of my white Southern militant view, mitigated by the compassion of my mother.

The world was becoming larger for me and for many others. No longer confined to the South, with television news coming in from around the country and from all over the world, I began to hear echoes of a deeper and larger world. That world would leap out at me in a place much closer to home: Oxford, Mississippi. In 1961, a bridge was completed from Helena over the Mississippi River towards Clarksdale and other places. Up until that time, a ferry was used to transport cars and trucks and even trains across the mile-wide Mississippi River at Helena. In the fall of 1962, I and many others would be drawn to Oxford, because a Black man named James Meredith had applied to attend his state university, the University of Mississippi at Oxford, known as "Ole Miss."

This event and process was the first time that I had really noticed the Civil Rights Movement raging in the South. I had engaged the Little Rock Nine in 1957, but the sit-ins and freedom rides had bypassed my consciousness. I do remember noticing the violence against the freedom riders when their bus was attacked in Anniston, Alabama. I told Mother that I felt bad about that, but that they deserved it because they were outside agitators. Mother replied: "No one deserves to have that happen to them, but I do wish that they would leave us alone down here in the South and let us work something out."

Because Ole Miss was so close to Helena, my perceptions picked up in 1962. This was close to us, both geographically and emotionally. Federal courts ordered the university to admit Meredith, but the governor, Ross Barnett, refused to permit Meredith to attend because it violated the state's segregation laws. Although reluctant to get involved, President Kennedy, through his brother and Attorney General Robert Kennedy, decided to force the issue. A confrontation was building, and the talk among us high school boys was that we should plan to drive over to Oxford (seventy miles away) to help protect Southern whiteness and segregation from the invading N-words and Yankees. I told Mother about the idea, and she ended my involvement right there: "Nibs, that is a stupid idea. Someone will get hurt and maybe even get killed over there. You won't be among them. Just drop that idea and that talk right now." I'm guessing that everyone's parents did the same—that conversation ended among us white boys. As I reflect back on it, I don't know that I would have gone over to Oxford, if it had been allowed. I did have just a little bit of sympathy for Meredith—why couldn't he go to his state university? A little crack in the wall of white supremacy in my heart was continuing, but I wasn't admitting it, and I certainly wasn't telling anyone.

My dilemma was demonstrated to me only a few weeks later, when I accompanied Brown and his dad Mr. Higgins (Gran's son) to the Ole Miss-Kentucky football game in Jackson, Mississippi. This was shortly after the violence at Oxford, in which many people were hurt, and one man was killed in the fight between white supremacists and Federal marshals. Mother did not want me to go to the game in this type of atmosphere, but Mr. Higgins guaranteed my safety, and being a huge Ole Miss football fan, I was itching to go to the game. Governor Ross Barnett showed up at the game, and during the halftime ceremony, he made a defiant speech supporting segregation. He also led us in singing "Go Mississippi, keep rolling along, Go Mississippi, you cannot go wrong." My cousin Brown and I felt uncomfortable in participating, but with all the white people shouting and singing around us, we stood up and sang too. I still have the program from that game, and I can still remember the words and the tune to that song.

During these months of the fall of 1962, we survived the Cuban missile crisis and the integration of Ole Miss by James Meredith, but the world had gotten so much larger to me by then. The month of May, and the summer of 1963, would become an important time for Mother and me in this movement. As I noted in a Chapter Three, I saw the movie *To Kill A Mockingbird* three nights in a row in May, 1963. It helped to open my eyes on several levels, on race and on parental presence. In that same month I learned that I had been accepted into a summer science program at that same Ole Miss. I would attend in mid-June, and it would be the first time that I had left home without my mother since I was a small child. Before that time arrived, I noted in my diary on May 29 that there was a rumor that "Negroes would attend the Delta Dance" that night because Bo Diddley was playing. I asked Mother about this, and she diminished the rumor: "They know better than that." She was correct—no "Negroes" attended.

On June 8, 1963, I wrote in my diary that "I begin my longest journey tomorrow." I was heading for the Ole Miss Summer Science Camp, and I did not want to go. I did not think that I could survive outside my small, known world, especially without Mother or any friends around. It would be the first time away from home on my own—no friends or family for eight weeks. I had just returned from a week at Boys State, the American Legion state camp that brought white boys together for bonding and indoctrination. Because of this, I did not have much time to sink into the doldrums prior to going to Ole Miss." Mother perceived my distress and asked me why I didn't want to go. My answer was that I would be lonely, that I would miss my friends, that I would miss her. She replied: "Nibs, this is part of growing up. You were honored to be nominated and honored to be invited. You can go on over there and find out if you really like science and math. You haven't been challenged much here, but you will be there. And you will meet people from all over the country. It's only eight weeks, and it's not far away—I will come to see you while you are there, and I am sure that some of your friends will come over."

Mother's thoughts were helpful, but I was still not assuaged. Since it was not our turn to have the car that weekend, our next door neighbors, Fannie and Mack Thompson, were going to drive us over there. That was a wise decision by my mother—having someone else involved in the trip would add to the pressure for me to go. On the day of departure, I remember sitting on the cedar chest in my room, looking out the south window at the backyard, with its flowers blooming and the rising of the hill into Crowley's Ridge. I simply did not want to go—I did not think that I could survive the science camp. I am not sure what I believed would happen. I knew that I could handle the academics, but I was not sure about all the rest, especially meeting new people and not being anchored at home. As I sat there on the cedar chest in a state of mourning, I tried to think of every excuse possible to postpone and even cancel the trip. As I sat there, Mother came into the room to say: "Nibs, we need to go. You will do fine over there. I am so proud of you for doing this."

I reluctantly picked up my suitcase and walked out the door, turning to the east to go next door to get into the Thompson's car. It would not occur to me until decades later that this was a big transition for Mother as well. Though I am sure that she looked forward to having some time on her own, I am sure that this was a fulcrum point for her also. I had been the center of her life for so long, and this departure for Ole Miss was the beginning of a significant change for her as well.

We arrived in Oxford at Ole Miss, and I stayed in Guess Hall there. I will always remember the smell of the dorm, especially the stairs, with its mixture of new rubber and concrete and metal. All the science campers were white, and most were from the South. Mother was right about the academics—I handled those. I also discovered, to my surprise, that I could handle the rest of life that summer. The first week was difficult because I was so apprehensive, and I remember expressing my woes in a letter to her. She replied in a letter: "Do hope you are settled in your room, busy and happier by the time you get this. . . . . We all miss having you at home, but 'this, too, will pass,' as the old saying goes. Be sweet and let me know if you need anything. All my love, Mother."

In one of the orientation tours that first week, one of the upperclassmen showed us around the Ole Miss campus, and he proudly pointed out the bullet holes, still visible in the Lyceum Building, where the white violence had erupted the previous fall in response to James Meredith's entry as a student. I felt a little bit of pride, but I also felt a bit uneasy—why celebrate this violence, even if it was protective of whiteness? It just seemed like macho madness to me. When I wrote Mother about it, she replied that she understood why white people would not want Black people in school with them, but she did not approve of the violence that was used in response. She also cautioned me to stay out of that kind of stuff.

I was among several students interviewed by newspapers from cities nearby: the Memphis *Commercial Appeal* and the Jackson *Clarion-Ledger*. Mother clipped the article from the *Commercial Appeal*, which we received at our home in Helena. I had not seen the one from the *Clarion-Ledger*, but we did receive it from a strange source. After I had returned home from Ole Miss, I got a letter from Jackson, Mississippi, with the return address written: "Stroupe, 2536 Woodbine, Jackson, Mississippi." My heart jumped when I saw the return address—it was from my father! It was the first time that I had ever received anything from him. I held the letter in my hand for a few moments, feeling many emotions—excitement, curiosity, fear. I opened the letter carefully and found a typed note. To my great disappointment, it was from his second wife Vivian, enclosing the newspaper article and congratulating me on my accomplishments and asking me to give the enclosed check to my mother. The fury grew within me, and I flung the letter across the living room and hollered out: "That SOB could not even bring himself to write me!!!! He had to have his wife do it." I added a few more curse words, and I was disappointed and hurt. I later shared the letter and the check with Mother when she got home from work, and I told her that it was strange to hear from them. I did not share with her the level of my fury and hurt. She told me: "I'm glad that they are proud of you. I sure am."

Mother was right on that and on the Ole Miss experience too. It did begin to build a bit of confidence in me, confidence that I could hold my own out in the world, confidence in my academic abilities, and confidence that I had an identity of my own. I also discerned at the Ole Miss science camp that math and science were not my passions. I was very good at them, but they did not move my heart.

As August rolled around, I began to focus on my senior year in high school, which would begin at the end of that month. Being at Ole Miss had gotten me to thinking about college, which I had only considered in passing in previous days. This was before the high-pressure, high-stakes time of today, when there is an entire industry built on getting high school students into their preferred colleges, and much corruption, as has been recently noted. Even though I broadened my world that summer, I still did not know if I wanted to leave home. Mother asked me what colleges I might want to apply to. I told her about my reluctance, but she made it plain: "You're going to college somewhere—you've got the brains, and I'll come up with the money. You'll be the first one in college. I wanted so much to go to college, but we could not afford it, so you are going. Just begin to think about where you want to try to go. You are going somewhere to college." I didn't have a choice. While I didn't want to leave home, I had gotten a taste of a larger world (even if it was Oxford, Mississippi), and I wanted to get out of the small town mindset and world of Helena, Arkansas.

Before I could move in that direction, events in August would open my mind and heart a bit wider. We had heard the news of a march on Washington in late August. In the white Helena world, thirty-four-year-old Martin Luther King, Jr., was a charlatan and/or a communist, who was determined to get money from unsuspecting "Negroes" and white people who were fools. Yet something was stirring in me—*To Kill a Mockingbird* and the summer at Ole Miss had begun to turn my heart to think about a larger and deeper world. The March on Washington took place a few days before my senior year in high school began, and I asked Mother about it. In her guarded way, she indicated that while they had the right to march, she did not agree with their point of view. "I know that some people treat Negroes badly, but most of us try to be decent. I just wish that they would leave things the way they are. You need to be careful with this stuff, Nibs."

On the day of the march, I decided to watch the coverage on television in the safety of my home, with none of my friends around. I did not want to be considered a "N-lover," but I was curious about the march. I listened to Dr. King's speech, and I was astonished! His eloquence and his passion were powerful, and I simply could not believe that all the 250,000 people attending the march were dupes and fools. There seemed to be part of another dimension, of another story that I had missed. I began to consider how I could find out more about that story. I didn't want to go too far, so I didn't share my reaction with many people. I did share it with

Mother, and she replied: "I've heard that he was quite impressive, Nibs, but you need to be careful. This is incendiary stuff." I wasn't planning to go very far with it, but I wasn't going back either. As I recall, I shared my awareness with three other people: my high school friend David Billings, my minister Harold Jackson, and my English teacher Vera Miller. David and I had a growing friendship, and he, too, had family roots in Mississippi. He and I would talk a lot about religion and about politics, and he, too, was intrigued with the March and with King's speech. Both Reverend Jackson and Mrs. Miller suggested that I read the book *Cry, the Beloved Country* by South African writer Alan Paton.

Paton's book was written in 1948, and it was about the dehumanizing effects of apartheid in South Africa. In that book, I met my first Black person. I had seen many Black people in Helena, but I did not think of them as people like me until I met the Reverend Steven Kumalo in Paton's book. Reverend Kumalo was an African pastor in a rural area who went searching for his son, who had gone to the city to look for work. It was a painful and scary search for him, and though I did not identify the connection with me at the time, I have since made the connection: the estrangement between father and son. I don't remember the page number when it hit me. Somewhere in the search for his son, Reverend Kumalo came alive for me in a way that no other person classified as "Black" ever had. I remember looking up from the page and thinking: "Reverend Kumalo sounds like me. Black people may be human beings like me." It is a sad but true admission—I met my first Black person as a fictional character in a book written by a white man. In the early fall of 1963, the idea that Black people were human beings was a revolutionary thought for me. I talked with Mother about it, and she agreed that she was wondering too, if Black people might be people like us. Yet she repeated her earlier warnings: don't mess with this stuff, Nibs. It is dangerous out there.

In just a few days, Mother's warning would be born out. Four little Black girls were killed in Sunday school in their church in Birmingham on September 15. It was as if the white supremacists were answering King's vision and speech from the August march on Washington. I noted to myself that they seemed also to be answering Mother's warning too. Mother was upset about the bombing, but she would not renounce the white supremacy in which we lived and had our being.

My senior year had begun. Changes happened almost right away. In mid-September, the principal of the school called me in on Tuesday, and I was concerned that I had done something wrong. He told me: "Nibs,

Mr. Hill [the math teacher] has a family emergency, and he needs to leave school today and will be gone the rest of the week. He and I have talked, and we think that you are the one to teach his classes for him this week. We know that you can do it. Is it something that you are willing to try? I will give you all the backing that you need, especially in the discipline area." I was shocked but also highly flattered, and I replied: "Yes, Mr. Christian, I will give it a try. If it is not working, can I let you know that too?" "Of course, but we don't think that you will have a problem at all. You let me know if you do. Of course, you will be excused from all your other classes this week."

When Mother got home from work, I told her the good and scary news. A big smile broke out on her face, and she replied: "Nibs, I know that you can do this. You know all the math already. You'll have to do a lot more work, but I'm so proud that they asked you, that they think that you are mature enough to do this." I went to work on it, and the week went surprisingly well. I taught all the math classes from beginner's math through trigonometry (we didn't have calculus in high school in those days). Having to master the lesson so that I could teach it to others actually deepened my understanding of the mathematics on all levels. Later, Mother would tell me about a conversation that she had with a woman who was one of her customers at the beauty shop. She told Mother that her son said that for the first time, he understood math when I taught it. She noted that I seemed to understand the struggles that students had, and of course I did because I was one of those students. It was another experience that continued to build my confidence that I could survive out in the world.

The Civil Rights Movement continued to break out all over the South, but my friends and I had little awareness of its depth. I do not remember being aware of the Birmingham Campaign in the spring of 1963, but as I noted, I was aware of the Birmingham bombing in September. In my diary on November 17, I wrote a line about a "Negro sit-in last night." I had forgotten about that until I began work on this memoir. In an article in the *Arkansas Historical Quarterly*, I discovered that the Student Non-Violent Coordinating Committee (SNCC) had come into Phillips County in late October, 1963.[1] SNCC had started in Little Rock and Pine Bluff in Arkansas in the early 1960's, and they had some success there. Because of that, they decided to test their mettle and move "toward areas

---

1. Randy Finley, "Crossing the White Line."

of more hard-core racism" of the Mississippi River Delta.² They chose Phillips County, the largest county in the Delta, focusing on Helena, West Helena, and Forrest City. Connecting with local Black churches and businesspeople, they targeted restaurants, the public library, and the public swimming pool for integration. They made it in some of the restaurants and in the library, but the swimming pool was too much. The white police chief indicated that "white and black adolescents would not mingle, scantily clad, in the pools of Helena as long as he was chief of police. He arrested the three young men. Ford and Allen were beaten while in jail."³

The same article also noted that John Lewis and Julian Bond had come to West Helena in 1965 to work on voter registration. None of this stayed in my consciousness, if it was ever there. I checked with my longtime friend and activist David Billings, and he did not recall it either. This process must have been the talk of the town, but I do not remember any conversations with Mother concerning this. By then I had left the public swimming pool because of the proximity of the Paines' pool across the street from our house. Perhaps if I had still been swimming in the public pool, we would have discussed it.

There was an event in the fall of 1963 that was a huge shock to all of us, no matter our political persuasion or our racial classification. On Friday morning, November 22, as our high classes were changing from one period to the next, the school janitor said to many of us in the hall: "The President's been shot." He was always teasing with students, so at first we thought he was kidding. He said, "No, no, President Kennedy's been shot in Dallas, and they are not sure that he will live." By then, the school was aflutter with murmurings and crying, and TV's and radios in the classrooms were turned on. We soon learned the awful truth: President John F. Kennedy had been shot and killed in a motorcade in Dallas. It was stunning to all of us. Just emerging from the placidity of the 1950's, shaken up by the Civil Rights Movement, and wondering about this new president—those of us classified as "white" still had a belief in the stability of the system, in the normal order of things as they were. The assassination of President Kennedy was a lightning bolt that told us that the world as we knew it was over. We did not process it that way on that terrible weekend, but as we reflected on it, it became clear: the world that we had known was changing.

2. Finley, "Crossing," 119.
3. Finley, "Crossing," 123.

As my ninth-grade civics paper proclaimed, I was not a fan of President Kennedy, but his assassination changed all of that. Seeing him as a martyr, experiencing that weekend of national mourning—these caused all of us to wonder what was real and permanent. For me and for many others, it was like an explosion that rocked the 1960's and sent many of us out into the world, seeking a new and different way. Mother and I discussed it when she got home from work. She was as shocked as I was, and she was even more shocked when his alleged assassin was also shot and killed. Conspiracy theories have spun out ever since, but whoever killed him seems less important than the total shock that it provided to the American system. It was as if the 60's had said to the 50's: "Your time is up."

Monday, November 25 was a day of national mourning that included the funeral for President Kennedy. Schools were closed, so I stayed home to watch the funeral on television. Mother went on to work, but "Miss Martha" was in our house, doing some ironing work for Mother. She was an African-American cleaning woman at the beauty shop where Mother worked, and Mother had hired her on a part-time basis to do some housework after Gran had died. On that day, she too was watching the televised funeral, and I noticed that she was crying as she ironed and watched. I was surprised that she was crying—I suppose that I thought that since she was Black, she did not have human emotions like those of us classified as "white" did. When Mother came home from work that day, I was telling her about Miss Martha and about my surprise at the crying, and she replied: "Well, Nibs, they do cry, they do feel, and many Negro people really liked President Kennedy. So it is no surprise that Miss Martha was crying. It's a sad day for us all."

During that eventful autumn, Mother and I were looking at colleges for me. I was not certain where I wanted to go, and we had severe financial limits. Our pastor, the Reverend Harold Jackson, suggested that I think about going to Davidson College in North Carolina—he still had visions of my becoming a pastor. I applied to Davidson and got accepted. It was surprising to me, because I had heard that it was good academically and was a tough place to get in. They gave me a good financial package, and Mother and I decided that Davidson was the place for me to go for college. It was relatively far away from Helena—almost 700 miles. We talked about the distance, since I had such a hard time leaving for the science camp at Ole Miss. She warned me that we could only afford one plane trip home, and that would likely be at Christmas. I was flattered to be accepted, so I decided to pitch my tent at Davidson.

We made it into spring 1964, and then my high school career was closing. In March, it was announced at school that I would be valedictorian of the graduating class. I was surprised, but neither Mother nor anyone else was. I began working on my valedictory speech, and Mother and many others helped me. I typed up my two-page speech and committed it to memory. I did not take any notes with me to the podium. Aunt BB, who had come down from Memphis for the event told me that she was really nervous because I didn't have notes. She told Mother, as I began my speech: "I'm so nervous, I don't think that I can enjoy the speech. Why didn't he take any notes?" She told BB: "Don't worry—he's got it down. He rehearsed it many times. He'll be fine." I quoted from President Kennedy's inaugural speech—by then, I had come around to support him after his martyrdom. I closed the speech with quotes from Thoreau and Emerson: "Thoreau once said, 'If a man does not keep pace with his companions, perhaps it is because he hears a different drummer. Let him keep step to the music which he hears, however measured or far away.' Thus, it must be with us. Our challenge is before us. Win or lose, we must be guided by Emerson's quote: 'The true test of a civilization is not the size of cities, nor the crops, nor the census—no, but the kind of man the country turns out.'"

I got through the speech without a hitch, and I had a great time that night at parties and dances—I wrote in my diary: "This was the best night of my life."

7

You Can't Go Home Again

It was sometime during my college years that Mother and I drove across the Mississippi River on the Helena Bridge. It was a hot summer day, with a blazing sun beating down on us. The humidity was so high that it felt like weather that we were wearing. I was a reluctant participant in what had become for Mother a new avocation. She had found some friends who loved to go to the sandbars of the River on the Mississippi side to search for rocks and other treasures. One of the friend's sons was an archaeologist, and he had nurtured them into it. They would bring picnic lunches and drinks, sit down in the sandy, rocky terrain and look for river rocks of different colors and shapes. They would go late in the morning or early in the afternoon so that the dreaded mosquitoes and other pests would not swarm them as much as they would later in the day. They traded freedom from mosquitoes for searing heat.

Mother had been asking me to go with her on several of these occasions, and I had declined to go. On this particular day, she prevailed on me, and I agreed to go. For her and her friends, it was an amateur archaeological dig—looking for arrowhead tips, small relics, and fascinating stones, sometimes an occasional agate. I did not mind the heat, for I had grown up with it—I still prefer 90 degrees to 30 degrees. What got to me was the boredom—the tedious turning over of the rocks, the sifting through various kinds of soils. Mother and her friends, however, were thoroughly enjoying it—joking and laughing, celebrating small discoveries, stopping for a drink and sitting back in their beach chairs. I was wise enough by this time not to obviously show my boredom, but it was a long trip. On the way back home, Mother said: "You were really bored out there today, weren't you?" I replied: "Not really, it's just not my thing—sort of like fishing for me. Lots of folks like to fish, but I'm not patient enough. I noticed that you and Miss Lorena and Miss Dorothy sure loved it, though. And that's a good thing." She dropped her voice a bit, "Well, I sure wished you liked it as much as I do." Trying to stem her disappointment, I said: "it's just not my thing—you know me, I like to be up and moving. But I'm sure glad that you like it."

As high school graduation approached, Mother and I had begun to split up, not so much on ideology yet, but in physical and emotional experience. My imminent departure for college meant that neither of us would experience each other on a daily basis. For the first seventeen years of my life, we had been the primary relationship for each other. This movement out of the nest happens to everyone. It is part of the maturing process, but it was especially true for us. She had been my guiding light all of my life, and now I would be moving out on my own. I was aware of this shift in my own life, and I was frightened by it. It would only be later in my life that I would reflect on the shifts in her own journey: who would she be now that I was leaving home?

She had already begun to make the necessary shifts to re-orient her life. Rather than turning to a man to help in this shift in meaning, she found other pursuits. She searched far and wide for furniture that she could re-finish. What had begun as a necessity had now become a vocation. She went weekly to the sandbar, and she deepened her reading. She found different sets of friends, almost always female-centered: her next door neighbor Sue, the sandbar group, a reading group at church. Through her sandbar friends, she would meet a Lyons, Mississippi native named Olive who would later pull her into the psychic world. She began to think about seeking to get her instructor's license in cosmetology so that she could teach students to be beauty operators. As it turned out, that move would lead her to work with these young women to help them develop their life skills, skills discerned from her "college of knowledge" that she had developed as a single mother in a patriarchal world.

First, however, she had to get me out of the nest, which proved to be more difficult than she and I might have imagined. I had applied to Davidson College and had gotten in, and I had surprisingly gotten a decent financial package. I had also gotten scholarships from the Rotary and

Kiwanis Clubs and from the church. During the summer of 1964, Mother and I packed up my trunk and shipped it off to Davidson late in August. The plan was for Aunt BB and Uncle Hart to come from Memphis to spend the night with us, as they often did. On Labor Day, they would take me to Memphis to catch the plane there for the flight to Charlotte near Davidson. I was loath to go, to leave home, but I did not have the same dread that I had the previous summer when I went to Ole Miss. Mother kept encouraging me, telling me that I could do it. She knew that I could do the academics, but she was concerned about the distance—it was too far to drive. She could only afford one trip home during the school year (for Christmas), so that would be a gigantic shift for me and for her.

On Labor Day weekend, BB and Hart came to stay overnight with us and to take me back to Memphis to begin what I described in my diary as "my longest journey." The time came to depart, and I hugged Mother and told her that I loved her. She told me: "I love you, Nibs, and I know that you dread this, but you will do fine. Go up there and show them who you are." We drove away with Mother standing in the yard, waving at us. I was sad to go, but I never gave a thought to what Mother might have been feeling as we left. Many years later she would tell me that she went back into the house and cried and cried, crying off and on all that day. It was a point of demarcation for us.

I went to Davidson for two reasons: the academic reputation and because Reverend Jackson had recommended it. I loved the academics and the ideas there, but I was anxious outside class. Part of it was my usual anxiety about being unworthy, but I also had not realized how an all-male school would affect me. It would be another decade before Davidson would welcome females as students. I had grown up in a world of women, and now I was moving into a world of men. I had also not realized how much women mitigate the tendency to toxic masculinity that we males have. I did not experience a lot of toxic masculinity at Davidson, but I did enter the world of overt male authority, especially the world of white, Southern male authority. At Davidson, it was genteel male authority, but it was that world nonetheless. For instance, I had not been aware that taking ROTC (military reserve training) was required of all entering Davidson students. Though this was never stated, it seemed to me that part of training males to be Southern men in authority was this teaching of the rudiments of military skills to us. I had already begun to grow my hair long, and I got demerits in ROTC for this. In an ironic twist, I would clean the rifles used in ROTC to make up points. I had not realized how much I needed women in my life, not so much for sex (though that was certainly on my mind), but for stability and balance.

I was definitely homesick, as many first year college students are. Mother kept up my spirits by writing twice a week and monthly phone calls (back when long distance calls were expensive and there were no phones in our rooms). I was not able to go home for Thanksgiving, but Mother noted in a letter, written on Thanksgiving night, "I'll bet you didn't have the noise and wild talk that we did. We had a good time as always but lacked one main ingredient—you! Dell said he bet you would like to pull your chair up under the table. Everyone missed you terribly, especially me. I can tell you now that they all will be back during the Christmas holidays to see you. Each one wanted us to come over there but I told them that all that you wouldn't want to go anywhere.....Cecil, Frances, Dell and Jimmie came in about fifteen minutes after I got home from work last night. You know we had bacon and eggs. Then Jean and her crew got here about 10 this morning, so this has been a full day—and food! Besides ham and turkey with all the trimmings, we drank a gallon of boiled custard, a quart of pickled peaches and so much else."

She also got others to write me to encourage me. Vera Miller, the high school teacher who had introduced me to *Cry, the Beloved Country,* wrote a letter to me that included these words: "I have pondered what to write you ever since I talked with your Mother last week...many of these boys have lost their childhood faith, and have not had your Mother or a Harold Jackson to lead them to a firmer faith in the Abstract God who does exist for us all. This is a trying time for you, and you must try to accept them as they are. Face it, Son, there are not many Nibs Stroupes in this world, and you had expected to find a lot of them in college."

By the time that I had made my one trip home for Christmas, I had decided to try to transfer to Southwestern at Memphis (now Rhodes College). It was closer to home and to Mother, and it had an urban and diverse environment. It was co-ed, so it would offer me the opportunity to take a few steps back from the dominating world of white men. I applied for a transfer, and I got in to Southwestern, but they gave me very little financial aid, which was a devastating blow. Their stated reason was that they did not want to compete with a sister Presbyterian college on issues of transfers. That evening I called Mother to tell her the bad news, and I wrote this in my diary: "I called Mother tonight, and she was disappointed as hell. She encouraged me, but I know that she was just as disappointed as I am. She said that she was going to call Mr. Rasberry and Reverend Jackson and get them to pull a few strings, but I doubt very seriously that they can do anything. It's a policy, and I know that they will not change their minds."

I had underestimated Mother and her determination. Mr. Rasberry was a prominent farmer who was a member of our church, and he was on the Board of Southwestern. She got to work, calling many of her church friends, and talking with Mrs. Rasberry, who was one of her customers at the beauty shop. In a few days, I heard the PA system come on in the dorm: "Long distance call for Nibs Stroupe." It was Mother, and she had great news: "You're in at Southwestern, Nibs—yay! Mr. Rasberry called this morning and told me that you'll get a $300 scholarship, a $500 loan and work-study for $200–300. If your record is good, they'll give you even more next year." That was back in the days when tuition was $500 a year. It was such great news to me, and I had an even deeper respect for my mother's ability to operate in the world. It was tough saying good-bye to Davidson friends at the end of the year, knowing that I would likely never see many of them again. Yet I was ready to go, and I headed home for the summer to look for a summer job.

I looked at the bank in Helena for a job, at the radio station, at the chemical plant, but none of those proved fruitful. Mother had been working again behind the scenes, talking with the bank president and with Joe Brady, a church member and the one who had comforted me when I was a boy in Little League baseball. She told me to go see Mr. Brady when I got home from college, and I went in soon after that to see him. Here's another entry from my diary about our meeting: "I went to see Mr. Brady this afternoon [Friday]. He said that I should not be discouraged about a job, and that whatever happened, I had a great mind and that would pull me through. He said not to lose my enthusiasm. He gave me a long talk about not giving in, and then he said that he was going to try to get me a job. He called me later this afternoon to tell me to be down at Delta Fertilizer Company at 7:30 on Monday morning and that I would have that job for the summer. That was surely nice of him—the work will be hard as hell, but I need the $."

The work did turn out to be back-breaking—digging ditches, painting huge ammonia and propane tanks in the hot Delta summer and generally working on all kinds of farm buildings. There were some other white college students working there, and there were some African-American men who did this kind of work all year round. I struck up conversations with some of them as we rode together in the back of pick-up trucks from one site to the other. They were the first Black men with whom I had conversations, other than polite ones in the world of white, male supremacy.

We kept the conversations "safe." We talked about male things—how hard the work was, how hot the weather was, who was best in baseball and football, relations to women in our lives. They knew better than I did how to negotiate such conversations across racial lines in the summer of 1965. The March to Selma had just happened, and the Voting Rights Act, the bill that would end neo-slavery, was just beginning to be formulated for presentation to Congress. We never talked about those kinds of things—I was too scared to ask them, and they naturally were careful not to broach such incendiary subjects in the Mississippi River Delta in 1965. I wish that I remembered their names, but in a sign of my racism (and aging), I cannot recall their names. These conversations, however, were more evidence to me, as the case was building in my heart and mind, that they were human beings like me. Such an insight—that we are all similar human beings—is the Jordan River for cracking the wall of white supremacy. I was not ready to cross it yet, but I could begin to hear the waters flowing on the other side.

I showed up on time and did not complain to the bosses about the work. At the end of the summer, our supervisor said: "Give me a jackhammer and Nibs and Jimmie (another white college student), and we will move the world." I was finally at home in the world of men!

My entry into Southwestern (fifty miles from Helena) for my sophomore year went well. The academics were good, but I still was uncomfortable with social life, especially with women. I had my share of lust and longing, but I was still in the grip of anxiety about dating. I did fall in love, though—with philosophy! I was good at math and science, but they did not speak to my heart like philosophy did. I was not quite as good at philosophy, but I loved it. It caused me to question everything, and one of those in question was religion. I couldn't quite give up my belief in God, but it was wavering a bit, as I considered so many various theories in philosophy. My new love also caused me to call into question the social order of the white South. Like belief in God, I still held on to the idea of white supremacy, but it, too, was wavering. Since home was closer, I was able to make several trips home in the fall, and both Mother and I were glad. I was noticing that "home" didn't seem quite as important in this second year of college as it had in my first year. An event was coming, however, that would make that distance even greater than I ever thought that it would be.

It began on a coolish night in January, 1966, towards the close of Christmas break in my sophomore year in college. My friend David Billings and I were sitting outside the local (segregated) late night hangout at the end of Cherry Street, the main drag in Helena. He was a student at Ole Miss, in the belly of the beast. We were discussing our future—we had both worked in physical labor the previous summer, and we wanted something different. We also were supportive of one another in our desire to find a different place to work—we wanted to stretch ourselves and our imaginations. There seemed to be a bigger and deeper world out there, and we wanted to try to look into it. We considered various options. I noted that when I was at Davidson, I had heard of a church in Brooklyn that hired college students for its summer work on the edge of Bedford-Stuyvesant. David's aunt Peggy Billings lived in New York and worked for the United Methodist Church, and that made it sound less formidable. We did not think that we had a chance at it, but we agreed that I would investigate the possibilities and get back in touch with him. In the meantime, two small-town Southern boys dreamed of the glamor and possibilities of a summer in New York City!

Before I made the contacts, I talked with Mother about it. She was very hesitant. She emphasized that I would need to make some money that summer in order to fund college. She agreed that there was a new world in New York, but she noted that there was great danger in the big city. Memphis was okay, but New York with its eight million people—that was something else. I initially understood her emphasis on "danger" to mean that there is crime in the city. I also thought that she meant that New York was a place where Black people were not totally controlled as they were in the South in 1966, even with the Civil Rights Movement breaking out. Though we did not discuss it, she also was thinking about my sociological view—what would happen to my view of the world up there? Would this summer experience in New York change how I viewed myself and the world? It was an interesting twist for us: Mother was usually the one ready to wade into the fray, seeking what she needed, as she did in the battle to get funding for me to transfer to Southwestern. I was usually the one who was timid and afraid, holding back and waiting for more clarity. On this subject, we changed places. I was excited and determined to try it. I told her that I would make some inquiries about it, even though I did not think that David and I had a chance of being offered positions for the summer.

I contacted Cecil Clifton at Davidson, with whom I had a good friendship on our hall in my year there, and he sent me the contact information. From that point on, it was an exciting and amazing journey. We contacted the staff of Lafayette Avenue Presbyterian Church in Brooklyn, and they invited us up to see the church and the program. New York City was stunning to both of us—the first trip there for either of us. We wanted to do it, and we were accepted onto the summer staff for LAPC that summer. Mother was still hesitant, but since I was so excited, she joined me in my enthusiasm.

Things got more complicated, as they tend to do. That spring I started dating a young woman named Margaret from Helena, who had been in my high school class and who was a college student in Mississippi. It was my first serious relationship with a woman, in which I felt that the feeling might be mutual. Because of this relationship, as the summer approached, I began to be hesitant about going to the program in New York, where she and I would be separated for two months.

David was also dating someone, but they had been in relationship for three years, so he was more secure. I had just about decided to stay in Helena for the summer, and it was only a few days before we were to go. I told David that we needed to talk, and I remember sitting on the hood of his car on a hot summer night in 1966, on a country dirt road deep in the fields of Helena. I told David that I did not think that I could go to New York, that I wanted to stay in Helena and be with my girlfriend. Love (and lust) had a strong hold on my heart, so I told him that I didn't think that I could go, that it would hurt my heart to be away from this woman. He reminded me of the excitement that we had felt initially upon acceptance, about the opportunity of seeing a new world, of perhaps finding a whole new reality that we had not encountered in life in the Mississippi River Delta. He spoke about being challenged and deepened by that new world. And: it was New York City!

On that night—I give thanks—David prevailed. We did go to New York, and we both left home forever that summer. I had thought that if I could stay in Helena with this young woman, my life would be deepened, and I would be feeling wonderful. Leaving home, leaving Mother—now I would find another woman to take her place. Yet I really didn't know what I thought I knew. I discovered later that summer that the young woman was dating another guy at the same time. She was not being duplicitous—I had simply misread the situation. My inexperience in dating, my longing for home, and for a relationship with a woman had blinded me to that reality.

Our time in Brooklyn changed our lives. For the first time ever, we worked with African-Americans as peers, and our supervisors were African-American. As Southern white boys captured by racism, we experienced the gift of a moment when those whom we had seen as "other" became people and indeed became our leaders. Our understanding of ourselves and of the world was changed forever. There were many miles to go in our consciousness, of course, but David and I would never be the same again.

My situation was also changed because I dated a young Black woman on the staff that summer. Though I did not notice it at the time, Deirdre reminded me of Mother in many ways—short, feisty, intelligent, humorous, determined. I was hesitant to tell my mother that we were dating, so I told her that we were just friends. She was not pleased with this news, and she gave me this warning in a letter: "Your experience will be enriched by your relationship with the Negro girl, but I am glad (and I sincerely hope) that you can keep it on a relationship basis. As you say, the barriers are very high and have never been overcome. So, play it smooth and even, and just remember when the fire gets too close, it blisters and burns and destroys."

When David and I came back South from Brooklyn that summer, we saw life differently. The dissonance between Helena and Brooklyn was so great that at first, I tried to believe that the Black people whom I had met and befriended in Brooklyn were qualitatively different than the Black people in Helena. I wanted to hold onto the white supremacist worldview that I had held for so long. My eyes had been opened in New York, however, and those former opinions could no longer hold me. A shift had taken place—the world did not look the same. I could not go back to my former consciousness—a new journey had definitely begun. I was now wading in the waters of the Jordan River.

Soon after I returned from Brooklyn, Mother and I sat in my bedroom, that same bedroom in which I had squirmed and fumed in the heat when I was four years old. On this occasion, I shared with her that Deirdre and I had become more than friends during the summer, that I didn't know if we were in love or not, but that I was going to pursue it. Mother did not take it well. She replied: "Nibs, I know that you have your own mind on this, but I don't think that you know what you are getting into. It is so hard to cross this barrier, and you could never live here in the South." It was not on my radar at the time, but it was one year before Loving v. Virginia made it possible to have interracial marriages. Mother continued: "I will support you in most everything, Nibs—you know that. But I don't know that I will ever accept it if you all get married. I will work on it, but right now, I just think that you are badly mistaken—you are infatuated with all that different world in New York. This will calm down. I don't know how much this summer changed you, but I know that it changed you. I don't think I can accept this part though—it will just be too hard for you and for her."

I am not sure how I expected Mother to take the news about this new relationship, but I was hurt deeply by her lack of support. I told her: "I hope that you don't make me choose between you and her. I'm not sure which decision I will make." She came back: "Don't do anything rash or foolish, Nibs. Time will tell on this." We left it at that. As I write these words now, I can only imagine how my ultimatum to Mother hurt her heart—she had nurtured and raised me and saved me for twenty years, and now I threatened to usurp her place with a young woman whom I had known for only two months.

I also went to share my Brooklyn experiences with the elders of our church. I was excited to do so because my time at LAPC in Brooklyn had such a profound effect on me. I felt that the church leaders had simply been ignorant in their view of Black people, and I knew that my revelatory experience would help convince them of a new truth. What a difference it would make! Instead of being met with the enthusiasm that I had expected, I was received with stern resistance. The most generous reaction was that I had gone up North and had been perverted by the Yankees—an old story for white Southerners. I was deeply hurt—partly because I felt the personal sting of rejection, partly because I simply did not perceive how deeply white supremacy was embedded in them (and in me). When I shared my reaction with Mother, she stepped back into protective mode and came around a little bit: "They are just a bunch of men who don't want to change and who don't want to know anything new. I wouldn't worry about their reaction—it is much more about them than it is about you."

I was worried about their reaction, because they had been one of my important parenting figures. They had rejected both the power and accuracy of my revelatory experience, and my soul was in turmoil. It felt as they were rejecting me, and in some way, they were. This rejection opened a deep chasm in my heart—if I had to choose between my church and this new revelation, I would be choosing the new revelation—the humanity of Black people and a new vision of myself as a human being. I was attentive to this process, but I felt that I had crossed over. I could not go back. It was the beginning of many new ways of seeing the world and seeing myself. David had the same experience with his Baptist church in Helena. We could not go home again.

8

Brave New World

"I IMAGINE YOU WILL adjust to living back in your old world. I am not saying that with my tongue in my cheek, as it might sound. More things are accomplished by understanding than any other way. Not many of us get the chance to do great visible things, but each of us who try can help. Right now, your main objective is to get an education, so you can help and be ready when the time comes (which it will in due time)." This was from a letter that Mother sent to me in Brooklyn in 1966. I had indicated to her that I thought that it would be hard to return to Helena with the same mindset with which I had left for the summer. We were both entering a "brave, new world," as Miranda quoted in Shakespeare's "The Tempest." As in that play, it would be a road filled with complexities and surprises.

I reluctantly returned to Southwestern that fall to start my junior year. I was pulled towards New York, but I was also excited to see what college looked like with my new eyes. When I came into the dorm room, my roommate Jeff Holder told me: "Wow, I was wondering if you would come back here. I thought that you might stay in New York." "Believe me, a lot of me wanted to, but I came back here for the time being," was my reply. I made it a point to get to know the first Black students at Southwestern, Lorenzo Childress and Coby Smith, who had become students a year earlier. In a manner similar to Brooklyn, they would open my eyes to many things on campus and off campus.

Mother was also wrestling with the changes in me and also in her own way of seeing the world. That fall she wrote me about a racial incident in the neighborhood. She was discussing her friend and next door neighbor, Sue, whose son Paul had been the subject of Mother's discipline: "Sue was in tonight, and they are fine. I caught Paul and his cousins throwing rocks at a Negro boy going by, so (me being me) I yelled at them to stop. To make a long story short, Sue called L.P. out of the backyard, and he tore Paul up. Sue said she bet he wouldn't throw any more rocks." Given Mother's kindness and compassion, it is hard to tell if this marked a shift in her racial attitudes, or if it was based on her general approach to life. Whatever the motivation behind that incident, she remained adamantly against the relationship between Deirdre and me.

In another letter, "I know from your lack of conversation that you don't want to discuss Deirdre with me, but if we are to stay as a team, I have to say a few choice words. Some of your confusion (now) is your relationship with her as a Negro girl. I know that burns you up for me to say this, but I can't express what I want to say. Please don't be mad at me, for I am trying hard to understand as much as you will let me. Before you decide anything, please look at your relationship aside of the physical attraction you obviously feel for her. You are both doing each other a grave injustice to get more involved. She is a world apart from your world, and in the end you would both end up hating each other and the whole world. Don't think that I am meddling, for I am trying hard not to, but just have to say something of what I feel."

I was resentful of Mother's words and what I perceived to be her intrusion on my love life. I chalked it up to her prejudicial ways, but I would later learn that from Mother's point of view, there would always be major drawbacks to any of the women whom I dated, no matter their racial classification. That is often the case with mothers and sons, but our close relationship added a deeper dimension. In one way, Mother was prescient in my relationship with Deirdre, because the geographical distance between Deirdre and me became a problem for our romantic relationship. We gradually drifted apart as romantic partners, but we remained friends.

My continuing movement into a new world would escalate dramatically in the spring of 1967. My friend Lorenzo Childress was denied service at a popular restaurant near the campus because the restaurant owner did not want to serve the N-word. I became part of the leadership team of those who organized a protest and a boycott of the restaurant's refusal to serve everyone, and we had picket lines and people standing with signs around the restaurant. Since it was a restaurant that was liked by many Southwestern students, our actions were controversial. Since it was off campus, the administration could not do much to diminish or support the boycott. Some of the students had contacts with the ACLU, and they influenced the U.S. Justice Department to become involved in investigating the complaint against the restaurant. To our great surprise, the restaurant owner refused to cooperate with the investigation and summarily closed the restaurant. It was a stunning victory! Some students thought that we had taken it too far, but my sense was that if he was not going to serve people, based on his racial profiling, then there should be a price for it.

I shared with Mother the good news of the success of our boycott and protest. She did not see it as a good development, and she warned me about getting involved with radical organizations. I had let her know that I had joined SSOC, the Southern Student Organizing Committee, who had come onto the campus when they learned of the boycott. As she had over the last year, she cautioned me about getting involved in such activities and about judging people like the restaurant owner too harshly. When I replied to her that she seemed too harsh about my changes, she wrote back in an April, 1967 letter:

> Next, I want to apologize for jumping at you about joining your organization—I truly am sorry! I always put my foot in my mouth without meaning to. It's just that I am 'big-mouthed' and bossy, and I try not to do that to you. I want you to live your own life, and I know you feel very strongly about these things. And, you are very capable of making your own decisions. Just ignore my remarks and try to remember that I love you very much. I guess I am nosy because I am interested in what you are doing. But, at any rate, just know, that I will go to hell and back for you. I don't mean to live your life for you nor do I want you tied to me through a feeling of owing me anything. I just want you to live, love, and to get a few of the things that will make you happy. Didn't mean to ramble on, but got started and couldn't stop.

I was glad to get that letter because it helped me to feel like Mother and I were still on the same side, at least as far as our history together went. My relationship to her was especially complicated at this time. She was a compass point for me, but like Miranda in *The Tempest*, I was finding new worlds, worlds that were pointing me in new directions. I was hoping that Mother would come along with me in those new directions, but I never really considered what I was asking of her. I did not want her to be stuck in the world of the "old white men" of the South, but I was beginning to experience her resistance to my new directions as her siding with them rather than me. She was still living—and even beginning to thrive—in small town Arkansas, and I was finding the excitement of the city. The small town was beginning to feel really small to me, whereas Mother heard that shift as a rejection of her and of those who had helped to raise me.

That tension reached a peak at the end of that year after I had gone home for Thanksgiving. After I had returned to Southwestern the next week, I received a letter from her, expressing her dissatisfaction with my seeming lack of interest in being home: "Have been intending to write but haven't. Just wanted to let you know I enjoyed having you home, even if it was dull and boring for you. I don't know any news except that Gladys told me today that she didn't want me to work over at the shop anymore. Said it was too hard on her and she's paying me to do what she tells me. I won't go into the neighborhood since I know that you aren't honestly interested in what anyone is doing here. Just wanted to let you know that I enjoyed your visit."

I was miffed and hurt when I received that letter—I felt that the root of it was that I didn't go visit enough of the people whom she wanted me to visit. In preparation for this memoir, I looked back at my journals for that Thanksgiving visit. I found that I was not bored, that I was busy with friends and not home very much. Mother's stinging letter was indicative to me of a break that was deepening. Some of the friends that she wanted me to visit over the holiday still used the N-word, and that made me less than enthusiastic about seeing them. I would have to be silent in my new zeal or take them on in a way that would have been unpleasant. Yet her antennae were strong—I was beginning to make a shift, not wanting to be so associated with the small-town people and mindset of those who had helped to raise me. There were times later when I was bored in my visits home—times when former high school friends were not home. The issue that she correctly perceived was that I did not want to engage those who were her friends and neighbors. To my regret now, I began to diminish their importance to me and especially to Mother—I was a "city" guy now, and they were "small-town-minded" folk.

The chasm was widening between us, and after Mother died, I found some of her journals. In one of those journals, she writes about a dream that she had. In this dream, she captures the essence of what was happening in our relationship:

> Was in this HUGE crowd at a concert, seemed to be outside (at times). Nibs as a young man was with me and Mary [Wetzel]—he also had a friend. We were all making our way out of the seats, and Nibs and his friend decided that they would do something. Seemed as if they wanted to catch the folk who had been in the concert. He was a grown young man now, not a little boy, as I usually picture him in my dreams. I was yelling and calling, because I realized we would never get back together—there were too many people. He wouldn't even turn around and finally went out of sight. I couldn't believe it and sat and sat, until the manager told the other woman and me that we would have to leave. Just the two of us left in that huge outdoor seating area. I got up, and the two of us left. I was so SAD because I realized that he was totally gone, and I would not be able to find him nor he find me.

I never knew that she had this feeling, but of course I was a young man, looking to chart a new course for myself. I was changing, but so was Mother. As the post-Thanksgiving letter indicated, she had changed employers earlier that year. She had switched to an employer, Gladys, who operated both a cosmetology school and a beauty shop. At the cosmetology school, people (the vast majority of whom were women) learned to be beauty operators, and then the advanced students would practice under Mother and Gladys's supervision. Mother wanted to get her instructor's license, so that she could fulfill her lifelong desire to teach in a cosmetology school. This would be a perfect opportunity to do that. She had been working at Becky's for a long time. She was hesitant to make the switch, but as always with her, once she made up her mind, she was taking action, as she noted in her letter earlier in 1967: "I went out yesterday to talk with Gladys. She wants me to come out there as soon as possible. Then this afternoon I talked with Becky and Johnny. I was gonna wait until tomorrow, but I thought that I owed it to her to let her know what I was thinking. They were nice to me, and I don't want them to be mad at me. I know that I would be a fool not to go because '8 to 5' hours and a five day week would be wonderful. But I have a funny feeling about it—I guess it is just the change." She did make the switch, and it was a good development for her.

I had perceived also that she was making incremental changes on the issue of race. Like many white Southerners, she would step up in individual situations, as she had done when the neighbor boy Paul was throwing rocks at the Black boys walking down the street. Yet she still seemed to be hesitant in the larger societal context. In my senior year in college, I had decided to apply to Vanderbilt Divinity School in Nashville, either to work on a PhD in religion or perhaps to go into the ministry. The raging of the Vietnam War and the power of the draft also influenced me to look more carefully at Divinity Schools—those young men approved for seminaries by their religious bodies got an automatic exemption from the draft. I needed to go to Helena to meet with the Session (the governing board) of First Presbyterian Church, in order for them to approve my going to seminary. I did not have a car, so a friend of mine from college, David Adcock, drove me down to Helena to meet with the church leaders. He stayed and visited with my mother while I was in the meeting. While my relations with the church had been somewhat strained after my summer in Brooklyn and the church's subsequent rejection of my new insights, I still remained a son of the church. They were happy to approve me to go to seminary—they wondered why it took me so many years to see that I was meant for the ministry.

On the way back to Memphis, David told me that he and Mother had a good visit, and that he really liked her. He was impressed with the depth and strength of our relationship, and he told me: "Your mother told me that you both influenced one another. She said that you had really helped to change her mind on race. While she would never march anywhere, she said that she was working hard on changing her attitudes about Black people. She said that you were the reason why she did it. I wish I could get my parents to do that." I was greatly surprised by David's revelation. I don't know why I had never considered that Mother might be paying attention to my journey on race in a positive way. All I had ever noticed were her cautions to me on race, and I felt that those were primarily out of concern for my safety. I was shocked but pleased to hear these words from David about Mother. In keeping with our tradition, however, I never mentioned the conversation to Mother, and she never mentioned it to me.

Mother also began to flex her power in politics too. Though she would never seriously consider running for office, she encouraged others to do so, including her friend Mary Wetzel, who ended up getting elected to the school board. She also encouraged her neighbor Sue Sellers to run for the City Council, and she also won. She and Sue worked together to thwart a McDonald's franchise from being built on a long-empty lot just down the hill from their houses on Porter Street. Both went door to door with neighbors, talking with them and getting them to sign a petition to protest McDonald's building a restaurant nearby. Their organizing worked—McDonald's withdrew their application and later built in a less residential area between Helena and West Helena. As she undertook that work, I was flattered that Mother would ask my advice about it, but in actuality, she had more experience and more courage than I did on such matters.

One of the reasons that I wanted to go to Vanderbilt Divinity School was that in my senior year in college, I started dating a young woman who was a sophomore. We had a serious relationship, and I dreaded being too far away from her after my graduation. Vanderbilt presented a reasonable alternative in that it was relatively close to Memphis, permitting us to see one another on a frequent basis. We started talking about marriage, and I brought her home to meet Mother. While Mother was nice enough to her, it became clear to me that Mother was not approving of our relationship for several reasons. First, she did not think that our relationship could survive the long distance between us, which proved to be presciently true. Second, she did not think that this woman was the one for me—there was a class difference as well, and Mother was not sure that I was more than a social experiment for the young woman. She also added what she had said in my relationship with Deirdre: "you are not ready for marriage, Nibs. Of course, I will support you if you get married, but I don't think that you are ready." This third reason would be given by Mother two more times until I did finally get married.

As I began my senior year in college, I shifted even more in my political thinking. My friendship with Lorenzo Childress and Coby Smith deepened, and I got involved that fall in the campaign of the first serious Black candidate for mayor of Memphis, A.W. Willis. I recruited students on campus to work in the campaign, and I would work in rallies for Mr. Willis. Some people on campus told me that I was being radicalized and needed to be careful. When I asked them what my offense was, they replied: "Working in a political campaign for a Black man." Reflecting back on that experience, it says a lot about the milieu of Memphis and Southwestern, that in the fall of 1967, I would be accused of radicalism for working in a political campaign. Even Mother approved it—because it was participation in a good ol' American tradition: seeking to get people elected to office. Mr. Willis lost by a considerable margin to Henry Loeb, but I had made a turn and would not be going back.

That political activity led me directly to a huge turning point: the sanitation workers' strike in Memphis, which began in February of 1968. The sanitation workers were mostly Black, and they had formed a union in the early 1960's, but the city of Memphis had never recognized them. In February of 1968, two sanitation workers were crushed to death in a trash compactor, and when the city's response was woefully inadequate, the workers went on strike for better wages and working conditions. Mayor Loeb, who had formerly been commissioner of Public Works, took a hardline response, and the struggle was on. I joined other Southwestern students in working to support the strikers. We went to white church services on Sundays and stood up in worship to shout "Support the Strike!" We participated in many rallies and gatherings in support of the strike. Having contacts through the Black students at Southwestern was an aid to me in keeping up with the work.

Through these contacts, I began to learn of the Invaders, a group of young Black students and adults who were militantly committed to working for justice in the strike and in the structures of Memphis itself. I had begun to adopt their attitudes toward Martin Luther King and other "established" Black leaders: the insistence on nonviolence was counterproductive. Many of us felt that there was a possibility of victory in the garbage strike, and when Dr. King agreed to come to Memphis to support the strike, we had ambivalent feelings. It seemed to us that he was only trying to capture the headlines, and the organizing seemed to be going well without him. When his first march was organized, it ended in violence, as Black youth and police clashed. Dr. King seemed stunned that the Black youth did not hold him and his principle of nonviolence in high esteem, and he was returning to Memphis in early April of 1968 to organize a bigger march that he intended to stay nonviolent. I had an opportunity to go to Mason Temple to hear what would be his last sermon on April 3, but to my eternal regret, my lack of respect for him and my cynicism kept me from attending.

I was working in the college library on the evening of April 4, and when my shift ended a little after 6 PM, I was walking out of the library, and one of my Black student friends came up to me to say, in anger and in disgust, that Dr. King had been shot and would likely not live. He then asked me: "Some of my friends are organizing for the revolutionary fight. We want to buy guns. Can you lend me some money to help buy guns?" I was stunned by his revelation and by his question, and I did not know how to respond. I have racked my brain, but I cannot remember whether

I gave him any money or not. I was a poor student, and I did not have money to spare anyway.

Violence followed in Memphis and throughout the country—the great apostle of nonviolence was gunned down by white people, and it seemed like all hope was lost. I remember the National Guard armored cars riding up and down the streets in Memphis, and I remember feeling lost and forlorn. Classes at Southwestern were cancelled, and all students were urged to go home, if possible. I called Mother about it, and though she was never a King fan, she was horrified by the violence. She was so very worried about me, and she wanted me to come home. She invited my girlfriend to come with me to Helena, which we did. It was a strange time—Mother gave her bedroom to my girlfriend, and Mother and I returned to sharing the same bedroom that we had shared when I was a boy. Indeed, my girlfriend and I both lost our virginity in that same bedroom during that visit, while Mother was at work. It was the same bedroom in which I felt trapped in the story at the first of this book—a lot took place in that bedroom!

At the end of the week, we returned to Southwestern during a tense peace in the city. The city had recognized the sanitation workers' union, but there were still so many problems. I thought about Martin Luther King often, and I began to think that I had been wrong about him for a second time. First I was wrong about him in my youth, as I wanted to maintain my racist attitudes. Now I was beginning to think that I had been wrong about him again in my young adulthood—maybe he was relevant after all!

Soon after I returned to Southwestern, I got a letter from Vanderbilt telling me that I had been accepted into their divinity school, thanks to the work of religion professor Michael McClain, who had gotten his doctorate at Vanderbilt. They gave me a scholarship that made it possible to go, so that was set. I graduated from college in May, as Phi Beta Kappa and a philosophy major. Mother came up for the graduation, staying at BB and Hart's house in Memphis. She told me that she was so proud of me—I had done it! I've often wondered what went through her heart in those moments. She so longed to go to college but could not, and now through her fortitude and feistiness, she had financed my college education. Her persistent and hard work, her scraping by, her saving money in envelopes in her dresser drawers, her dedication have given me (and her) the dream that she had been unable to fulfill in her life: a graduate from college.

9

A Hard Rain's Gonna Fall

SEVERAL DAYS AFTER CHRISTMAS in 1969, I was sitting in Mother's living room in front of the big space heater. I was in the middle of my second year at Vanderbilt Divinity School. All my life, I had warmed myself many times in front of this gas heater. It was the same heater by which I used to chase away the fears of the dark in early mornings in my youth, while Mother prepared breakfast in the kitchen. Now on this day, I was engaging more demonic powers. I was sitting in front of the heater with a loaded .38 pistol in my hand, thinking seriously about killing myself because my girlfriend had ended our engagement and broken up with me the night before. She had come down to Mother's to be with us after Christmas, and I knew that something was wrong. When I asked her about what was going on, she indicated that she was also dating another guy in college, and that she had strong feelings for him. She indicated that she still loved me, but she did not know which of us she would choose.

I did not want to deal with the ambiguity and anxiety about what her choice would be, so we decided to end the romantic relationship. It was painful to break up and then have to be together for a couple more days, especially at Mother's home. On the day that we ended the relationship, Mother came home from work and found me crying in the bedroom. She tried to console me, but I asked her to leave the room, and I cried a lot more in that same bedroom where I had spent much of my youth—from feeling trapped on that hot Sunday afternoon in the story that began this book, to staying near my mother for 12 years in that room in order not to push away the feeling of being abandoned, to losing my virginity with my fiancé in that room.

On this day as I sat in front of the heater with the loaded gun, my ex-girlfriend woke up and saw the gun and gradually talked me out of the gun. I don't know if I would have actually committed suicide, but I was deeply hurt and felt so abandoned yet again. The gun had belonged to Gran, and after Gran's death, Mother had kept it deep in her closet. Mother was not a fan of guns, but she had kept it just in case she needed it to protect us. I knew where the gun was kept, so I got it on that day. When Mother came home from work that day, I told her what had happened, and she was terrified and deeply concerned. She talked to me many times over the next day or so, and she also talked with my housemate, David Kidd, at Vanderbilt, who arranged for me to go into the mental health services unit at Vanderbilt for a couple of weeks. David met me in Memphis and took me to that unit in Nashville, and I stayed there for ten days as I began to work through the pain and loss. The psychiatrist put me on Thorazine to calm me, and I mainly remember the deep pain and feeling of being lost. I was not sure that I could stay enrolled in Vanderbilt Divinity School, but I had a few weeks to think about it. I went back to Mother's in Helena to try to figure things out.

I can only imagine how scary this was for Mother. She mailed the gun to her brother Bud in Chicago, and she and I had many talks about the value of life and the value of my life. Though I was not telling her or anyone else, I was still thinking about suicide. With the gun gone, there was no easy method—the pills, which I was still using, were not helpful for suicide. On one occasion, I told Mother that I was thinking about writing a long letter to my ex-girlfriend and telling her how much pain I was in. When I told her this, she laughed and replied: "Nibs, I wrote the same kind of letter to your father after he left me. It didn't do any good, but if it makes you feel better, go ahead and do it. You are not the only person who has had to go through something like this—believe it or not, you will get over this and will come out stronger for it. Believe me, I know what I am talking about."

On one level, Mother's laughter offended me because I thought that she was belittling my struggles. Yet as she explained her meaning, I began to feel better, feeling that even though things had fallen apart, I might be able to get to the other side. That year of 1970 would be one of deep wrestling for me, and I am so glad that Mother was a powerful rock for me.

Her steadfastness for me came as things began to fall apart for her, too, in that year of 1970. She had to contend with my struggles and thoughts of suicide, and later that month her brother Bud called her from Chicago to tell her that he and his wife Flossie were getting a divorce after twenty-seven years of marriage. Bud and I were the two main men in her life, and now both of us were struggling. Mother and Bud had been distant from one another for the previous year. That distance was usually a result of Bud's pulling back from Mother, who as his big sister had acted like a surrogate mother after their own mother had died. She had experienced a closeness to him over most of their lives, but he had also had times when he was hesitant to let her in. They had reconnected earlier in the fall, as she noted in a letter before things fell apart for me at Christmas:

> But the most exciting thing happened on the phone about 10:30 last nite—Bud called me just to talk, and we are communicating again for the first time in years. Told me how awful his life had been, and we arranged to meet in Memphis one day in January! He is gonna fly down just for the day, and I will meet him at the airport. Then I was so excited that I couldn't go to sleep.

Within a month of the excitement of that letter before Christmas, she would have to help talk me out of suicide and then go through her beloved brother's divorce in the same year. It was a difficult year for both of us. At the end of January, I decided to return to Vanderbilt, but my heart was not in it. I was still deeply wounded over the break-up, and I was dismayed by the developing Vietnam War and feeling a general sense of lostness. As I struggled over whether to stay in school, Mother sent an encouraging letter that included these words: "It has been such a pleasure to send you to school, so don't worry about that part. Of course, it has been hard, but isn't everything worth having? Life itself is difficult! So we will just keep plugging along, as we always have, loving each other, and for heaven's sake, let's not lose one another again!" I don't know if Mother realized it at that point, but that encouragement helped give me the courage to think about becoming a conscientious objector to the Vietnam War.

I had begun to think about it on a personal level at a conference for seminarians in New Hampshire in the summer of 1969. I had just completed my first year at Vanderbilt Divinity School, with the intentions of either going for a PhD in theology or becoming a minister. As a seminary student, I was automatically exempt from the draft that fed the Vietnam War. Seminarians and ministers were exempt by the nature of our calling. Every man in my age bracket who grew up in the United States will have their own story of relating to the draft at that time. There was no way around it, because the war machine was eating young men up, especially poor men and men of color. And, when I say "men," I mean males, because women were not allowed as fighters in the military at that time and were not eligible for the draft.

The leaders of the conference in New Hampshire challenged all of us to think about giving up our draft exempt status, while challenging all ministers in religious bodies to do the same. The idea was that if all ministers and seminarians could be drafted to fight the war, then the religious bodies such as churches and synagogues would rise up in opposition to the war and end it. Mosques were not yet on that radar, though there were certainly many of them, and some of the strongest opposition to the war came from them (e.g., Malcolm X and Muhammad Ali). It sounded like good strategy to many of us, but few of us were willing to risk it. If we gave up our draft exemptions, there were only a few choices to prevent us from being drafted to go into the army and perhaps be sent to kill Vietnamese people in the war. Those options were a high lottery number in the draft, a conscientious objector status, a medical exemption, fleeing the country, or going to prison. Of course, that was the point. Would there be enough people willing to go into that risky status in order to end the war? I was not one of them.

Now, with the break-up, I was uprooted, and I was deeply troubled by the Vietnam War. The call from the 1969 conference began to resonate in me, and I began to consider the alternatives: I had a low draft number, so a conscientious objection (CO) or prison or flight were the only options if I gave up my draft exemption. I am so grateful to Don Beisswenger on the faculty at Vanderbilt and to Ed Loring, who was finishing up his PhD in American church history at Vanderbilt at that time. Both of them were friends and counselors and assisted me in working out my thoughts. The CO seemed to me to be only an educated man's exemption, but they helped me find its rich tradition in American history, and I began to think about it. Could I give up my draft exemption? Did I have the courage and stamina to do it?

Mother was troubled by all this, especially the idea that I might go to prison as an anti-war protester. She wrote me:

> But let me throw in one idea for good measure. Jail is not the place for you. You are like I am when it comes to absolute confinement. I HAVE to be able to wander outside and look around, if nothing else. Boredom would be your deadly enemy, and there would be no side trips to break the monotony. If I had to choose for you, I would pick the army. But, of course you must do what you consider the best thing to do. I can't see that you would do much for anybody's good in jail because four walls would be too confining. I'm off the soapbox!

Then, another set of events—the USA officially bombed and invaded Laos and Cambodia in May, 1970, and National Guard troops killed protesting students on Jackson State campus in Mississippi and Kent State campus in Ohio. Those events did it for me and for other seminarians. At a mass protest in DC (in which I joined others in being tear-gassed), some of us formed a pact and agreed to give up our draft exemption and to challenge the Vietnam War head on. I was near making a decision, but Mother tried another approach in a letter from May 5:

> It's a normal procedure that you gradually get past these depressions, so stop trying to hold on to them. You don't need to retreat behind a cloud of gloom. Play a little in God's sunshine with a grateful heart. So you try to relate to one person and fail, or are rejected! So what? Life is made up of failures, rejections, and a few successes. So, forget about your own self and start looking at people as lonesome, anxious people who want you to like them. Stop trying to solve everyone's problems and feeling that you are defeated when you can't. Even Christ didn't try this. So take a positive approach and see what happens. There's no key or map to go by, so you sorta make up your own route as you go along. Not DRIFT along, but GOING along—Class Dismissed!

I dropped out of Vanderbilt Divinity School at the end of May, 1970, and I joined the faculty of the Roses Creek Folk School, near LaFollette, Tennessee, for the summer. It was an experimental idea based on the Danish model of folk schools, where people with formal education joined with locally-educated people to develop one another and learn from one another. In this case, it was college and graduate students joining with Appalachian Mountain people. During the summer, I continued to wrestle with my options: conscientious objector (CO), prison, or flight to Canada. None of them were good options. I did not think that I would survive prison, and my Southern rootedness would not allow me to imagine life in Canada, uprooted forever from my family and community. So I decided to seek CO status and serve the country in that capacity rather than going to kill people in Vietnam.

In September, 1970, I joined with my long-time Helena friend, David Billings, also in seminary, and several other seminarians, in informing our draft boards that we were giving up our 4-F draft exemptions and would seek alternative service as COs. We were hoping to challenge the draft exemptions of ministers and seminary students—in doing so we had hoped to get churches to rise up against the war. We learned, however, that not enough of us were doing these actions, and that the draft boards were only too glad to add more fodder to the grist mill of young men sent over to fight in an immoral war. David and I both applied for CO status with our local draft board in Helena, Arkansas. I got several people to write letters of recommendation for me to the draft board, and Mother's was one of them. Her letter was powerful and moving to me, so I will quote it in its entirety:

> My son, Gibson, is making application before your board for status as a conscientious objector. As his mother, I would like to undergird this serious decision with my whole-hearted approval. Gibson has no choice other than the one he has elected to follow. As a very young child, he was influenced by my own conviction that all people are created by the same God, and that situations are better for having been settled in peace through understanding. Thus he grew up knowing that all men are his brothers, and that he is his brother's keeper. In later years, Gibson became the teacher and I the pupil. His experience with all types of people and his seminary training carried him far beyond my own small scope. Knowing that this earnest young man considers himself a part of the world-wide community of Christ, in my opinion, it would be impossible for him to undertake any training that would be in direct conflict with his deep-seated beliefs. I am extremely proud of my son for taking this stand. It has been a difficult decision for him, and he has finally come to this conclusion that he feels is in accordance with the teaching of Christ. I will be more than willing to appear before your board to testify in his behalf. Yours truly, Mrs. Mary E. Stroupe.

I had not read this letter for many years, and as I researched my files for this book, I came across it. It still gives me a warm and powerful feeling of support and love. I moved back to Helena to live with my mother at the end of the summer, while I began to look for alternative service positions. I had heard from CO counselors that it would be much better for me to find a position rather than allowing the draft board to assign me somewhere. The draft board would still have to approve it, but I was told that they usually did because they already had their hands full with meeting quotas to send young men to fight in the war. I checked into several places in Arkansas, but they were based in rural areas, and although I grew up in a small town, I could not see myself serving in such areas, especially given the hostility that I knew that I would find there with my CO status.

I got a call from Don Beisswenger in late September, telling me that he had been talking with Father Jim Zralek in Nashville. Jim was a Catholic priest in east Nashville, and he was very interested in prison ministry. He wanted to start a halfway house in Nashville for men getting out of state prisons, and he was looking for a staff person who could direct such a venture at a cheap cost. Don had recommended me for the job, and he wanted to know if I was interested in it. My first reaction was that while I had rejected going to prison as an alternative to serving in the war, now I would be going in and out of prisons. I said "yes," and called Father Zralek, and he hired me over the phone. I went to Nashville to start working there at Opportunity House as its first director. I was waiting on the Helena draft board to respond to my request for the CO status.

In the meantime, I was ordered to report for the physical for service in the army, but since I had applied for the CO status, I skipped it. My mother called me to tell me that I had made the local paper with this headline: "Two Are Sought." The article read in part: "One man failed to show up yesterday at the local Draft Board to go to Memphis for induction, and another failed to appear for his pre-induction exams...Failing to report was Gibson Stroupe. Both are asked to contact the Draft Board at once." I contacted the draft board to let them know that I would go to the Nashville draft board for the physical, but I never did it. I wondered if the MP's were coming for me, but I figured that they had bigger fish to fry.

In late October, I heard from the Helena draft board that my application for service as a CO had been approved and that my work at Opportunity House had also been approved. My good friend David Billings was turned down by the draft board. Much later I found out from one of my mother's friends why his application was denied; he had been on that draft board. He indicated that all of them knew that I was always going to be a minister, so it was within the bounds that I would be a CO. David, however, had a less than stellar reputation in high school, so the friend indicated that they knew that he was just trying to get out of the draft. As we all scrambled to assist David, he was almost drafted. In the meantime, showing God's sense of irony and humor, he was convicted of "malicious mischief" on trumped-up charges (that word "trumped" has added meaning now) related to racial justice issues, while he had been a student at Ole Miss. He was given probation and exiled from Mississippi for five years. But it was a felony, and his status as a felon made him ineligible for the draft! David's story made me realize how arbitrary the draft was, and how many young men had been sent to their deaths because of such capriciousness—some of them who were killed were my friends.

The work at Opportunity House changed my life. I got a first-hand look at another system that ground up people: the prison system, based on arresting and convicting and incarcerating people with no financial resources, especially people of color. It was not quite the prison-industrial complex that it has become today, but the same root issues were there—poorer people and people of color used as fodder to make us all feel better and to keep control over those who feel the weight of injustice and inequity all their lives. In my two years at Opportunity House, we never had anyone come through who had any material resources—those kinds of folk never made it into the state prison. From then on, I had a different view of race and of prisons, and I've tried to live out of that calling for justice and equity ever since.

Although Mother breathed a sigh of relief because I was settled for the moment, her family heartaches continued. Her uncle Dell was dying of emphysema and lung cancer, and his wife had called Mother and BB to come see him. She wrote of this sorrow in a letter to me: "The doctors have only given him three or four weeks. It is almost a cruel joke that four members of our family are all dying at the same time. As you can tell, my heart is sore and troubled. As you said, I am not cheerful and full of pep as I usually am. I am disturbed about you and all those I love...You are more to me than life and breath, so when you are unhappy, I am too. You are my reason for living, and all my love goes with you, where you are and whatever you do, I am a part of it."

Dell would die within a few weeks, and the next family death would be five months later. It would rock my world, in March, 1971. On the first Saturday in March of that year, I got a call from Mother telling me that Bud's estranged wife Flossie had died of cancer. My aunt Flossie had been one of the four people that Mother had noted were dying in her letter of mourning. Flossie had always been good to me and attentive to me, so I told Mother: "I am sorry to hear this, but I know that she is glad that the suffering is over. When is the service? If it's in Byhalia, I will plan to come down for it." She replied: "Nibs, I would love to have you there. Are you sure that you can get off work?" "I can do it, Momma. When is it?" She replied again: "Well, there is one thing that you need to know before you decide to come. Your father may be there."

I was shocked and puzzled, and I replied: "Why in the world would my father be at Flossie's funeral? I didn't even know that they were friends." Mother then said, "No, Nibs, they weren't just friends. They were brother and sister. Flossie and your father were siblings." I had seen my aunt Flossie many times because she was married to Mother's beloved brother Bud. Yet in all that time, no one, including my mother, had ever told me that my aunt Flossie and my father were siblings. I felt a long pause in my consciousness, and the silence was heavy. I felt a bit faint and woozy, and the world began to spin. I was shocked. I told Mother: "Why have I never known this?" She replied: "I thought that you knew it, but I guess that you did not. I am sorry that you are just learning this." I wanted to say more, but I was unsure of myself and my feelings, and I did not want to strike out at Mother in anger for never telling me this. "I'll be there," I said. I'll meet you in the funeral home in Byhalia." I hung up the phone, and my mind and heart were in a whirl. How could this be? Why did I not have any knowledge of this relationship? It was hard to believe—I would be meeting my father, finally, under very weird circumstances. I drove down to Memphis and spent the night there with a friend before driving to Byhalia the next day for Flossie's funeral.

Here's my description from my journal of the day of the funeral for Flossie, the day that I met my father. "I finally met my father. Damn, it's strange. The whole damned service was weird. I came in late with the Burrows and Mother, and I perceived that many of the Stroupes were there. I wondered muchly, of course, if ol' dad was there. After the service, lots of the Stroupes introduced themselves to me. I couldn't stand the pressure, and I went outside for a few minutes. I was talking to Mother and Bud and Jean when the man walked up. He shook hands with Mother, and just before she said 'Gip,' I knew that it was him. Indeed, he looked like me. I can recall what I felt in the split second between my realization and the actual introduction—anxiety, embarrassment, repulsion, and anger ran through me. Mother said to him: 'Gip, this is Nibs.' I shook hands with him, but I don't remember what I said because Bud interrupted us and said (I don't know if he was referring to me or my father): 'You mean this is the first time that you've ever met him?' I was mortified, and we parted quickly. I did notice that I was taller than him!

I drove back to Nashville that night, and it is probably a good thing that I did. I was too angry and hurt to talk with Mother in a helpful way about that day. Meeting my father—wow! A moment that I had earnestly desired for most of my life—now it had come and gone in a few moments of embarrassment and shame. As I drove back to Nashville, I alternated between anger and sadness and bewilderment. In my earlier days, I had imagined that if we ever met, it would be like the meeting in Genesis 46 between Jacob and his long-lost son Joseph, where they greet one another and lament the past hurt and pain, all the while celebrating their reunion. In my meeting my father at his sister Flossie's funeral, our reunion was filled with the intrigue of my just having learned that my Aunt Flossie was my father's sister! Our meeting was brief and perfunctory, as if I were meeting a distant cousin. Many years later, I would contact him and hear that he, too, felt badly about the way that we had engaged one another that day at Aunt Flossie's funeral.

I do not remember having any conversation with Mother about this meeting with my father. I participated in continuing that cone of silence about these relationships between my father and my mother, between my father and me. It would take me a long time to process this meeting with my father. I was so stung by Bud's comments because I thought that Bud meant that it was my responsibility that I was just then meeting my father. Deep in my heart, I had always felt that it was my fault that we had never met, just as I had thought for so many years that my father's absence was my responsibility. It took me years and lots of therapy to come closer to what is likely the truth. Bud meant his comments for my father and not for me. He was not saying to me: "Why haven't you gone to see your father before this?" He was saying to my father: "Why haven't you come to see your son before this?"

The "conspiracy of silence," as one of my therapists later put it, about the relationship between my aunt Flossie and my father, was equally not my responsibility. Why had no one ever told me that? Why had my mother never told me that Flossie was my father's sister? Why had Bud never told me? Why had Flossie never told me? I still do not know the answers to these questions, and though they remain important questions, they are no longer central to me. Even still, I will never forget that day. It would be our only meeting, but there would be more contact.

10

Where Do We Go From Here?

I ENCOUNTERED ALL TYPES of people at my alternative service at Opportunity House—all except people with material resources, who usually did not go to prison. I also learned during that time about the hierarchy of prisoners. At this time in 1971 before the drug onslaughts drove the murder rates up, those who committed murder as an act of passion or in the course of another crime were considered trustworthy in the prison hierarchy. Those on the bottom of the trust scale were check forgers and those who committed fraud. One of those on the bottom of the trust scale was a man named Sam, an Anglo man who came to finish his prison sentence at Opportunity House. We had many rules in those days—no alcohol, no drugs, no theft, no women allowed. The residents also had to have jobs. Sam pushed the boundaries on many of those rules, and he and I were in constant conflict.

One day during the lunch hour, I came back to the House after running some errands, and Sam was in his room naked with an older woman with very few teeth. I told him that he would have to get up, get dressed, and get the woman out of the house. He was drunk, but he jumped out of bed, pulled a long knife out of his dresser, and came at me to stab me. He was much bigger than I was, and he slammed me up against the wall, put one arm over my throat, and jabbed the point of the knife at the edge of my stomach. He roared at me: "Nobody tells me what to do, Nibs, especially not a little pipsqueak like you!" I was terrified, but I managed to say as calmly as I could, "Sam, don't do this. You'll go right back to prison. Just get that woman out of here, and then we'll talk." He shouted: "No, I'm cutting you right now—stay out of my business!" He raised the knife to stab me, and I instinctively covered my face and upper chest with my arms, but in mid-air he stopped. To this day, I do not know why he stopped. He slumped back into the bed, cursing and telling the woman (who was also terrified) to leave. I went downstairs to try to regain my composure, and I went back up to get Sam to be on his way, which he was. I called Jim Zralek to tell him about it, apologizing for being so scared, and he comforted me: "Nibs, no apologies needed. I would have been scared to death. You go on and leave the house, and I'll bring some help over, and we'll get Sam out of the house. He won't be coming back. I am so glad that you weren't hurt." Jim came over late that afternoon in his Catholic priest's clothing, but he also brought some men with muscle power from the parish in case he needed them. Sam left and never came back, and although I was frightened of him for weeks after that, I have never heard from him again.

I never told Mother about this incident, because I did not want her to be worried about me. The incident came in the middle of many struggles that I was having at Opportunity House. We had very little funding, and I was both the director and resident house manager, with an ex-prisoner as live-in help and cook. I was learning so much about myself and about the criminal "injustice" system, but I was also wrestling with exhaustion, with high anxiety about my future, with whether or not I could ever become an adult. I would write Mother about some of this, and on one occasion, she replied with powerful words in a letter:

> My first guess is that you are tired and discouraged. There are few I know who have set their path as early as you, so forget about the "directionless" part. Think of how you have fought against being pushed into some "niche" that you didn't want to sit in. You may be searching for the road to get where you are going, but all of us have made many detours and have had to muddle through rough dirt roads. So, accept yourself as a decent human being, faulty and all that stuff, but quite a guy! Like yourself a little—everyone else does! You aren't perfect and you never will be, so stop trying not to make mistakes. Go on and live!

Part of the issue that Mother was addressing was the anxiety that dwelled deep in my heart. It was an anxiety that had been nurtured by my father's absence, an anxiety that told me that I was not worth much because my father never bothered to contact me or come to see me. He knew where I was, but he had never made contact with me. My "little boy self" reasoned that if I had been a worthy son, my father would have made an effort to contact me. It would take my years to mitigate that anxiety, and I am grateful to Mother for sticking with me and for helping me to hear a different voice, a voice that told me that I was loved, that I was valuable.

Later that same year, Mother would fly on an airplane for the first time. Her brother Bud's income had grown, and he paid for her to fly up to Chicago to see him and to meet his new lady friend, Violet. Mother had been to Chicago by train and by bus, and now she would go on an airplane. Mother's mom had been named "Viola," and Mother and Violet, the new woman in Bud's life, hit it off very well in that first visit.

Mother and Mary Wetzel also traveled to Nashville to see me. By that time, we had gotten a federal grant for Opportunity House, and I was able to move out as house manager and live somewhere else. My longtime friend David Billings had also moved to Nashville, and through his aunt Peggy's United Methodist connections, we had been able to rent a house of a former United Methodist Center in north Nashville. The plans were to tear the house down, but in the interim, the Methodists allowed us to stay there to give some human presence to an otherwise abandoned house. The place was enormous, and Mother and Mary stayed there while they toured Nashville. In a move that surprised me, Mother took several dishes and other items from the Methodist house. When I playfully teased her about stealing from a church facility, she replied: "They are just going to tear this down anyway, and this stuff will be destroyed. I can put them to much better use." Her taking of the items did surprise me, because she had always taught me that stealing (or taking without permission) was wrong. I had always seen her as a paragon of virtue, and while this incident did not shake my faith in her, it did make me think that Mother was more complex than I had previously thought. She still had her honing instincts for finding valuables where others saw only trash. She took several bowls and dishes, and she proudly displayed them in her home, telling everyone where and how she had obtained them, as if the taking of the dishes opened up another side of her.

Bud decided to get married to Violet, and he wanted to have the wedding ceremony in his and Mother's home church, First Presbyterian, in Byhalia, the same town in which he had buried his first wife Flossie seven months earlier. Mother and I both had mixed feelings about Bud's getting married so soon after Flossie's death, but in the same way that she was in her relationship to me, she was loyal to her brother. She also really liked Violet. I drove down from Nashville to meet her at Byhalia for the wedding, and I saw many people in the Armour family that I had not seen in quite a while. My grandfather and his brother Dell had died by then, but three of the other siblings (Bernice, Ila, and Cecil) were there. The fourth, Thurman, had moved to Florida and was not able to return for the wedding. I spent the night at Dell's daughter Jean's house in Byhalia. She and Mother were the oldest of the children of the six siblings. It was a huge regathering of the Armour clan, the biggest since Dell's funeral a year earlier. Everyone was a bit on edge because of the closeness to Flossie's death, but Mother was glad to have both of her favorite guys together in one place.

Mother was still renting her house in Helena, as she had been doing since 1959. Gran's heirs had indicated to her that they wanted to sell the house after all these years since Gran's death. They gave Mother the right of first refusal. She began to think about trying to buy the house, but she did not have enough money to make a down payment, so it seemed like a fantasy on many levels. I was sorry that I did not have any money either to assist her in making the down payment. She turned to the other important man in her life, her brother Bud, because he did have the money. I give thanks that he decided to buy it for her—she would not have to move from her primary residence of almost thirty years.

His decision to assist her was not without drama. He indicated that he did not have the cash right away, but that he would work on it. He loved to gamble, and he often escaped the brutal Chicago winters by going to Las Vegas for shows and gambling. As Mother tells the story, Bud organized the cash to buy the house for her, but he told her that he was going to take it to Vegas to use it for a gambling stake—if he won, all the better. If he lost, they would have to start all over again. Fortunately, the numbers were right on the roulette wheel, and Bud multiplied his money, put the amount for Mother aside, then went on gambling. He would purchase the house for her (in his name for tax purposes), and she would be set. Though Bud could be unreliable in many of his close relationships, to my knowledge, he rarely failed Mother. For that, I give him great praise!

I was still wrestling with Opportunity House and with what to do after I finished my alternative service there. The working conditions were not conducive to my staying there beyond my two years, but I was not sure what I would do after that. Would I return to seminary? Would I get another job? Could I grow up to finally be an adult? I didn't have a job or a wife. In my mind those were some of the categories that I would have to fulfill in order to be an adult. As I look back on it now, it's clear that unless I had a strong woman like Mother in my life, I would not consider myself to have reached adulthood. Some of these questions are reflected in my journal entry over Christmas holidays in 1970–71: "I feel very strung-out, very intense, but I can't seem to put it into words. It's a dimension that I've admitted ever since we broke up, an intensity that first surfaced when I cried so much after that. Even now I don't know what it is, or what it means. It usually expresses itself in sentimentalism, but that's only because I don't know what to do with it."

As I thought about it, I began to connect the dots between my sense of abandonment by my father with the break-up of my engagement. For both of them, I had attached so much meaning and even salvific power. This now became a powerful force in my life, so I decided to seek some counseling so that I could talk about it with someone trained to listen and to give me insights. I first decided, however, to broach the subject with Mother, a subject that I had avoided with her for most of my life. I wrote her a letter, telling her that I was thinking about seeing a counselor, especially to discuss my relationship with my absent father. As I have noted, neither she nor I were interested in talking about my absent father, but now I felt that I needed to do it, with her and with a therapist.

When I heard back from Mother in a letter, I was pleasantly surprised to hear that she felt that my desire to see a counselor was a good idea:

> The counseling sounds great! You would know better than I do about your feelings. The fact that you feel guilty about the lack of a father would be my fault and not yours. Unfortunately, children always pay most of the price when parents decide to split. A divorce is always the fault of both parents and not the children. You had nothing to do with our separate ways. Hope that you can realize that you are a fine human being with many talents to offer.

Mother did not often talk about her divorce from my father, so I was intrigued when she said that divorces often were the responsibility of both partners. I had not really heard this approach from Mother—the divorce story on which I was weaned was that his infidelity and choosing the other woman had caused the divorce. Part of my development as a mature person was in discerning that the divorce story that I had learned and affirmed might have been too simplistic. When I later got married and had a family of my own, I saw my mother from a different perspective. I began to notice that she might have been hard to live with as a marriage partner. She was a very strong woman and would bow to no man. That quality was rare in the 1940's just after World War II.

I would dither around quite a bit longer in my lostness and struggles, delaying seeing a counselor until I could get better insight into myself. Of course, if I had gone to a counselor earlier, I would likely have gained such insights into myself. Part of my hesitancy was a sense that seeing a counselor was a sign of weakness, a sign that I could not work out my problems on my own. I envisioned that my counselor would be male, because I was still held in the grip of believing that males were the center of humanity, and because I instinctively knew that I would need to do my psychic wrestling with a male, a father figure. An equally important hesitation came from my sense that if any male counselor got involved with me and my story, they would laugh at me, reject me, and then confirm that my father had been right in leaving me in the first place.

I did talk with my friend and my mentor Ed Loring a lot about these issues, and he urged me to seek therapy. By this time, he had decided to accept a position on the faculty of Columbia Seminary in the Atlanta area, and he and his family moved there in 1971. He also began to nudge me to consider moving down to live with them and to return to seminary at Columbia rather than returning to Vanderbilt. As I considered my options, I decided definitely to resign as director of Opportunity House when my CO time was completed. I told Jim Zralek, who was saddened but not surprised. I recorded this in my journal about my resignation: "I officially resigned from Opportunity House last night at the Board meeting, and they gave me a standing ovation. I was humbled, but I also felt that I deserved it, because I had put up with a lot. So, it is downhill from here for me and Opportunity House. I have no idea what I'll do after Oct. 13 except to go to Atlanta. As I wrote earlier, I had a long talk with Ed, revealing fears and anxieties that I rarely reveal."

Later on in that same entry, I shared an anecdote that is revealing, as I read back over it. I was on the board of a halfway house for women in Nashville, and the director, Eugenia Moore, and I had a good working relationship. I wrote: "Eugenia Moore told me an interesting thing today. Someone had asked her about me, and she told them that while she was a married and settled lady, if she were a bit younger and free of obligations, she would move in with me in a heartbeat if I would have her. That humbled me. It also depressed me because it is the same old story with me—I try to impress people, then I do, then I feel as if I have deceived them."

It took me years of therapy to understand why I worked so hard to deflect such compliments: to accept them would mean that I would have to take responsibility for myself, that I was finally becoming an adult, that the "little boy" story of abandonment and unworthiness could no longer work for me, if I was going to be a mature adult.

I did move to Atlanta for a brief time in the early winter of 1973, but Eugenia asked me to come back to Nashville to work for her on a temporary basis because her chief of operations had resigned suddenly. I was not getting anywhere in looking for jobs in the Atlanta area, and the Lorings were having marital issues, so I moved back to Nashville. I moved in with friends from my college days, Harmon and Ginger Wray, who were living with several other people in a big house in Nashville. While there I decided that I would give seminary another chance. It was in this house that I would meet the next woman who would move to the core of my life. One of the other residents at the house in Nashville was Les Davis, who was married to another former college classmate.

In early June, 1973, the Nashville house was host to the wedding of Robin and Linda Williams, who later became acclaimed bluegrass and folk singers. Robin and Les Davis were first cousins, and also attending from Atlanta was Murphy Davis, sister of Les and cousin of Robin Williams. Murphy had been named after Robin's father, Presbyterian minister Murphy Williams. Accompanying Murphy on the trip was her friend the Reverend Caroline Leach, who was a campus minister at Georgia Tech. Caroline and I connected immediately at that wedding, and as she and Murphy left to return to Atlanta, we made a pledge to get in touch with one another when I moved to Atlanta in the summer.

I not only wanted to get in touch with her. I wanted to date her—I was smitten. Although I won't say that she was the main reason that I moved back to the Atlanta area later that summer, it was a strong motivating factor in making the decision to enroll in Columbia Seminary in that fall to resume my seminary career. I also give thanks for a scholarship that Ed Loring and the Dean of Students Erskine Clarke got for me. Caroline and I began dating, and it did not take long for us to decide that we wanted to get married.

That fall I let Mother know that Caroline and I were dating, but I did not let her know how serious the relationship had gotten. By the time that

Christmas rolled around, we were very serious, and Caroline planned to come to Helena after she had visited her parents in Chattanooga. She and Mother met, and we also took her around to visit some of the neighbors, including the Armour family in Byhalia. Caroline and Mother hit it off, and more importantly, Caroline made a great impression on BB, my most important relative in the family. Mother put it this way in a letter: "I thoroughly enjoyed meeting Caroline, and having her here was a real pleasure. Maybe she can come back soon! (You, too, of course)."

Later in January, Caroline and I decided to get married, and I wrote Mother to tell her the news. She had not reacted positively to the previous women whom I had dated seriously, so I chose to tell her about our engagement in a letter rather than calling her on the phone. I was pleasantly surprised to get her reply in a letter: "Am delighted that you and Caroline are making plans. It sounds very exciting to have an outdoor wedding, and you are right about the 'surprise" part. I am looking forward to knowing Caroline better, so keep me posted. She seems just right. So, all the struggling through other situations has proven worth the effort. Let me hear from you, and tell Caroline that I will be more than happy to have a daughter to go along with you. I'll drop her a note this week."

As Caroline and I were developing our relationship, Mother was expressing frustration with her other main man, her brother Bud, as she put it in a letter to me: "I have written Bud and Puddy [his wife's nickname], but had no reply. So, I called them. Strange and sad, too. Almost as if I had never met either of them. Nice and polite but no depth of feeling! I almost knew that all this would happen. There is such a gulf between Bud and me. Without a deep love on the part of both of us, a situation such as this has to develop. You know that I love him dearly, but you also know how afraid he is of any opening in his suit of protection. So, the next letter and phone call will be on him and from him."

It took me a long time to make the connections underlying the dynamics of Mother's frustration and loneliness. Both of her men—Bud and me—were now relating to women intimately in a short time span, and I can only imagine that these were threatening times for her personally. Bud, however, redeemed himself quickly in her eyes. He and his wife came down South from Chicago to celebrate their wedding anniversary, and they stayed at Mother's house, which delighted her. Bud also went to the local bank in Helena to talk with the president of the bank, looking to finance the loan on Mother's house but also to lay the groundwork for a future favor. Bud was now president of a company in Chicago, and he was looking to expand the company. I called Mother while Bud was there, and she described the call and the bank visit in her letter:

> I so appreciated your call and so did Bud. He was delighted. The three of us went down to the bank on Monday morning to talk with Bill [the bank president]. Not just about the house but about a location for a plant in Helena or West Helena. Bill was excited (to say the least) about the plant plans and said that they would loan me the money to buy the house.

Bud would later dangle the possibility of putting a plant in the area as a lure for an even bigger favor for Mother, his big sister.

Caroline and I made plans for our wedding, which we planned to do outside in May in Atlanta. Caroline did not want to be a June bride, so we chose May 18, a date right in the middle of my seminary exams. Caroline was the 21st woman ordained as a minister in the former southern Presbyterian church, but it had been a struggle. Her home church in Chattanooga had rejected her request to be endorsed as a ministerial candidate, so there was no desire to have the wedding there. For wedding gifts, we asked people to make monetary donations to one of four non-profit organizations that we had chosen—if they didn't care for those, we asked them to pick one of their favorites and make a donation in our names.

As part of the ceremony, we decided to ask our parents to say something about each of us and to acknowledge that we were all starting a new journey. Since I would not be wearing a suit or a tie, I asked Mother to make me a shirt for the wedding. She replied to these requests in a letter:

> What type of thing do you want me to say at the ceremony? I have never been to this type of thing before, so I am sorta feeling my way around—you will have to elaborate on the idea. I also have to know several things about the shirt. As you know, I will be delighted to do it. But you failed to tell me what kind of shirt. Long sleeves or short? Knit or cotton? Why don't you and Caroline draw me some sort of design?"

In that same vein, she also asked: "What am I gonna wear? I know that it is informal, and that is an excellent idea! But, make a suggestion! Better yet, ask Caroline since you will say it doesn't make any difference to you." Mother's radar was on target on my approach to fashion issues—her suggestion to consult Caroline on clothes and fashion would continue throughout our marriage!

The wedding would be what our kids now describe as a "hippie" wedding—outside at Ed Loring's home, no formal dress, with covered dishes brought by the guests for the meal. Ed officiated, along with Caroline's longtime mentor Sandy Winter. Mother and Mary Wetzel drove over from Helena for the wedding, as did David Billings and his wife Meredith, who had made our wedding rings. There were circles of friends from my days in Nashville, from Caroline's hometown of Chattanooga, from Columbia Seminary (where Caroline had graduated before I entered), and students from her campus ministry at Georgia Tech. When the part of the wedding came for the parents to speak, Mother stepped out of the larger circle towards Caroline and me and said: "Nibs and Caroline, I am so glad to be able to be here for this wonderful event. I have spent most of my life trying to raise Nibs to be the fine man that he is. And I am so glad that he has found such a wonderful partner in Caroline. I pledge to work just as hard to support you two together as I worked to raise Nibs himself."

While Mother was speaking these words, I was thinking to myself that I was blessed to have these two strong women in my life. Though I did not realize it at that time, I had relied on strong women throughout my entire life. Mother and Gran had gotten me through the perilous days of childhood and adolescence, and now Caroline was joining in this great cloud of women who would sustain me for the rest of my life. We did not use the "traditional" vows of "in sickness and health, to honor and cherish," in our wedding, but I felt their power on that day from Mother and from Gran and now from Caroline. The wedding party lasted from 10 AM to 10 PM in various forms. Since I was in the middle of exams, we took a "quickie" honeymoon to Montreat, North Carolina, thanks to Erskine and Nan Clarke's allowing us to use their apartment there.

That summer we would make a tour of Chattanooga, Helena, and McKenzie, Tennessee, to have each of us meet all the family and friends who we had not been able to meet prior to the wedding. Caroline's paternal grandmother, Sophie Leach, lived in McKenzie in west Tennessee, and though I had met her, she wanted all of her neighborhood friends to see Caroline again and to meet her new husband. Sophie had been born in 1882 (near Gran's birth year of 1880) in Texas, and she shared stories with me of riding in a covered wagon as a girl, as her family moved east (not west) to west Tennessee from Texas. In our visits prior to this summer gathering, we had talked about women's rights issues. Caroline asked her if she remembered women getting the right to vote in 1920, and Sophie replied: "Yes, I do. I did not think that women should have the right to vote, but once we got it, I always voted—I never missed an election. And I always voted Democrat." That remained true until her death in 1978, even after her "yellow dog" Democrats had begun to switch to be Republicans after the passage of the Voting Rights Act.

On this day in August, 1974, she hosted her lady friends (mostly widows like her) to renew their acquaintance with Caroline and to meet me. It was a pleasant gathering, and Sophie asked us to talk about ourselves, especially me, since no one there knew me. She was especially proud of Caroline, her first grandchild, for her perseverance in getting ordained. Most of the women there had never met a woman minister, and they were all astonished at the little girl who used to make summer visits to her grandparents in McKenzie. About 2 PM, Sophie made an announcement: "Thank you all for coming—this has been such fun. I want you to stay here with us, but I also want you to know that the Watergate hearings are starting up on television, so I am going to turn those on, and I want to listen to those. You're welcome as rain to stay, but we are watching these hearings." It was easy to see where Caroline got her spunk and her political orientation.

We received good news and bad news when we got to Helena. The good news was that Mother was welcoming of Caroline into the family of "Mother and me." Mother had not been welcoming to the three women whom I had seriously dated. The first one, Deirdre from Brooklyn, did not have a chance because she was Black, and because Mother never met her. Mother met the other two women, but she had quickly dismissed them as suitable mates for me. Part of her dismissal was her own good judgment, but I also began to feel that part of it was that she did not want to share me with another woman who would move to the core of my being, where Mother lived. Her reaction to Caroline was different. She wrote Caroline a welcoming letter after we got married, and in that letter was included a locket that Mother had made from an earring that had belonged to my grandmother, Mother's beloved mother. That sense of welcome continued during our visit to Helena that summer.

The bad news was that the beauty school where Mother worked was struggling. The original owner was having family problems and had sold it to someone else who did not have the personal ties to Mother. When we arrived in Helena, Mother shared the bad news. She had been fired. Mother said: "How could they do that to me? I worked hard for them? I'm 54 years old, and I have never been fired in my life. What a mess." I was so sorry to hear this, and Mother was so hurt by the firing. She had gotten her instructor's license to be able to teach at the beauty school, but now she was fired. She knew that she could go back to being a beauty operator, but she would miss the teaching, which she loved. She would now have to return to the eight-hour, six-day grind of the beauty operator's life, at the starting point where she had begun her career. The money would be tight, and I was so sorry that we could not assist her financially. We talked about it, and as I stewed about her difficulties, she stepped right back into the "momma" role: "Me and the Lord have been through too many valleys together, so I have decided that things will work out. Maybe not the path that I would choose, but I will find the window that opens when the door closes. I always have, so no reason to try to direct traffic now." She went back to work at another beauty shop, but a window would begin to open as the next six months developed.

Caroline and I returned to Atlanta where I began my final year of seminary. We, too, would begin to think about our own vocations and jobs. Funding for the campus ministry at Georgia Tech had been cut by the church governing body, and to no one's surprise but to our great consternation, it was the woman, namely Caroline, whose job was cut. Now, Mother and I had switched places. She had been worried about the two men closest to her in her life—Bud and me—and now I was worried about the two women closest to me—Mother and Caroline. Where would we go from here?

11

Finding New Paths

BOTH MOTHER AND I were unemployed, and now Caroline had lost her job as a campus minister. Mother at least had a skill upon which she could fall back, which she did. She returned to working as a beautician in a shop, as she had done when she began working in 1941. She was able to go to work in Helena in the shop of one of her former students, which was awkward. Mother had been the instructor to the student, and now she was under the authority of the student who owned the shop. I asked Mother how she felt about that situation, and she said that while it wasn't ideal, she had a job, and she was grateful. I remained impressed with her resiliency, and I felt bad for her, but I had very little money to assist her.

Because of my transfer from Vanderbilt Divinity School, I was scheduled to finish at Columbia Seminary in December, 1974. When Caroline and I returned to student housing in the fall of 1974 at Columbia, we began looking for calls to churches in the southern Presbyterian denomination. When her job as a campus minister was cut because she was a woman minister, we began to look for a church where we could be ministers together. This idea was basically unknown in our southern Presbyterian church. There were no clergy couples who worked in the same church, mainly because there had only been a short period since women had first been ordained as ministers in 1964.

In 1983 the former "southern" Presbyterian church (called "PCUS") reunited with the "northern" Presbyterian church (called the UPCUSA) in an historic meeting in Atlanta. The denomination had split in 1861, when the white Southern Presbyterians pulled out in order to support slavery. But, for now, in the fall of 1974, we were working in the confines of the PCUS, the Southern Presbyterian Church. Fortunately for us, the headquarters for the PCUS was in Atlanta, so we had access to their offices and staff. We went to see Don Campbell, the head of the national personnel office for the PCUS—that office was still called "The Minister and His Work." We met with him to discuss possibilities of our finding a church together as a clergy couple. His reply was: "There's no such thing as a clergy couple in the PCUS—you'll never find any churches open to that. My suggestion would be for Nibs to look for a church and for Caroline to work around whatever church Nibs goes to. I know that things have changed a bit with women's ordination [in 1964], but this idea of clergy couple is revolutionary—don't try to take things too fast." We thanked him for his time, and we told him that we would continue looking as a clergy couple for a while.

Mother returned to working as a beauty operator. It was hard work, and she had trouble making financial ends meet. She thought about taking a second job, but she recognized that she was getting too old for such work, especially considering that she was on her feet all day as a beauty operator. Her neighbors across the street, the Paines, offered her a second job cleaning the doctor's office every day after the beauty shop closed, but she turned them down, adding these words in a letter to me: "Your going to the auction makes me green with envy, but in my financial strain, I am staying away from old furniture. As you know, I am addicted to it and have no will power. My life is sorta plugging along—have sorta managed to make ends meet. Had an interesting offer from Jimmie Paine to work at their office from 7 PM cleaning as a six day a week job. I was sorely tempted to take it, but I know I am not physically able to hold two hard jobs. And, as you know, I need more than work. I am not geared to just work—I need other things."

We helped Mother financially as much as we could, but our finances were limited, too. Mother did find something in which to invest her passion that did not cost a lot of money. She became interested in psychic phenomena. I am not sure where or how this began—her sandbar buddies had some interest, and a friend across the River in Lyons, Mississippi, had a keen interest, so perhaps it began with them. She especially focused on angels and began to read all that she could on angels. A decade later, she would reflect back in her journal on this journey into the psychic: "This journey was started about ten years ago in Chicago. I went to a psychic there, who informed me that my mother was right over my shoulder. She has been there for a long time (I am sure) pushing me on, so the title of this trip is 'Angel Over My Shoulder.'" She searched for her mother for a long time, but I do not believe that she ever participated in any seances trying to contact her mother. Her main interests in the psychic world seemed to be to establish that this extra dimension existed and to discover her own guardian angel. Given what she had been through, and what she had to do, she no doubt thought that a guardian angel had assisted her. Back in the prosaic world, she continued to work in the beauty shop of a former student.

Caroline and I did not heed the advice from "The Minister and His Office"—rather we began aggressively looking for churches that would be willing to consider a clergy couple. As Don had indicated, there weren't very many of them. We finally found two possibilities: a yoked call of two congregations in the mountains of western North Carolina, and a small congregation in Norfolk, Virginia, which was being funded as a Presbytery mission ministry in a housing complex of many low-income families. The first one meant that we would have two congregations to pastor, with the main qualification being the possession of a four wheel drive vehicle (which we did not have). We talked with the Presbytery leaders on the phone, but we never visited the locale.

The other one in Norfolk was initially interested in a woman pastor, which was highly unusual at that time. The search committee wanted a woman pastor because the housing complex had many Navy families in it. Many of these families were young, and the husband was often out to sea for six to eight months. The church did not want any male pastors coming around to visit the young wives with their husbands gone for so long a time. I don't know which the Presbytery mistrusted more, the Navy wives or the male ministers! They also felt that most of the ministry would be with young women, so that strengthened their desire to have a woman pastor doing the work. This sounded intriguing to us because it was so unusual to have church looking for a woman pastor. We contacted them to ask them if they would be willing to accept me as an add-on in order to make it a clergy couple. We were so desperate for a job that we indicated that at the start, we would be glad to come for one salary, so that they would get two for one. Norfolk Presbytery said that they would be interested in interviewing us as a clergy couple, and that they would check with the small church called St. Columba (twelve members) to see if they were willing to consider such an idea. The church indicated that they were willing to consider it—there was enough work for two people anyway!

We went up to look over the situation in Norfolk, and we liked the possibilities. Not every member at St. Columba was thrilled to have a woman as pastor, feeling that the Bible forbade such a thing. Desperation works wonders, however—they were willing to call us as a couple at one salary, and then we would go from there. We accepted the position as co-pastors of St. Columba Presbyterian Church in the winter of 1975, the first clergy couple working together in the old southern Presbyterian church. It was located in a 1500 unit apartment complex known as Robin Hood Apartments. Robin Hood had originally been built for Navy families but by then also included other low-income families. As we prepared to move up to Norfolk, I wrote these thoughts in my journal: "Caroline and I have accepted a call to Norfolk, beginning May 1. It is very far from all the folk we love, and that is depressing. It is a good job, but I have been fighting depression all day. It is a combination of leaving Atlanta and of being away from everyone way up there. Also, I suspect that the deepest cause of the depression is that I am now finally on my own (age 28), with career training and all. I am now an adult and will be expected to act like one. Now it is truly up to me." It would also be the first move really away from home for Caroline also—she had gone to college in her hometown of Chattanooga, and she had gone 100 miles south to seminary at Columbia.

Mother was happy for us, though she was not thrilled at the distance from her. She did note, however, that the Edgar Cayce Center was at Virginia Beach, Virginia, and that she would look forward to visiting it whenever she was able to come up. Edgar Cayce was a well-known psychic, and she had been reading a lot of his books. Her job prospects were also beginning to look a bit brighter. In 1964, the state of Arkansas and Phillips County had established the first community college in Arkansas, located in Helena-West Helena. It was developing a school of cosmetology there, and Mother began to have designs on becoming the director of that school of cosmetology. Like many positions in those days, it was highly political and was dependent on whom you knew. She did know the dean of that part of the college, the Applied Technology section. There was already a director of the cosmetology school, but she made contact with the dean and indicated her interest in the job when it became open.

He replied that he would put her name in the running for the position if it came open.

Caroline and I arrived at St. Columba in May, 1975. The church was named for the saint who brought Christianity to Scotland. We quickly went to work to help grow the church membership and to develop the community ministries. We set up a summer program for kids in Robin Hood Apartments. My ordination as a minister was set for June 8, and we paid for Mother's flight up to be present for that. Her good friend Mary Wetzel also came to the ordination. We had a formal ceremony at St. Columba Church, with Norfolk Presbytery presiding over the ritual.

I don't remember much about that service except how mad Mother got at one of the ministers, who was part of the commission to ordain me. He gave me a charge as a new minister, telling me about various delights and pitfalls of the ministry. During that time, he strongly emphasized that if I wanted to get out of the ministry at some point, that I could do so. It was a weird time to say such a thing, but he was older, so I chalked it up to his own relationship to his ministry. Mother took it another way—she heard him saying that I should not be in the ministry, that I would soon find that I made the wrong decision—and she was mad! "You were meant for the ministry," she said, and added "how dare him bring such an arrogant attitude." She wanted to call the minister and give him a piece of her mind, but I talked her out of it, telling her that Caroline and I would have to work with him, especially to raise funds for the community ministry. We talked her down, but she never forgot that pronouncement. And, in the end, she was right—though I am now retired, I'm still ordained after these forty-six years.

While Mother was with us, we took a tour of Colonial Williamsburg, and we also saw Jamestown before it got expanded and renovated. We were there on a rainy and coolish day, and I remember feeling the despair of the Indigenous people who were being pushed out and of the English settlers who were obviously in over their head. While we were in Norfolk, we did a lot of that kind of exploring. Caroline and I had both grown up with the Civil War as the center of life—history began and ended there. In the Norfolk area, we re-learned that there were significant milestones in the nation before the Civil War! In 1976, Mother joined us for the Bicentennial celebration, with tall sailing ships coming into the Norfolk harbor.

Mother's economic woes continued, as she tried to rebuild her client base after being in the beauty school for several years. We helped her financially, as did Bud. She kept angling for the director position at the Community College, but she was getting discouraged, as she wrote in a letter: "I called the College and talked with Mr. Jumper [the dean over the cosmetology department] about the director's position. He told me in so many terms that as far as he was concerned, the job would go on as it was. He said that Mrs. Ryall planned to stay on indefinitely. So, guess I'll turn that loose and turn over a new page, wherever that takes me." I was sorry to hear this and was wondering what we could do to help her, when Bud intervened and took it to another level. He called the bank president Bill, whom he and Mother had visited a year earlier in Helena. He told Bill that he wanted to come down to look at land that might be available for him to consider in thinking about building a factory in Helena or West Helena. In typical Bud fashion, though, he added a qualifier. "I won't be able to think about the plant unless I can get my sister settled so that I don't have to worry about supporting her. I would feel a lot better if she were able to get an instructor's position at the community college. Can you help me out on that?" The bank president responded that he would look into it, and he and Bud set a date for Bud to come down to look at land for the factory.

By the end of that year, Mother had been offered a position as instructor at the college cosmetology school. She was delighted and soon moved into being a co-director of the cosmetology school with her African-American colleague Jessie Weston. She put it this way in one of her first letters after getting the position: "The school is leveling off, and some say that the problems are insurmountable, but I don't see it that way. Have finally learned info on all thirty-six girls—their names, addresses, and who the ring-leaders are. Could not have done this without Jessie Weston, the Black instructor. I spent two weeks sending the Black girls to her for answers to their questions." Mother and Jessie Weston made a good team in the diverse school of cosmetology, with both Black and white students there. She and Jessie became friends also. Mother would stay at the Community College until she retired ten years later. And, oh yes, after several years of stalling, Bud never built the factory at Helena-West Helena.

Caroline and I began to make progress at the church and in the community ministry of St. Columba. We discovered that there were plenty of what we then called "battered women" in the Navy families. It often happened that a young couple would get married, then the husband would join the Navy, and they would be stationed at one of the Norfolk bases. The husband would go out to sea for six to nine months, and while he was gone, the wife had to be the manager of the household and of any children in the marriage. When the husband came back from sea duty, the wife was often no longer the same young girl that he had left behind. She was now a young woman, capable of handling herself and her family. This clash sometimes led to domestic violence, and sometimes the wife and her children would show up on the doorstep of St. Columba.

There were no shelters for the victims of domestic violence in the Norfolk area, so we had many of them staying at our home until we could get the situation stabilized again. I was often the one who had to go talk to the husband to seek to get him to calm down and act more equitably with his wife. As many of us know, domestic violence cases are scary because they are so volatile. I knew that I needed to try some kind of intervention, but it was always a scary situation. In those moments when fear would make me hesitant, I would remember that I had survived the violence of Opportunity House. I also remembered how courageous Mother had been in going into difficult circumstances, and I gathered my courage up. Although it did not always work out for the wife and family to return, often it did, and most of the time the domestic violence ceased. One of the husbands whom I confronted became a friend of mine, and after we developed the friendship, I asked him if he was threatened by me when I came to talk with him about the domestic violence. He replied: "No, Nibs, not much. You are such a little guy that few of us feel threatened by you when you show up. And you offered us a way out with some dignity." Caroline did not want our home to become the permanent shelter for victims of domestic violence, so she worked with the YWCA, the Junior League, and others to organize and open the first shelter in Norfolk for women victims of domestic violence.

The church also began to grow and change. As co-pastors, we would rotate preaching one month at a time, and whoever was the preacher for the month also moderated the monthly meeting of the Session, the church's governing board. The church had been all white, but we declared that we were open to everyone. We began to attract people of other racial classifications: Black, Latinx, and Asian. Unbeknownst to me, we also began to attract gay and lesbian persons, who were not making a declaration of their sexual orientation, especially in a military town. As I have stated so often, I grew up with a huge captivity to homophobia. Actually, the idea of a person being sexually attracted to a person of the same gender identity was so far-fetched in my young mind that it was not even on my radar. As I began to change on race and gender issues, I also changed a bit on sexual orientation issues. I was willing to go to "Don't ask, don't tell," but I was still troubled by what seemed to be clear biblical mandates against "same-sex" relationships.

Our pastorate at St. Columba would be a time of conversion for me on LGBTQ issues. Two women started attending the church—one was civilian worker in the Navy, and one was a housewife with young children at home, whose husband had served in the Navy. The housewife, named Alice Taylor, was an astonishing person at the church. She jumped right into activities at the church—helping in the summer programs, teaching Sunday school, visiting in the apartments, visiting shut-ins, helping to lead worship. She was a kind, compassionate, hard-working church member, the kind of member that ministers long to have in our churches. Because of her work and example, we asked her to allow us to nominate her to be on the church's board of elders. She replied that she would need to come in to talk with me about it. I thought to myself that she was really taking this seriously, and that I appreciated her coming in to find out more about the position.

When she came in to talk about being an elder, she indicated that she was interested, but that she would have to decline the offer. When I asked her why she was declining, she replied: "Nibs, I can't do it, because I am a lesbian. I don't think that the leadership of the church should be so out of line with the biblical teachings." Her reply stunned me, and I thought to myself: "How can Alice be lesbian? She looks like a regular person to me? She is married to a man and has children. How can she be a lesbian?" Yet I also knew that she was one of the best Christians whom I had ever met. She had all the qualifications to be a leader in the church. That knowledge led me to a conversion experience, right then and there. If Alice can't get in, who can? Would God say to her, "You know, Alice, you have been such a good servant—you have loved others and served them, you have fought for justice, you have lived an exemplary life, but you just have one problem: you love someone of the same gender. Too bad!" I could not believe that God would say that, so I said to myself: "This is not her issue—this is your issue, and you need to change on this."

My reply to Alice was this: "Alice, I don't think that God cares about someone's sexuality. God cares about loving and justice and compassion, and you fit those categories—you have been on fire here at St. Columba, and we think that you would make a great elder. We want you to say 'yes.' I appreciate your sharing this with me, but it makes no difference to us."

Alice smiled and said, "Okay, let's do it." We did it, and she became an elder at St. Columba in 1978. Later, after Caroline and I left St. Columba, Alice would become the director of the St. Columba Ministries which had been established there, and it grew and flourished in ways that we could not have imagined.

In 1977 our friend Lena Clausell, who was an Associate Executive on the Presbytery staff, suggested that we apply to receive the Birthday Offering of the Women of the Church in the PCUS. It was a one-time grant of $200,000+ (the equivalent of $800,000 now) to start or to strengthen a ministry project. We did not think that we had a chance, but Lena encouraged us to apply. I had written a federal grant for Opportunity House, and I felt like we could at least write the grant. With Lena's encouragement, we wrote the grant, submitted it, and in early 1978, we received notice that we would receive at least $225,000 from the Presbyterian Women Birthday Offering for that year. We established St. Columba Ministries as an outreach program in the immediate Robin Hood Apartments and in the larger community, and with the money we would establish a preschool for neighborhood children, hire a youth worker (Alice), and begin community organizing in a much stronger way to develop an advocacy for those who were poor. After the award was announced, Caroline and I traveled around the Southeast to meet with Presbyterian Women's groups to help raise the funds.

We also did some traveling that was not so pleasant and which forced me to make a difficult decision concerning Mother and Caroline. Caroline's grandmother Sophie, who had hosted us in west Tennessee, had begun to fail in health. She moved in with Caroline's parents in Chattanooga. At the same time, the health of Mother's beloved aunt BB (Bernice Green) had continued to fail. In March, 1979, Mother called to tell me that BB was in the hospital and that she did not have long to live. I agonized with Mother because BB had been her best friend in the Armour family and a stalwart supporter of mine. Later that day, we got a call from Caroline's parents that Grandma Sophie was in the hospital at age ninety-six with a massive tumor on her lung. Both of these matriarchs died within one day of one another, and I had to decide whose funeral I would attend. The stakes got higher when Caroline's family asked me to deliver the eulogy for Sophie at her funeral. I decided to support Caroline, but I remember the sadness in Mother's voice when I told her that I could not attend the service for BB. Though she told me that she understood my choice, I know that her heart was hurting, and so was mine.

I felt like I was back being that middle school kid, standing in Gran's bedroom after Gran's death, disappointing Mother yet once again. Here is a journal entry that I wrote in regard to BB: "Most of all what I remember about BB is the richness and love she gave me. A scrawny, insecure, pimply kid loved and even (dare I say it?) adored by her. She was a great gift to me. Her love was a great gift to me—she enriched my life. Her great sense of humor, her toleration, her loyalty—they were gifts to me. So, to you, BB, wherever you are, I celebrate your life and your gifts to me. You were the personification of the love undeserved and the love much needed—you were indeed a vehicle of grace for me." And, though I didn't write it in the journal, I know that her love for me was because of her love for Mother.

In that same year, in the summer of 1979, Mother came up to visit us with the purpose of taking a longer trip to see DC, Boston, and Amish country. We drove for the trip, and on the first night, we stayed together in a motel in Virginia outside DC. I had forgotten how much Mother snored, and for that first night, Caroline and I felt like we were in the room with a freight train. She and I moved into the bathroom, her in the tub and me on the floor, trying to get some sleep.

The next day I had to be the bearer of the bad news, telling her that we would have to get separate rooms so that we could get some sleep. She took it personally and indicated that we needed to be tougher, that she had snored all of her life. She also pouted and said, "Let's just cancel the trip and go back to Norfolk, then I can go on back home where I can snore by myself." I was surprised by her reaction, but I said: "Mother, nothing has changed. We're so looking forward to this trip with you. We're planning on covering the cost of the trip—we'll just have two rooms rather than one. No problem from our point of view. Don't be mad—we just want to be rested." She grumped around, muttering that it was too expensive to do separate rooms, but finally she agreed to continue the trip. I would not realize until later, when I found her journals after her death, that part of her negative self-image was her snoring, from a 1991 entry: "Have I been in my unconscious mind telling myself I am unlovely and therefore no one can love me? All my life I have been teased about being a little girl who snores and a big girl who snores."

We did have a great time on the trip, with many memories established. We visited Gettysburg, and Mother enjoyed it, but she was miffed that the statues for Southern states were not as prominent as those for Union states. I reminded her: "Well, Mother, the Union forces did win the Civil War, so naturally their memorials will be more prominent." She replied: "Yes, but they could have given us a little more credit—minus Pickett's charge, we would have won the battle here and maybe even the war." Always a loyal follower of the white South.

And yet, a follower in contradiction. She and her co-instructor Jessie Weston became friends, and by "friends," I do not mean "acquaintances" as people classified as "white" often mean when they say that they have Black friends. Mother and Jessie actually became friends, crossing racial lines to visit in one another's homes, taking trips together, and bonding together to make the diverse school of cosmetology work. Indeed, it was Jessie Weston's visits to Mother's house in the 1980's and 1990's that gave Mother the reputation of being a radical on race. What had she done to demonstrate her radicality, according to her white neighbors at the time? She had welcomed Jessie into her front door, invited other white friends over to visit with them, and generally acted like they were friends, which they were.

When we returned to Norfolk from our trip to the Northeast with Mother, we were greeted with the news that the city of Norfolk planned to buy Robin Hood Apartments, tear them down, and disperse the 5000+ residents. The purpose of this was to build an industrial park in its place, in order to attract more businesses to Norfolk. We lobbied hard against this proposal, seeing it as absolute nonsense to take low-income housing without replacing any of it. What would happen to the families? The city's answer was that the existing housing stock would absorb them, but what they actually meant was that they were hoping that the surrounding metro areas of Portsmouth, Virginia Beach, Newport News and Hampton would absorb them. We organized rallies at the church, and we led marches on the city council as they prepared to make their final decision. We had some hopes because three of the seven council members were Presbyterians, including the mayor. The final vote was disappointing—we lost by one vote, with two of the Presbyterians voting to tear down the property. In our immediate reaction, we thought that it was only the stupidity of the Norfolk city council that caused this. Later we found out that this was part of a nationwide "urban renewal" trend, to take housing where low income people lived, tear it down and re-purpose it in order to benefit middle and upper class people.

We had been trying to get pregnant for several years, and finally on the trip with Mother in 1979, we discovered that Caroline was pregnant. Our son David was born in late January, 1980, on a night when it snowed six inches in Norfolk. Caroline was dilated four centimeters quickly, so we thought that it would be a quick birth. David's head was big, however, and that slowed things down, so eleven hours later, he came out, snorting and breathing with difficulty. The doctor let me hold him, then let me cut the umbilical cord, then take him to the special neonatal nursery to have his breathing checked. It turned out to be fine, for which we have been eternally grateful. Mother could not get off work right away, but Caroline's parents drove in from Chattanooga, beating a huge snowstorm which closed bridges across the rivers and brought us forty inches of snow! David claims that he has been trying to get warm ever since (he now lives in Utah!).

Mother came in March for a week, and she and David were delightful together. Photos from that visit show Mother holding him tenderly, and she helped us to take him on his first outing since birth—to Williamsburg, of course. We had named him David Armour Stroupe, including Mother's birth name as his middle name, and she proudly wrote that fact in her home church bulletin. When she got home from her visit with her new grandson, she wrote to me: "Tell my little friend that I miss him! Thoroughly enjoyed my stay with you all, and I am delighted I came home on Saturday instead of Sunday—it poured rain here all day yesterday—didn't stop all day. I did find out some sad news when I got home. My friend, Tennie Logan, died while I was with you, so I didn't have to fix her hair at the funeral home. I will really miss her coming to get her hair done every week, especially since she had been following me around town for thirty years. Give David a kiss for me!"

Though we had been feeling defeated and dissatisfied after we lost on the Robin Hood vote, David's birth gave us great joy! It also made us feel the distance even more from our families, especially Mother, who was now almost a thousand miles away. We had not realized how long the states of Virginia and Tennessee were! We decided to move to Nashville, where I would work for the Southern Coalition on Jails and Prisons. I would be working for prison reform in the state legislature and visiting people on death row, and Caroline would be staying at home for a while to care for our new baby. We also were trying a new communal living situation—sharing space and income and life with former seminary friends in a house in Nashville. I would be back in Nashville for the third time—perhaps I should have become a country music singer!

12

New Horizons

WHEN I STARTED WORKING for the Southern Coalition on Jails and Prisons in Nashville in 1981, one of my primary duties was to work in the Tennessee State Legislature for prison reform. My friend and supervisor Harmon Wray told me: "This will be a tough job. There are two things that no one wants to see how they are made: sausage and laws." I found that to be correct. The business of lobbying to get laws passed or amended is a messy process, and at times, it can be a sleazy process, especially in those days. There are good and effective lobbyists for justice and for social change, but I was not one of them. I was too hesitant and too cautious to jump into the fray, as I needed to do.

My mother would have been a good lobbyist, because she was accustomed to fighting for herself and for what she wanted, such as when she lobbied heavily for me to get a scholarship when I transferred to Rhodes College. In 1981, though, the sexual innuendos and demands of lobbyists were even much worse than they are today, so I am glad that she never had to work in that way. And, of course, as I have noted, my uncle Bud was a powerful lobbyist, and, although he was always so supportive of Mother, his ways were not my ways.

I did find fulfillment in visiting in jails and prisons, as I had a decade earlier at Opportunity House. I can't say that I enjoyed going to visit those imprisoned—I will never get accustomed to that jail or prison door slamming shut, whether it is done by human hand or by computer. There is a finality to that, and it is one of the things that I never felt comfortable with—that, of course, is one of the points of prison, that closing of the door, that ending of freedom. Yet those very feelings made me commit to doing prison ministry. I would be in and out of jails and prisons, visiting people for the rest of my career.

While I was struggling in my new job, Mother had found her groove in her job as instructor in the community college. She had wanted to be a teacher when she left high school, but the financial circumstances never permitted her to go to college to achieve that goal. She was now in her element in teaching these young women (and a few men at that time), to get their beautician's license. Mother took it much further than that, however. She had to do remedial work: teaching students to read and to comprehend what they were reading. In order to work on people's hair, the students would have to learn some chemistry in order to mix dyes correctly. This was especially true in doing Black women's hair, and in this sense Mother and Jessie Weston had indeed crossed the color line—the students would learn to do the hair of all kinds of women. She also began to teach the students life skills, learned from her own school of hard knocks. In many ways, she had lived their lives, and she wanted to share her wisdom. She taught health classes, and when HIV/AIDS came along, she made certain that they knew how the disease was transmitted and how to prevent it. She and co-instructor Jessie Weston wanted to help their students develop and celebrate their humanity, as well as learning how to be good hairdressers.

Mother also wanted to teach them how to be citizens in the basic meaning of that word. She insisted that her students get registered to vote and that they vote in elections. Our daughter Susan especially noted this kind of work by her Grandma, and here is a Facebook post that Susan sent out to her friends on the confluence of the Day of the Dead and the elections in November, 2014.

> Since we are still near Day of the Dead, here is a Voting Day story about my grandma, Mary Stroupe, who died almost exactly ten years ago: after working for many years as a hairdresser and beautician in Helena, Arkansas, and raising my father as a single mother in the 1950s and 60s, she changed from being a practitioner to teaching at the local community college. The majority of her students were black—men and women who were working toward their beauticians' licenses. My grandma was a product of her time—raised in an entrenched and (to her) unnoticeable

segregation that firmly defined which races of people were worth more than others. My father was also raised in this system, but as he came of age, his mind was transformed toward justice, and my grandma, because of her own intelligence, her devotion to my father, and a friendship with a Black woman, who was her peer and fellow teacher at the community college (Jessie Weston), began to change as well. Grandma was insanely stubborn: a trait which allowed her to be a single mother, and a trait which also served her students in community who would rather conserve the ways of fearful separation than become vulnerable to change.

On every election day, my grandma would only let in students who brought proof that they had voted before coming to class. In her early years of doing this, she had students come in saying they were being prevented from voting by election officials. The story goes that Grandma stopped class and led all of her students and her five-feet-on-a-good-day self over to the polling place, demanding of the men blocking the door that her students be let in to vote, as was their constitutional right. They relented, and her students voted. So I have my sticker, and I think of my grandma. We don't take enfranchisement lightly in this family.

As Mother was finding her good place at the cosmetology school in the community college, I was struggling with our situation in Nashville. Our communal living situation was not working out, and we moved out of the house that we shared into a duplex nearby. Our finances were tight, and I worked part-time as a supply pastor at Second Presbyterian Church in Nashville. It was a great place for our whole family, and I also learned there how much I missed being a pastor in a local congregation.

I also began to wrestle more consciously with my relationship to my father. I had previously checked in with Mother about it and about contacting him. I wrote Mother and told her that I was thinking about contacting my father. Part of me wanted to withhold this information from Mother, but just in case things got weird with my father, I wanted her in on the initial stage. She wrote me back: "The contact with your father seems to be a good idea. You have been trying to do this for years, and I agree with you that you should do it now. I appreciate your telling me about your plans. It honestly doesn't have any effect upon me now, and it certainly would help you close that chapter." I was glad to get her permission, and years after meeting him at his sister Flossie's funeral, I decided to write him a letter to announce myself in his life. I struggled with it for a time—it was a huge demarcation for me. I finally wrote the letter, and even the writing of it was tough. I wrote in my journal: "I sweated like a hog when I was writing it." My long letter to my father, the first contact that I had ever made with him, included these words:

> So, let us begin, you and I—we who carry the same name and blood, we who are strangers to one another, we who haunt one another and shall for years to come. I've often wondered why you never came to see me, why you never acknowledged my existence, why you never let me be a son. I still wonder, and I hope to hear from you some reason. I do not mean to imply that you are bad or evil, or that my mother is innocent. Yet the fact remains that you never came, you never wrote, you never said a word to acknowledge that I was and am your son. The only communication that I received from you was a note from your wife—no word from you, as if you could not speak or write.

About six weeks later, I did receive a letter, but not from him. It was a letter from his wife Vivian—once again she stepped into the breach. Her response was a long, single-spaced typed letter, telling me that my father had not responded yet because he had been in and out of the hospital for mental depression and that he was in the hospital as she wrote the letter. She asked me to stick with him—and I remember thinking as I read her words: "Ha! Stick with him? He is all up in me, but he has never acknowledged me." I wrote back to her, mainly wanting to know if my father had read the letter that I wrote to him. She responded in a second letter: "Now to answer some of your questions, which was not clear in my first letter. Gip did read your letter, and it did have an effect on him. Not sure just what was going through his mind, but he had been crying when I got home the day your letter arrived, then when I read your letter, he started to cry again. We talked, and I asked him would he please write to you, and he promised he would, but not that day. Then when your next letter came to me, I showed it to him when he came home. He didn't have too much to say, only again he promised he would write you."

This process would go on for about one more month—Vivian and I wrote a couple of more letters, while my father stayed silent, in and out of the mental hospital. Finally, a year after my letter to him, I finally heard my only words from my father in a letter that he had written by hand. I was glad to hear from him, but the only things that he shared was asking my forgiveness for his neglect of me. Here's the first paragraph of his letter to me, the only communication that I would ever have from him:

"My dearest Son, Nibs, I don't know how to start this letter after all these years of no communication. All I can say now, Nibs, is that I have asked the Lord to forgive me, as I didn't stop to think during all these years that what I was doing was not what I should have done. Again, the Lord has forgiven me for that."

As I read that last sentence, I thought to myself: "Yes, but I haven't forgiven you." I wrote him back a letter, indicating that I would like for us to continue writing, but I never heard from him or from Vivian again. My immediate response to his only letter to me was a sense of anger, resignation, and accomplishment. Anger—that he did not seem to really own what he had done to me. Resignation—that this would likely be all that there would be between us, because he seemed very weak emotionally and mentally. Accomplishment—because I had finally done it. After all those years of absence and neglect, I had finally forced him to acknowledge me and to admit (a little bit) that he had done me a great disservice. I waited in anticipation for a while after I had written my letter in response to his letter, but after a time, I decided that it was over for me. I would not pester him to respond to me. He obviously was choosing the path of least resistance between us, and I decided to let it go. I forgave him in my own heart for his absence, although I did feel a bit of sweet revenge that my letter had seemed to put him back into the mental hospital. I am not proud of that feeling, but it was there—and it still remains on a smaller scale, as I have discovered in re-reading these letters for this book.

I never told Mother about this exchange of letters, and she never asked me about them. We kept up the code of silence and even the "conspiracy of silence" that had existed ever since my father abandoned Mother and me. Though my absent father will always remain in my heart and my psyche, I felt good that I had written him and had been acknowledged by him. I preferred to put my energies where they needed to be: with Caroline, with our children, and with Mother. Mother and I rarely spoke of my father after that.

Though Mother and I did not speak of this exchange, it felt like a turning point for both of us. I had wrestled with the legacy of my father's abandonment, and with overcoming the fears and lack of self-confidence it caused. Mother's support played a large part in my overcoming these. She also was recovering her sense of self-worth through surmounting her own challenges as well as nurturing me through mine. I had finally turned around to confront the bogeyman who had dogged me through each major step I had taken, sowing doubts about my self-worth. That bogeyman turned out not to be my actual biological father, but rather the absent father that I carried at my core—an absent father whose voice had gained strength way out of proportion to his actuality. I could now think about cutting the shackle on the chain that I had been dragging all my life. And when I did this, I did not know it at the time, but the last shadows for Mother seemed be released too.

Mother continued her inner, psychic journey also. She had achieved one of her major goals—to get me grown, into college, married, employed, and into fatherhood—and now she could continue and deepen her own identity—who was she, other than the powerful woman who raised her son as a single mother in a patriarchal, racist, homophobic world? Who was Mary Elizabeth Stroupe? She turned to the psychic world to seek some answers. She began to record some of her dreams and her thoughts a journal. I never knew about these journals until I found them in her papers after her death.

One of the dreams that she recorded was one in which she had gone to a party across the Mississippi River. She had driven over there and had a suitcase, making her assume in her reflections on the dream that she had stayed several days. In the dream, she decided to go home, but the hostess of the party insisted that she meet someone before she left. Here are Mother's reflections about that part of the dream:

> The hostess called to this man and introduced me to him. We were instantly attracted to each other, but I told him I was on my way home. He walked along with me, trying to persuade me to stay, but I wouldn't. There was a slight embankment that I had to cross to get to my car. He insisted on helping me. As usual, I refused, but he took the bag anyway. Then, he held out both arms to me and swung me down to the bottom. With that, he began to turn flips and somersaults, laughing fit to kill! He finally persuaded me to stay until morning. I could see the sun shining on the water in the river on my way home. On awakening from the dream, I felt that I had known a total pure love. My whole body and countenance were glowing and warm. It was a wonderful dream (the man had short black hair—I did notice that.)

As I read this dream in her journal after Mother had died, I was so glad that she felt such joy, and I found myself hoping that she had found that kind of joy from outside her own psyche. I did note several themes in the dream that seemed to touch the images that I had of Mother. She noted that she at first refused the man's offer to help, and added "as usual" to her declining his offer to help. The idea of her own agency—of her reluctance to allow others, especially unfamiliar men, to assist her—came to mind. Given the joyful nature of the encounter with this man in the dream, I wondered if he was a projection of Bob Buford, her fiancé who had been killed in World War II. She did not venture into this kind of musing, but that image came to me, as I read her recording of the dream. The man's assertion into her life, bringing great energy and joy, made me think of that earlier reflection where she felt unloved and unlovely, as a little girl and a big girl whose identity was in snoring. Here in this dream, she was desired and welcomed into laughter and joy and intimacy. She did decide to stay over for the night, and her reflections on waking up from the dream sound like a lover in her beloved's embrace. Although I had wished for this kind of experience in her life, I was so pleased that she could affirm her own self in this way in such a dream. She was made for loving!

We had found a wonderful circle of friends in Nashville, a circle that we had missed in Norfolk. I continued to struggle with the work, however. It was good work, and it was a good working situation, but it became clearer to me that I was not good at it, nor was I fulfilled by it. I still felt the pastorate calling back to me, and I began to look around for churches where I might be called as pastor. In the midst of this, Caroline and I decided to try to conceive another baby. Our son David was still young, and my ambivalence about having children came out once again. Caroline reminded me that it had taken us three years to conceive and birth David. It took us a long time to get pregnant, and she had a miscarriage during the first pregnancy. In the fall of 1981, she was 34 years old, and she could hear the biological clock ticking. I certainly enjoyed trying to make a baby, so we got off birth control and began to work at getting pregnant. In a big surprise to us, Caroline got pregnant in a couple of months, sometime during the Christmas holiday. In September of that next year, Mary Susan Stroupe popped out of Caroline's womb.

And, I do mean "popped out." By this time, birthing methods had improved a bit, and Nashville has always been a place where birthing was seen in a holistic way, rather than just a hospital event with the mother isolated from the community. We chose a woman OB/GYN, Dr. Betty Neff, who encouraged us to think about a home birth. Given that we had an active two year old, we chose the birthing room at Vanderbilt Hospital. On the Saturday night when the contractions began, Caroline had been playing balloon ball with our son David. I was working on my sermon for worship at Second Presbyterian the next morning. Thanks to Caroline, I had asked Nancy Ramsay, an ordained Presbyterian minister, to be on standby for the sermon. Caroline had suggested this, but I had indicated that I did not think that the baby would come that night, since the due date was still a week away. Caroline had wisely and firmly replied: "Nibs, I'm the one who is carrying this baby, not you, and I'm feeling like the baby is coming out this weekend, so get someone to fill in, just in case."

While Caroline was playing balloon ball with David about 10 PM, the contractions increased in frequency and intensity. We went into action. I called Nancy for the sermon, and I called Paul and Susan Robinson next door to come and stay with David while we were gone. He was a medical student at Vanderbilt, and she was a nurse, so we felt that David would be in good hands. They also loved to play with him. Caroline and I arrived at the hospital about 11 PM, anticipating a long night of birthing. We had a birthing room to ourselves, and the nurse left us to ourselves, checking in every now and then. Caroline had not used drugs in the birth of David, but about 12:45 AM, she told me, "The pains and contractions are just too great. I think that I will need some drugs this time—I can't hold out all night with this level of pain. Please go get the nurse to get me something." I went to get the nurse, who came right away, looked at Caroline's vaginal area, and said: "Wow, I can see the baby's head—she is coming out soon—that's why you are in such pain. But, hold on just a little longer. This is Dr. Neff's first birth in her new private practice, and she wants to be here for the birth—I'll get her right away!" We were stunned—Caroline was pleased to hear that the baby was about ready to be out, but she was not pleased to hold back a few moments.

Dr. Neff came in and helped to usher our baby out of Caroline's womb, and Dr. Neff said: "Welcome to the world, Mary Susan." At that pronouncement, Caroline almost jumped off the table because she had so wanted a girl. We had chosen not to do the amniocentesis to find out the gender or the condition of the baby—we would just take what we were given. We named her "Mary Susan," getting the first name from Mother, and we ended up calling her "Susan." Both of our children had Mother's name in their names: "Armour" for David's middle name, and "Mary" for Susan's first name. Mother was delighted by this turn of events.

As we were counting down the days for Susan's birth, I got a call from my longtime friend and mentor, Ed Loring. He was now the co-founder with his spouse the Reverend Murphy Davis, of the Open Door Community in Atlanta. He called to ask me if he could put my name into the pool to be the next pastor at Oakhurst Presbyterian Church in Decatur, Georgia, a part of the Atlanta area. I agreed for him to do it, and he gave me the name of the person at Oakhurst who chaired their pastor search committee. Caroline had worshipped on occasion at Oakhurst while she was a student at nearby Columbia Seminary. It was a famous church in the denomination because it had been one of the first majority white congregations to call a Black person as its Senior Pastor: Dr. Lawrence Bottoms, in 1973. Dr. Bottoms later was elected Moderator of the Presbyterian Church (PCUS) in 1974, the only Black person ever so elected.

He had come to Oakhurst in the beginning of its downward spiral from 800+ Anglo members to its nadir of 80 members in 1983. It had suffered such a rapid and dramatic loss of members because the city of Atlanta had taken Black housing in the 1960's to build major league sports venues. Many of the displaced Black people moved into the east Atlanta area, including the Oakhurst neighborhood in Decatur.

To no one's surprise but to many people's dismay, white flight from the Oakhurst neighborhood began immediately. Only two white churches stayed: Oakhurst Presbyterian and Oakhurst Baptist, and both became anchors of the changing neighborhood. The membership loss for Oakhurst Presbyterian was devastating, especially in terms of building maintenance. A space that had been built over the years to accommodate almost nine hundred members now needed to be maintained by one hundred members, with a rapidly dwindling budget.

Soon after Susan's birth, the chair of the Oakhurst search committee called me to see if I would be interested in interviewing for the position of Senior Pastor at Oakhurst (actually, the only pastor and only fulltime person). I told her that we had just had a baby, and I would have to think about it. She called back in six weeks, and I indicated that I was interested in talking with them. I was interested in getting back into the church as a full-tine pastor, but I was also interested in Oakhurst because it had a significant number of Black members. One of the hardest barriers in creating multiracial ministries is getting people of other racial classifications to step over the line and join in the church, especially if the dominant racial category in the church is "white." Oakhurst had already crossed that line, and that intrigued me. The search committee came up to Nashville to hear my preach and to meet with me after worship to talk about the possibilities. In this event, I would get a glimpse of how much I had to learn about race and its power in myself and in our culture.

In our initial discussions, I had asked the Chair of the search committee what the racial makeup of the committee was. I was pleasantly surprised to learn that of the five people on the committee, two were Black. I had already experienced plenty of white institutions who had claimed to be sharing power with Black people, but when decision time came, only those classified as "white" made the decisions. This composition of the search committee heartened me that Oakhurst might have broken that pattern. On the Sunday that the search committee arrived at Second Church to worship with us and to hear me preach, I kept looking out at the congregation to see where the Black faces were. Second was all white at that time, so any Black person would have been easily identified. As I scanned the assembled multitude, there were no Black faces, and inside myself, my heart fell. Either the Black members of the committee were not interested or not permitted to come, and neither alternative was a good one.

After worship, we went out to lunch to talk and to discuss the possibilities of my becoming pastor at Oakhurst. At this point, with a two-month old baby and a three-year-old, Caroline was not interested in being part of the pastoral team, although all those in the church will recognize that in those days, the pastor's wife was an unpaid member of the pastoral team.

When we sat down, I asked where the other members of the committee were, and they replied that one of the committee members was sick and was unable to come up. When I asked where the other Black member was, a very light-skinned woman spoke up and said: "Oh, I'm here. I'm Black." She looked white to me, and it was the first of many lessons that Oakhurst would teach me about my own captivity to race and about its continuing and abiding power in our hearts and in our culture. After that awkward beginning, we had a good discussion, and the committee indicated that they were very interested in my becoming the next pastor at Oakhurst. I indicated that we were interested in coming there, too, and we would like to come down to Decatur to look at the building and the community.

We dropped David off at Caroline's parents' home in Chattanooga and went down on a cold winter day with baby Susan to look over the situation. Much of that visit is now a blur, but I do remember how cold the big, old building was, because the congregation could no longer afford to heat it during the week. I also remember that every door on the inside and the outside was locked. The building person who gave us the tour had a huge ring of keys, reminding us of medieval buildings and all the keys required to open their doors. There was definitely a fortress mentality in the building and in the heart of the congregation, a mentality that we knew that we would have to break if the church were to survive. Despite these difficulties (and many more that we would learn after we came), we decided to accept the position if it were offered to us.

The initial positive impression that I had made on the committee on the Sunday visit to Nashville seemed to hold, and the congregation voted to call me as the next pastor at Oakhurst Presbyterian Church. We were sorry to leave our circle of friends in Nashville, but we packed up our stuff and headed south down I-75 to the Atlanta area in early February of 1983, not knowing if there would be enough money in the church budget to last more than two years, taking a three-year-old David and a five-month-old Susan in tow with us. As it turned out, we would be at Oakhurst almost thirty-four years.

13

The Rutted Roads of Life

WHEN CAROLINE AND I and David and Susan moved to the Atlanta area, we first rented a house because we did not have a lot of money, and because Oakhurst Church was in such precarious shape, we did not know if it would survive more than a couple of years. The Presbytery executive who approved funding for the church indicated that he would give us two years to show some possibilities. Mary Reimer and Wilma Franklin, members of Oakhurst, found us a house to rent, and it had a swimming pool! We enjoyed hosting many people at the pool, and it turned out that we had more friends and family than we thought, once they found out that we had a pool! On a hot summer day in July, Caroline's parents were down from Chattanooga. We were all cooling down in the pool when we heard the phone ring in the house—this was 1983, before the advent of cell phones. Caroline was in the house, and she answered the phone. She motioned out of the window for me to come into the house.

"It's your mom—your father has died," she told me. I took the phone, and Mother gave me the news: "Nibs, I got a call from Doris today, Gip's sister. She wanted to let me know that your father had died of a massive heart attack on Thursday. I wanted to make sure that you knew, and also, the family wanted to know if you wanted to be listed in the obituary." My reaction was hard to pinpoint. For a split second, it did not register—I didn't have a father. Then, it sank in, and I said: "Mother, I appreciate your calling to let me know, but I don't have much interest in this. His family can put whatever they want to put in the obituary." She replied: "They also want to know if you will be coming to the funeral." My spiteful, inward reaction was "I bet they do wonder that—some of them probably don't even know that I exist." Instead, I said: "No, Mother, I won't be going to the funeral, so they can all exhale at this point. He was the prodigal dad, not me as the prodigal son. How are you doing with the news?" She said: "I'm much like you, Nibs, it is water under the bridge a long time ago, but I just wanted to make sure that you knew. I am sad at his passing, but I won't be going to the funeral either." Though she did not seem to be posing the question of attendance at my father's funeral as a loyalty oath, for a moment I felt it that way. If the issue of choosing sides was involved here, I did not perceive it, but even so, I was glad that I had chosen my mother's side of not attending the funeral.

I wrote in my journal that day: "I'm sad for him but have experienced no great regret for me. So, my father, the 'flesh and blood' anyway, is dead. The more powerful, absent, mythical father still lives inside me, though—the one who could have blessed me but didn't; the one whose love I'll always search for, the one who will always be elusive—that father is still alive and well. Perhaps that would have been the one benefit from talking with him about our relationship—the myth of the great, all-blessing, all-loving father would have been shaken a bit. But, myths are indeed powerful, and I'll still be wrestling."

Speaking of wrestling, there was plenty of it at Oakhurst Presbyterian, as we entered our first year there. The church building was huge and old and needed a lot of work. The eighty or so members who were left did not have the energy or money to do maintenance for a building constructed for almost nine hundred members. The infrastructure of the organization also needed a lot of work. Although there were Black members, those classified as "white" still held all the power. We had many fights in the first couple of years, as we sought to shift the church from a majority white church that had Black members to a multicultural church in which power was shared among the leadership and membership and in worship. Because of how deeply those of us classified as "white" are captured by racism and white supremacy, this was a continuing struggle beyond the scope of this book.[1]

---

1. For more information on our particular journey and suggestions for change, see *O, Lord, Hold Our Hands* by Nibs Stroupe and Caroline Leach and *Passionate for Justice* by Catherine Meeks and Nibs Stroupe.

The wrestling that stung me the most, however, was my own discovery of how deeply racism was embedded in my consciousness. The white supremacy that I had learned at my mother's feet is imprinted in my ways of perceiving the world, and I was confronted with that over and over again at Oakhurst. As I arrived at Oakhurst as pastor, I considered myself a liberal on most issues, and I also felt that I was mostly over the racism that I had learned as a child. There might be some residuals left over in me, but for the most part, I had overcome.

My teachers at Oakhurst were many, and they all taught me the same lesson: racism and white supremacy were buried deep in my soul.

Early in my time at Oakhurst, one of our Black members called me on the phone to express her concern over a decision that I had made as pastor about asking a white couple to be the leaders of our growing youth group, a group that included our son David but which otherwise was mostly Black. As we disagreed about this on the phone, I asked her: "Why are you so angry about this?" She replied, "I'm not angry. What makes you think that I am angry?"

"Well, you sound angry to me." Her reply again: "No, I'm not angry. You don't know me well enough. Believe me, if I am angry, everyone in the room will know it. No, I'm not angry." I said: "Well, I'm not sure—you sounded angry to me."

She then made a huge decision to take me on as a white man, as her white pastor. "No, I'm not angry. But I think I know the reason that why you thought I was angry. Do you want to hear it?" I thought for a moment, then said, "Okay, why is that?" She came back: "You thought I was angry because you are not accustomed to Black people calling you into question. So instead of admitting that, you tried to put the problem on me by accusing me of being angry, when all the time it was you who was getting angry. Y'all white folks do that all the time to us. You projected your anger onto me because you are not accustomed to dealing with us as peers. Am I right?" There was a long silence as I pondered my options. Was it true? Was my racism showing? Should I acknowledge it? Should I deny it? How much would it cost me if I acknowledged it? I decided to jump in, as she had done with me: "I think that you might be right. I don't have much practice with Black people as peers. I'm accustomed to being in authority." To my surprise, she thanked me for my honesty and said, "Now, I can work with this. Most of you white folk want to deny that you have any racism in you, but you are saying that you do, so I can work with that. I still don't agree with you about the youth leaders, but let's see what they can do."

There were many other stories and engagements that demonstrated to me the continuing power of racism in my life, and I have related a lot of them in the books noted above. Out of these came my approach for those classified as "white" in how we would acknowledge our captivity to racism and seek to diminish its power in our lives. It is my sense that those of us classified as "white" are like addicts in relation to the idea of race. We have breathed it in, and it will require a daily practice and accountability to begin to lessen our captivity. I call it "the Seven Steps": recognition, repentance, resistance, resilience, reparations, reconciliation, and recovery. I am grateful to the congregation at Oakhurst, especially the African-American members, who engaged me, challenged me, and helped to inspire me to acknowledge my captivity to race and to seek a different way. I'm also grateful to Mother for teaching me the resiliency as a child to be able to work in this kind of system.

Mother was also a valuable asset in her many visits to Oakhurst. It was a long drive from Arkansas to Atlanta, and most of the time I would catch the bus in Atlanta and take it to Birmingham, where I would meet up with Mother and drive her car the rest of the way to Atlanta. By this time in her life, Mother had developed friendships with several African-American people in Helena. When she came to visit at Oakhurst, she fit in naturally and even had a great advantage because the African-American culture that we experienced at Oakhurst highly valued mothers and grandmothers, of which she was both. One of the Black women laughingly commented on observing Mother and me in a Bible study that I was leading at Oakhurst—"it was like watching a tennis match. You would serve something up, and your mother would waste no time in returning the serve, sometimes even getting in a corner shot where you had trouble returning. I see where you get your oral skills now—the nut didn't fall far from the tree. But as your mother said in the study, 'the largest oak tree is just a nut that held its ground.'"

We would also make several visits a year to see Mother in Helena, with the most exciting ones being at Christmas. Mother loved Christmas and decorated everywhere. She also loved buying presents for our children—she usually shopped year-round. Our kids loved going to her house at Christmas time, though it was a hard trip for Caroline and me. The Advent and Christmas season are hard on pastors in a church—so many activities, so much pressure to do the season right. Our pattern for many years was to be exhausted following the Christmas Eve worship service at night. We would then go home and finish wrapping presents. On Christmas morning we were up early with David and Susan—when they were little, the rule was not to wake us before 7 AM, but when they became teenagers, the rule was that they had to be up by 10 AM. We would get up on Christmas Day, open our presents, then take the two-hour drive to Chattanooga to be with Caroline's parents, then head out in a day or so for the nine-hour drive to Arkansas through many two-lane highways in north Alabama and Mississippi.

Upon arrival in Helena, the kids would be greeted with Mother's long Christmas pantyhose stockings filled with presents, and they would be thrilled. Mother showered presents and food upon us, and those Christmas trips are among their favorite memories of Mother. By that time, Mother had lived by herself for almost twenty years, and her house had remained the same small house in which I grew up. She was glad to see us, but it was a tight fit. David and Susan would occupy the bedroom in which I had grown up, the same bedroom that Mother and I had shared when I was a boy. Mother would be in her bedroom, and Caroline and I would be on the fold-out couch in the living room. Before Mother retired from teaching at the community college, she would be up making coffee and having a morning cigarette at 6 AM, and Caroline and I could hear and smell it all on our couch-bed in the living room.

In the early years of our visits to Mother's, we would survive because of the Christmas buzz. In the summer, the swimming pool across the street, where I had learned to swim at the Paines' home, was a welcome respite from the oppressive summer heat of the Delta, as well as from the cramped quarters. As our kids got older and more mobile, the tensions began to rise on our trips home. Mother would never say it, but it had to be quite a shock for her to have us four descend upon her space and her solitude. We learned why the three-day rule applies to fish and company! David was a very active and busy child, which we affirmed, yet when he was about eight years old, Mother decided to focus her irritation about our crowding her upon him rather than on the adults in our family. She would criticize just about everything that David did while we were visiting her. She never focused her discomfort or anger on Susan, but rather chose David as her focus. Indeed, to this day, Susan has great admiration for my mother, whom she called "Grandma." The tensions between Mother and David would build over the next few years.

The early 1980's would be significant years for Mother. She was now the lead instructor at the Community College School of Cosmetology, which fulfilled a long dream of hers to be a teacher. In September, 1984, her Aunt Ila died, the last of her father's siblings to pass. Ila was the relative who lived in West Helena and was the relative with whom Mother had shared the car in my youth. Ila's death left Mother as the oldest of the Armour family, but she did not seek the role of the matriarch—that fell to the next oldest Armour person, Jean Armour Burrow, Mother's first cousin, who lived in the home village of Byhalia. Though Mother did not seek the matriarch role, she did perceive that Jean wanted to use her familial authority over her, and there were always tensions between them. I perceived Jean differently—I perceived that she was seeking to be the channel of the family stories and heritage for the next generation, including me and the other grandchildren of the six original Armour siblings, who had been the foundational matriarchs and patriarchs. Mother was more of an "outsider" in the family, because her views on race had changed and because she was becoming more outspoken on social issues. Mother seemed to prefer it that way.

Mother continued her journey into the psychic realm and began to believe that she was a reincarnated spirit. She sought to be hypnotized, but it did not work. She had been referred by one of her cosmetology students to a doctor who did hypnosis work in Brinkley, Arkansas, which was about sixty miles away. Here is how she put it in a letter to me: "The weekend has been full. We went to Brinkley to see the doctor, and wouldn't you know it, I was so excited he couldn't hypnotize me. Anyway, I made a tape of the girl, Martha, who was hypnotized. She came over with me because she wanted to see and hear what I said. As it turned out, I said nothing. When you come home, I want you to listen to the tape—very interesting! Mary and I decided that we were going back later." Mother made at least two more trips back to see the doctor in Brinkley to seek to be hypnotized, but none of them were successful. Neither Caroline nor I nor the kids were surprised at this. Mother had such an iron will to survive, and it was hard to imagine her yielding that control to a doctor who wanted her to give herself up and probe her inner self in hypnosis.

Mother was so interested in hypnosis because she believed that she was living in the karma of other peoples' lives from the past. In one of her journals she wrote: "Listened to 'Golden Angels' tapes and got the name Sarah as my angel's name. Things are moving fast—was told that I was a concubine in Abraham's camp, and now my angel's name is Sarah!

Strange! I have felt so pulled by angels. Will have to go on with my quest of them. Thank You, Father, for angels and the healing of my mind!"

Mother continued her search for angels, for her past selves, and for the meaning of these messengers for her life. She recorded this dream in her journal: "I saw Mary Wortham, who actually had been dead for 3–4 years. I was so GLAD to see her and told her 'I never was so glad to see someone.' When she asked why, I told her that she had confirmed something that I had believed in for years: Reincarnation. I realized that she had died and had come back. We walked down the street to get some food, and there was a huge wolf behind her with weird eyes. In front of us there was a doctor who had fallen out with a spell. I realized that it was a demon so I cast it out. Got him to go to bed and told him that he would be well when he waked up. Then I was in gorgeous sunshine again on a picnic. People were in small groups of 4–5 people, and Mary Wortham was in one, sort of in the roots of a tree. I stopped to tell her again how glad I was to see her, and I put my hand out to touch her, but there was the wolf, with his teeth now showing. I took my hand back and waked up."

In 1985 she began to write about her increasing sight difficulties with macular degeneration. Hearing from her ophthalmologist in Helena that there was not a lot to be done to cure it, she began to search for alternative remedies. Losing her sight, or having it greatly diminished, would threaten the independence that she had worked so hard to create and maintain over forty years. Part of her journey into the psychic realm was intensified by the desire to heal the degeneration in her eyes, or at least to stop it where it was. She wrote this prayer in her journal: "God, I need some encouragement. I know that all this is an 'I' thing, but that's where I am right now. God, you are moving so slowly (and I know that the impatience comes from me). You know that I need someone to say 'Let me help, let me take you to the shore.' Loneliness is no joke! Thank You, God, for my healing of my eye. I am claiming the promises You gave. I keep hearing in my mind the healing of the blind man in Luke 11:34–35 and connecting it with me."

Mother never would find a cure for the macular degeneration in her eyes, a fact that gives me pause as I age. Her sight still enabled her to drive to places that she knew, including places like Byhalia, but she knew that she was beginning a long decline. Since she had been working as the lead instructor for the School of Cosmetology for ten years and was thus invested in the state retirement system, she decided to retire in the early spring of 1986. It was right in the middle of the Lent and Easter season at the church, so I was not able to attend her retirement ceremony at the school. In her typical pattern with me, Mother brushed off any potential hurt at my absence from that occasion, but I have always felt bad that I did not make it. They gave her a great party, and her picture was on the front page of the local Helena paper, with the caption "Mary Stroupe, lead cosmetology instructor at Phillips County Community College for the past ten years, is retiring this Friday. Yesterday cosmetology students and faculty had a party in her honor. Here, she and cosmetology instructor Jessie Weston pose with a cake which said 'Cosmetologists never retire—they just curl up and dye.'"

As one of her last acts as lead instructor, Mother recommended to the Dean that Jessie Weston be promoted to be the lead instructor, and the Dean wisely followed her advice. Jessie also was a believer in the psychic realm, and she and Mother continued their "front door" visits at Mother's home, talking about psychic phenomena and gossiping about the happenings at the School of Cosmetology. It was a friendship that lasted until Mother's death, and if Mother and Jessie were correct about the psychic realm, their friendship resumed after both of them entered the next realm. I don't know if Mother ever knew how much she had scandalized the neighborhood by welcoming Jessie into her home through the front door. Knowing Mother, if she had known, she would have thumbed her nose at the neighbors and even would have delighted in scandalizing them in this way.

Now that she was retired, Mother was able to travel more and enjoy not having a schedule. One of her first trips was to Chicago to visit Bud, who was now beginning a long decline in his own health. Tensions had developed between him and his four children after he had divorced his wife Flossie, but two of them, Bonnie and John, had stayed close to him. Mother had become friends with his second wife, Violet (nicknamed "Puddy"), but Bud later divorced her too. He was now with his third wife, much younger than him, but he had also developed emphysema and the beginnings of lung cancer from all the smoking. Lung cancer was a huge issue for the Armour side of the family—my grandfather had died of it; his brothers Dell and Cecil, and Thurman had died of it. Indeed, the anecdote in the Armour family was that only one male, Cecil, had lived past age 63 in the last few generations. Bud felt that pressure, too. At age 61, he had surgery in 1986 to seek to mitigate the lung cancer and to relieve the symptoms of the emphysema.

Since she was retired, Mother went up that year to take care of Bud after the surgery, and she was shocked at how much his mobility and his stamina were affected by the lung diseases. She decided to stop smoking so that she would not irritate his lungs and would not tempt him to resume smoking. While she was up there with him, he told her that he felt like he was dying slowly one day at a time, and that he hoped that she would be able to avoid that fate, the same fate that had affected their father. He also let her know that he had set up a trust fund for her and for the two children who had stayed loyal to him. That fund would go into effect at his death, and it would continue for her until her death. He wanted to make sure that he had taken care of his big sister who had done so much for him, after their mother had died in 1934 when Bud was only eleven years old.

By the time that Mother had returned home from that Chicago visit, she had decided to quit smoking. Not wanting to tempt Bud, but also being alarmed to see what the lung disease had done to his vitality, she decided to quit cold turkey. Mother had begun smoking when she was a young adult. I am not certain what caused her to begin smoking, other than all her male adult relatives did it. When I was in high school, it was still considered "unlady-like" for women to smoke, so I am intrigued that Mother entered this male world of smoking in the late 1930's. Few of her female relatives smoked, although her favorite aunt BB smoked, and that may have been her original motivation. Smoking also may have provided some of the few moments that she had to relax for a bit and to let the nicotine sink in to assist her. That she took up smoking so early is another indication to me of her refusal to accept the boundaries set for her as a woman by a patriarchal world.

I was aware of her powerful will, but even I was surprised that she simply stopped smoking, without assistance, after smoking at least two packs a day for fifty years. When I asked her about it, she demurred and said that she just decided not to do it. She also noted that she had a great desire to smoke until she decided to try one at home after she had returned from Chicago. As she was smoking the cigarette, her body revolted—she got nauseated and went to vomit in the toilet. Mother always hated throwing up, so I knew that she would be able to keep away from cigarettes after they had made her vomit. She had direct evidence of what cigarettes did to her body. I knew this evidence first hand because I had tried smoking in the sixth grade with a couple of male friends in the hills behind our house. Word got back to our baseball coach, and he made us run laps until we were ready to puke. "Now, boys, this is what cigarettes do to your body. Smoke if you want to, but you won't be playing baseball on this team anymore if you do." That was enough for me—I didn't like smoking anyway.

Bud lasted two more years—he was determined to make it past his 63rd birthday in October, and he made it. Just a few days after he turned 63 in 1988, he died, and his oldest child Bonnie called Mother to let her know. Mother then called me, crying, and said: "Nibs, Bud just died. What am I gonna do? He was the last one who cared anything about me!" I was sorry to hear about Bud's passing, for I knew how important he was to Mother. Yet I was also hurt when she said that he was the last one to care about her. I told her: "Mother, I know that this hurts so bad. But don't worry, I care about you, and I will always take care of you. Plus, Bud left that trust fund for you, and that should help with the money." She caught herself, and replied, "No, Nibs, I know that you love me and will take care of me. I meant that he was the last one of my generation to die, who cared about me—Daddy's gone, Dell and Cecil are gone, BB's gone, and now Bud is gone. It just hurts so much."

Caroline and the kids and I drove over to Byhalia for Bud's funeral, and at that funeral we met Doris, my father's sister who had called Mother about my father's passing. We also met Phil Stroupe, my father's brother, who turned out to be one of Mother's best friends as a youth. The revelations just kept coming! I also do not remember Mother crying at Bud's funeral. Such vulnerability was not part of her public persona. I don't know that she had the male perspective that crying shows weakness, but she seemed to have adopted the view that crying in public did show weakness. Even for her beloved brother, she would not cry in public, although she had certainly cried with me on the phone.

In 1985, three years prior to his death, Bud and Bonnie and Bud's third wife Lynn had flown down to Helena, and Caroline and I took the kids over to meet them. As we left Bud's funeral in 1988, I was glad that Bud had met David and Susan before he died. Bud had always appeared to be a rough and tough man, but I had often perceived him as a little boy whose gruffness sought to cover his deep hurt at the loss of his mother when he was eleven years old. In that sense, I knew his heart—fortunately, my mother had stayed, and I thank God for that.

14

Hard Times

As our kids got a bit older, we saved up money for a beach trip every summer. We often went to Tybee island, off the coast of Georgia near Savannah. We chose it because it was relatively close, and it was a beach that had not yet been totally commercialized. We usually stayed at a condominium complex near the mouth of the Savannah River, where it met the Atlantic Ocean. I remember seeing for the first time the two currents flowing together, the river flowing east and south, the ocean tides coming in from the east, flowing west. It was such a primordial feeling, to see such elemental things—I felt like I was privy to some secret ceremonies of nature.

Sometimes we went to other beaches, and for spring break of 1990, we went to Edisto Island, off the coast of South Carolina, near Charleston. Mother went with us to Edisto. We had taken her with us to Tybee a couple of times, and she enjoyed the beach immensely. She loved looking for shells, and she especially liked cutting a few sea oats to take back to Arkansas with her. We reminded her that taking the sea oats was a crime because they were federally protected, but she indicated that she would take the chance. We did not accompany her when she would make her sea oats forays on the beach, and I told her that I did not want to know anything about it. She would take the sea oats home, dry them out and cure them, and then use them as flower arrangements. I must admit that after her death, we packed up a few remaining sea oats from her house

Hard Times

and brought them back to Georgia with us. They now sit in our house in a vase engraved with sea oats, which we had given her for her birthday.

On this particular visit to Edisto, we rented part of a duplex about a block off the beach. It was paneled with dark wood, and it had a long hall perpendicular to the beach. When the ocean winds blew onto shore, they seemed to roar right down through that hall. Since it was April, the air was still cold at times, so the first few days were spent trying to stay warm on the beach. The tensions continued to grow between Mother and David. David and Susan and I often played what we called "hall ball," a game that had many variations to it, including dodge ball and a modified version of baseball. We made a lot of noise, and on the days when it was too cold to enjoy the beach, we were stuck inside for most of the day. Mother would start making edgy comments like: "Can't y'all take that game down onto the beach?" and: "It's a little too loud for an inside game—can't David hold it down just a little bit?" The truth was that all three of us—Susan, David, and I—were making noise, but she had singled David out, a discrimination that David and I especially noticed.

Mother also began sniping at Caroline. She would indicate that we were too permissive in our child-rearing and that the source of our permissiveness was Caroline, because Mother had raised me and was strict. She also made comments about Caroline's failure to make lunches for me, even though I told Mother that I preferred to make my own lunch. She also felt like I washed the dishes too much, seeming to forget the fact that she had taught me and even coerced me into the habit of washing dishes, which I still do to this day. Mother and Caroline had seemed to me to be pretty solid until the kids were born, and Mother and Caroline were both strong and independent women. I was surprised by Mother's zingers at Caroline, and Mother's attacks on both fronts of David and Caroline were surprising to me. Caroline and I discussed the situation, and I told Caroline that I figured that she could take care of herself in relation to Mother.

I began to think, however, that I would need to talk with Mother about her relationship with David. Caroline and I both agreed that we were concerned about the damage that Mother might do to David and to their relationship. I was reluctant to talk with Mother about David because she was a heroine of mine and because I was so shocked that she would be so negative towards him. I had thought that she would appreciate her grandson—my son—who she helped into existence by her fierce dedication to me. It did begin to dawn on me that the same fierce dedication that enabled Mother to save me might now be focused on continuing to protect me (and her) from the same kinds of dangerous forces in the world. I had thought that Caroline and David were inside Mother's circle of protection, but obviously that was incorrect. For some reason the "outsider" status that Mother had given to Caroline and David did not apply to Susan. I'm not sure why this was the case—maybe it was because Susan was just too young in these days, and Mother did not think that Susan had agency yet.

On this beach trip to Edisto, I decided to try to be with Mother alone a bit more. She and I took a trip around the back roads of Edisto Island, looking for cabins where people held as slaves were forced to live. We did not find any of those, but we did find a refurbished plantation where Lafayette once stayed. It was now owned by a family in Philadelphia, and the groundskeeper stopped us as we sought to walk around the grounds, telling us that they did not allow tourists. We also went to see the movie "Driving Miss Daisy." I enjoyed the acting but was a put off by once again seeing a noble Black man redeeming a cranky white person. What interested me most about the movie was Mother's reaction to it. She said that she was a lot like the cranky white woman in the movie. I wanted to push this further, but I was afraid to open it up, given the family tensions. One of the dynamics at the end of the movie is that the woman ends up in a nursing home, and I knew that this was one of Mother's great fears about the end of her own life. I thought to myself that she also seemed intent on driving away those who were close to her, as the character in the movie had done, except that her son had stayed loyal to her, as I would.

Things came to a head the next year on our summer visit to Mother's. As usual in family discord, the event that set it off was trivial. We never brought our dogs to Helena with us, but when Mother came to see us in Georgia, she often criticized us for allowing our dogs and cats to go anywhere in our house. We only had one pet when I was growing up—a dog named Spotty, who never was allowed inside the house except on the coldest of nights. Mother often had stray cats and dogs show up at her doorstep, and the Sellers' dog Nosy would often sit on her back stoop. Mother did develop affection for one of the cats who came around, a cat she named "Mrs. Hargraves." She occasionally let Mrs. Hargraves come in the house, and on this visit we teased her a bit about letting the cat indoors, after she had raised such an issue about our animals being in our house. The next day David found a flea in Mother's rug, and he teasingly told her: "Grandma, you've got a flea in the house!" He meant it in a kind and joking manner, but she took it as a capital offense. She huffed and puffed and immediately went to the phone to call the pest service and told them: "Y'all have got to come out here immediately because my grandson found a flea in the house, and he doesn't like it." It was a hurtful gesture and an attack on David, and he understood that. He ran into the bedroom and cried and cried, and I felt that little, sad boy stir in me as I witnessed this episode.

That night the tensions in all of us, especially me, were powerful and palpable. I was now caught between my mother, whom I loved deeply, and my son, whom I also loved deeply. As Caroline and I lay on the couch bed that night, I was furious, and I had trouble going to sleep. I got up and went out on the screen porch and wrote this entry in my journal: "I am tense and unable to sleep because of the tremendous tension with Mother, David and Caroline, combined with Susan's getting the croup/pneumonia that David had. My back has such a huge knot in it from the bottom of my shoulder blade to the top of my neck. I go to sleep, then wake up almost immediately. I'm also afraid that I may be getting the pneumonia, too, but I think that the main issue is my tension and anxiety over having to be peacemaker. I am totally exhausted from worrying, trying to keep Mother off David and Caroline. We plan to head back to Atlanta day after tomorrow. It has been a hellacious vacation, and I hope that I will learn, once and for all, that coming to Mother's is not vacation. She seems worse than ever this time, more difficult, more argumentative. She got into it with David this morning over the flea, and she was more childish than he was."

I had been stalling on having "the talk" with Mother, but I could do it no longer. I told Caroline that I would talk with Mother that afternoon, and Mother and I went out on the back porch attached to her workshop—it was a lovely place to be for a very tough conversation. I asked Mother: "Why are you being so hard on David, especially yesterday over the flea?" She looked up with a steely stare: "I was not being hard on him. I was just trying to respond to his finding the flea—I didn't want to ruin y'alls' trip by having fleas." "Mother, you know that is not what happened. I don't know if you meant to hurt him or not, but you did." She took a drink of her vodka and orange juice. While I was growing up, Mother did not drink at all, as far as I knew. I never saw her take a drink at home. Sometime after I went to college, and especially after she retired, she would have a late afternoon drink, and in the warm weather, she loved going out to the porch by her workshop to have her afternoon drink. She was doing that now as we talked, and she replied: "I didn't mean to hurt him. He, and apparently you, took it that way."

There was no easy apology coming, and while I knew that there would likely not be, I was hoping for one from her. I had to step up my game, and I decided to probe and even escalate it a bit: "Mother, you've been hard on David lately, and I don't know why. He is a good and kind kid, and though he makes mistakes, he has done nothing to merit the reaction that you have been giving him." She replied quickly: "I don't think that I have been hard on him. Perhaps he feels that way because you all are too easy on him." Now, I had to step it up again, and I wanted to avoid a conversation on how permissive we were with our kids, her grandchildren. "Mother, we are raising David and Susan just about the same way that you raised me—firm but loving. We do allow some silliness at home, but we would rather that he show out at home and be courteous out in the world, just like you taught me." Her retort: "I was never as easy on you as you all are on David. He could never get away with some of the stuff that you allow him to do."

I had no intention of going down that road with her. I wanted to keep it simple and direct. "Mother, you and I can talk about parenting philosophy another time, but I need to make this clear now. I simply cannot tolerate your harping on David like you are doing now, whether you think that it is warranted or not. You have got to change your approach with him, or at least tone it down. You are important to me, and I want you to be important to David, but right now your relationship with him is in danger, and you are the one who can change that, not him. If things don't get better, we'll have to think about how often we can come over to visit."

She gave me a fierce look, and for a moment I was not sure what she would say or do. Then she said, "All right, I will try to do better. I want David to have a good relationship with me." I sighed to myself and said: "Okay, thank you. This will make it a lot easier on me." After that, there was silence, as we both thought about the conversation and about all that had led up to it. In a little while, Mother got up and said, "I need to go in to see about supper."

She went back in to the house, and I let out a big sigh. I had not had that kind of conversation with her in a long time, perhaps since we had disagreed over my dating Deirdre from Brooklyn. She was true to her word, however. She did ease up on David, but her months of attacks would sour their relationship for a long while yet. Things were less tense on our subsequent visits, and one of the reasons was that Caroline had gotten insights from Mother's neighbor Ann Lewis, who was part of the Paine family and now lived in the house across the street with the swimming pool. While Mother and I were having the talk, Caroline wisely took the kids over to the pool. Ann came down to the pool for a visit, and Caroline was thanking her for allowing us to use the pool so much, because things had gotten pretty tense between Mother and the kids, especially with David. Ann was a little surprised, saying: "Gosh, she talks about them all the time and shows me the letters and photos that you send to her." Caroline added: "Well, we do sort of invade her space when we come over for a visit, but it is really tense this time." Ann gave us a good suggestion: "You know, here's something for you all to think about. I think that Mary E [Ann's name for Mother] would just like to have Nibs visit her by himself once in a while. She loves all of you, but she just wants some time with him by himself every now and then. Maybe you can try that and see if that helps."

As Caroline and I lay on the couch bed that night, our last night for this visit, we shared the content of our talks with Mother and with Ann. We were both glad to have those done, and we wondered if Mother would hold to her word on David. We also wondered if Ann's advice was right, and we decided to try it. It turned out that Ann was right on target. I would visit Mother at least once a year by myself, and that seemed to perk her up and to lessen her need to grind on David. After her death, I did discover one residual from our talk on David from that afternoon on the porch. In her dream journal, she recorded this dream: "I was going to London with Jean. Was all packed and was to catch the bus to meet her somewhere. It was time to drive to catch the bus downtown here in Helena. I could not catch the bus because I was not dressed. Could not find a pair of hose without a huge runner in it (she put in ALL CAPS): I TRIED TO GET NIBS (WHO WAS A TEENAGER) TO HELP ME BUT HE ONLY WANTED TO KNOW WHERE I WAS GOING TO LEAVE THE CAR SO HE COULD USE IT. I was positively frantic trying to get to West Helena to stop the bus."

In that dream, anyway, I guess that I had fallen out of the inner circle of Mother and me. I did begin making visits to Mother by myself. On one of those individual visits, we had another hard talk, but this time I had no personal stake in it. It was during the winter because Mother had a fire burning in the fireplace (she had replaced the big gas heater with central air and heat and had put in a fireplace where the coal chute used to be).

On her wall by the fireplace was an oil painting, which had been done by BB's oldest son, Hart, Jr. As I have noted, BB ("Bernice") was her aunt but was more like a beloved sister than an aunt. Hart Junior (as he was known in the family, since he was named for his father—he'll be "Hart Jr.:" for this story) was quite a talented musician and painter, and Mother liked his work. His paintings tended to be on the abstract side, but Mother preferred his still life work. On a summer visit to BB's in Memphis when I was still in high school, Hart Jr. noticed an afghan that Mother had made for BB. "You know, Sug [the family nickname], I really like that afghan that you made for Momma. Why don't you make me one for Christmas?" Mother replied, "Why, Hart Jr., I'd be glad to make you one. Let's make a deal. I'll make you an afghan, and you'll paint me a picture. But I want just an ordinary picture." Hart Jr. asked: "Well, I don't do many of those—what do you have in mind?" Mother asserted: "I just want a painting of a bowl with some yellow flowers in it, a painting that anyone can tell what it is when they look at it. Can you do that? Deal?" He answered, "I really want that afghan. So, you'll get your bowl of flowers!"

As the year progressed toward Christmas, Mother was diligently working on the afghan for Hart Jr. She began to get alerts from BB, however, that Hart Jr. was not making much progress on Mother's painting. BB indicated that he might not have it ready for Christmas, and Mother might want to slow down in her work on the afghan. Mother finished the afghan for Hart Jr., but she also had a back-up plan. That year for Christmas we went up to BB's and Hart's house in Memphis, and Mother had wrapped a big box nicely with Hart Jr.'s afghan in it. When Hart Jr. came over on Christmas Day for dinner and for opening presents, he was especially glad to see that box. We ate dinner, and the time came for opening presents, and Mother noticed that there was not a present for her from Hart Jr.

He picked up his brightly wrapped big box from Mother, and said: "Sug, I have a confession to make. I did not get a chance to get your painting done—I've just been so busy at the store. But I will get it to you soon! I am glad to get this present, though!" As he began to open the present, Mother replied: "Hart Jr., I think that you'll find that this present is just right for you!" He opened the present, and inside the big box was one small square from the afghan quilt, with a note for Mother that said: "Here's the beginning of the afghan, and the rest is waiting for you when I get my painting of the bowl of flowers. Love, Sug." Mother and BB had obviously been in communication, because they both fell out laughing at the look on Hart Jr.'s face when he pulled out the one square from the afghan. "Okay, Sug, Okay," he said, as even he began laughing, "I'll get the painting to you by early spring."

He did get the painting to her, and she gave him the completed afghan, and it was that painting that I noticed on that winter evening on one of my trips to visit Mother by myself. We recalled the story together, telling it again and laughing. Then Mother turned serious and took the story to another level, and she asked: "Nibs, why do you think that Hart Jr. has never gotten married? He is such a nice guy, and he is so attractive." Hart Jr. was now in his mid-fifties, and while he had dated women seriously in college, he had never dated any women after that. I knew why Hart Jr. had never been married, but I was hesitant to go down this road with Mother. My antennae were up, but I decided to step into the dangerous path.

I told her: "Mother, I actually know why Hart Jr. has never been married." She took a drink of her vodka and said: "How would you know? Did he talk to you about it?" I got up from the couch and walked towards the fireplace to sit on the hearth because I expected this to be another tough conversation, and I wanted to be able to look directly at her but not be too close to her. I said: "No, he has never talked with me about it, but do you remember when I spent the night in his house in Memphis on one of my trips to see my girlfriend? He had a man sleep over with him, and he introduced him to us as his friend, but they slept in the same bedroom." Mother answered: "Why didn't you tell me about this?" I remembered my conversation with Alice Taylor many years ago at St. Columba, and I exhaled and told Mother: "I wasn't sure how you would react to it. I didn't talk with him about it. I didn't even know if BB and Hart knew it. I didn't want to start something that would cause a big conflict."

She replied: "I always suspected that he was gay, but BB and I never talked about it. I wish that we had. I wish that he could know that I still love him, that I don't care who he loves or sleeps with." I had not thought of this until then, but I told her: "Well, you can write him and let him know that his sexual orientation is his business and that you will always love him." She replied: "I think that I will do that. I won't tell anybody else in the family, though. They would not be able to handle it and would condemn him." The parents, BB and Hart, had both died by this time, but there were cousins left in Mother's generation. I reflected to her: "Yes, our family is very conservative, but I think that some of the people in my generation might surprise you."

Mother did write Hart Jr., but as far as I know, he never replied to her. By this time, he had moved to Florida, and I suppose that in terms of family, he decided to keep his sexuality buried in the closet. He never engaged Mother on this issue, which I saw as a significant loss for both of them, since they had strong love for one another. In many ways they were both outsiders in the family, Mother with her divorce and he with his sexual orientation, and I wish that they had been able to make that connection and support one another. The role of secrecy in the family had reared its head again, and this time, it would end in a lonely and painful way for Hart Jr.

About a decade after our conversation on that winter evening, Mother heard from Armour family members that Hart Jr. had contracted HIV/AIDS and was not doing well. I contacted his younger brother to get his address, and Mother and I separately sent him letters of encouragement and love. Neither one of us heard back from him, and about a year later, we heard that Hart Jr. had died of pneumonia brought on by HIV/AIDS. He would allow no family members, not even his brother, to come to see him. I have often thought how terrible it is that we live in such a cruel world that forced Hart Jr. to live and die in such secrecy. I think of him a lot in these days, as I look at his painting of the bowl of flowers that he gave Mother, a painting that now hangs in our dining room.

15

On To Writing

I CONTINUED TO BE fascinated by the life and witness of Ida B. Wells. I began to think about writing a book about her, but for many reasons it would take me thirty years to do it. David Billings suggested that I seek a sabbatical to work on a book on Wells, and he had a contact at the Fund for Theological Exploration who funded sabbaticals for pastors. Thanks to David's help, I was able to receive a grant in the summer of 1992 to begin work on a book on Ida Wells.

As I began my sabbatical study, I tried to talk David into writing something on Wells with me, but he felt that it was not a good idea for two white guys to write a book on Ida Wells. I also noticed right away how ignorant I was in regard to the development of the construct of race in American history, and I decided to put the book on Wells on the back burner. Instead, I would do something on race in America, and I oriented my sabbatical work in that direction. I attended a workshop on "Undoing Racism" by the Peoples' Institute for Survival and Beyond, of which David was a trainer. I became acutely aware of how I had learned racism in my life: my mother, my family, my church, and white Southern society had all taught it to me. I had breathed it in and accepted it as truth long before I had any capacity to consider whether it was true or not. I was taught racism by white people who were wonderful to me, who raised me and nurtured me.

Those teachers included Mother, and on one of my individual trips to see her in Arkansas, I decided to talk with her about it. I had learned enough not to ask her why she had taught me racism. Rather, I asked her about her father and his siblings. I asked her if she perceived racism in them. She said: "Yes, Nibs, I did. It was just the way that the times were back then. We had some Black people whom we knew and whom we loved, but there just was a line that you could not cross." Her father Maurice Armour, my grandfather, had a reputation in the Armour family for being the kindest and the most loving of the six siblings. I remember BB's husband Hart telling me when I was a child, "Maurice, your grandaddy, was the best of the siblings—he was kinder and more generous than any of them. It looks like you have some of his blood." I took that as a high compliment, and I had Hart's words in mind when I replied to Mother's description of the racism of the six siblings: "But, Grandaddy, he wasn't like that, was he? I know that Hart told me one time that Grandaddy was the best of the siblings."

Mother replied: "Nibs, you know that I love Daddy more than anything, but I have to tell you that on race, he was the worst of the six. When he ran the store, he would treat Black people okay, but when he got home, he described them in horrible terms, using the N-word all the time. Some of the Black people would occasionally come in the front door of the store, and he would come out from behind the counter and get in their face and tell them that they better get out and go around to the back. He was loving with all of us, but there was only one way to do race in Daddy's life—white people were supreme." When I heard these words from Mother about my beloved Granddaddy, my stomach churned. How could such a loving man be such a racist? How could my grandfather, with his overly generous heart and his great belly laugh, my grandfather who cuddled me as a boy and told me that I was his favorite, how could he be a racist? It was difficult to acknowledge, but it was true—I heard it from my mother, his daughter.

That revelation changed some of my thinking on the issue of race. I began to understand why a powerful structure like race was so difficult to combat in my own heart and mind. Although I had begun to change my mind on race, my ways of perceiving the world kept popping up with these old ways of race. I tried to repress them, but they kept presenting themselves!

I got on the train at the subway station near the church. At the next stop in another Black neighborhood, several young African-American men got on the train, joking and clowning and speaking loudly. I noticed a bit of tension beginning to build in myself. At the same time, I noticed that someone had gotten on the train and sat behind me. This person was reeking of alcohol, and I found myself putting these two occurrences together. I thought to myself "Black males really need to get their act together—they shouldn't be dissipating their lives in this manner." I pondered these things and solutions to them as we rode on the train together, knowing that I was the only white person in that train car. Then, a couple of stops later, the man behind me, who had been reeking of alcohol, got up and exited the train—he was a well-dressed white man. I was reminded of how much of my ways of perceiving the world were still rooted in my childhood of Helena, Arkansas.

Previously, I had been thinking about racism and white ignorance being connected, just as I had thought when I returned from my summer in Brooklyn to tell our white church elders that there was a whole different world of which they (and I) had been ignorant. I learned from that experience that ignorance was only partly to blame for racism, that there was a much deeper issue. When Mother revealed the deeply-held racism of my loving grandfather, my heart hurt, but the revelation helped bring clarity to my thinking and work. If ignorance was the issue, it was willful ignorance. The deeper issue was not ignorance but captivity. Those of us classified as "white" were captive to the power of the system of race. It had taken over the way we perceive ourselves, the way that we perceived others (especially Black people), and the way that we perceived the world. The way out of this captivity was not just knowledge but rather a journey to liberation, a conscious and conscientious work to undo our bondage to the power of race. It is a journey on which I am still traveling.

As I finished up my sabbatical that summer, I knew that I would write a book on the power of racism, on its history and development in America. I was thrilled to think about writing a book, which had been a goal of mine for a long time. I loved reading and its power in my life, and I wanted to share in that power as an author. I knew that I would need to enlist an African-American to be a co-author with me on the book. I recruited my Oakhurst colleague, Inez Giles, who had engaged me on the phone conversation mentioned earlier. I knew that she was outspoken and fierce, and that I could count on her to be both honest and strong on the issues of race. She was not interested in being a co-author, but she agreed to write a chapter and to review my chapters in order to see if they were true in regard to her experience of race. Through friends and networks, we got the manuscript to a publisher known for its strong stands on progressive issues. They were initially interested, and one of the founders called me to say that they wanted to publish it. It was wonderful news, and I wrote this in my journal in November, 1993: "Great news! They want to publish my book! Great news! One of my dreams fulfilled—a book in print."

As they got the manuscript and began to work with it, they were also surprisingly hesitant. Like many of us white liberals in those early 1990's, they agreed that there might be some lingering injustices that were racially based, but they felt that the issue of race was just about over. I remember a telephone conversation with an editor, who told me that they felt that race was now just a sub-category under class, because class was the biggest problem in America now. I was shocked to hear this, but I wanted to get this book published. As a compromise, I agreed that I would delete most of the historical work in the manuscript that compared the post-Reconstruction period to the 1990's.

They also wanted some stories from life at Oakhurst, and we added a chapter on that. That satisfied them, and the book finally came out in April, 1995, entitled *While We Run This Race: Confronting the Power of Racism in a Southern Church*. I was not pleased with the subtitle, and it is clear to me now that they had hoped to confine the power of racism to white Southerners. As the events of the last twenty-five years have shown us, the power of race is everywhere in American culture, and it is both resistant to change and resilient in shape-shifting when change does come.

Mother was proud to hear about the book developments, telling me: "I knew that you could do this. You've always loved reading, and you are an excellent writer. I'm glad that you have stuck with it and gotten this book ready. I know that you will do more, too!" As she aged, Mother's journey hit some major bumps in the road. In 1990, Mother had driven over to Byhalia to see cousin Jean. Just when she was leaving Jean's house to begin her trip back home, Mother pulled out from a stop sign right in front of another car. Miraculously, no one was hurt, but Mother's car was totaled. Jean was concerned about Mother's health and eyesight, and she wrote this description of her reaction to the car wreck: "Nibs, I was totally weak when I got to Sug's car. I could not believe she was not even bruised. There is nothing left of the car from bumper to windshield. I believe that can be considered a modern-day miracle."

The car wreck also shook up Mother, and she wondered about it in her prayer journal: "Thank you, Father, for sparing me in the wreck.

While I was saying my morning prayer today, it was revealed to me that the total wrecking of my car represented the total wrecking of the person I know as me. The fact that I was not hurt is proof of that idea. Thank you for your huge blessing. Could I ever practice mental telepathy?" I'm not certain what she meant by the "mental telepathy," but she saw herself beginning to build a new self after the automobile wreck.

In a series of journal entries, she revealed that such re-building was difficult work. Part of her frustration was that her vision continued to deteriorate rather than improving. Earlier she had written: "Bad day!!! Can't find myself. Who am I? Where am I going? Have to consider going back to work because I am running out of money. Bud's family only sends the check when they feel like it. I deeply resent having to ask for something that doesn't even belong to me. I have to re-organize my life. That's not hard, but it's hard to find a starting place. Bought the marble top from Maxine and went to library doing angel hunting." She was despairing about her life, but she still loved to read and to re-do furniture!

The tensions with David were diminished to a degree, but by 1992 we were making only two trips to Helena each year to see her: Christmas and summertime. I would make a couple of other trips by myself to see her, and that seemed to lower the tensions. Mother continued her psychic work, and she began to focus it on God and on God's healing of the macular degeneration in her eyes. She wrote in her journal early in 1991: "Heard God SPEAK TO ME while in my quiet time, asking God for the strength to do something, and God said, 'Lean on me; I'll do it.'"

This was exciting to her at first, but as the months dragged on without any improvement to her eyes, she began to wonder about herself and about God: "God, I need some encouragement. I know that all this is an 'I' thing, but that's where I am right now. And you are moving so slowly, and I know that the impatience cones from me. You know that I need someone to say 'Let me help. Let me take you to the show, etc.' Loneliness is no joke!!! Thank you, God, for my healing. I am claiming in advance the promises you gave me."

I talked her into coming to see us in order to meet with the eye doctors at Emory, and I made an appointment for her. For her it was a combination of wanting to see us and a desire to check out other medical possibilities for healing, or at least stopping the degeneration of her sight. The doctors at Emory told her that they could not do anything to heal her eyes, and here is what she wrote about it in her journal in 1991: "Have been to Nibs' home for two weeks. No time for meditating or reading or writing. Mary and Bob took me up on Saturday and met me yesterday at the airport. Went to the doctor at Emory while I was in Atlanta. He said he had nothing to offer me about my eyes. I was not disappointed because I already felt what he was gonna say. That leaves it to God and me. So I will really begin my journey on healing myself through God's instructions. Have to work on my impatience and how to avoid worrying and trying to fix things by myself."

Mother had relied on herself for most of her life, from her mother dying when she was a teenager, to her fiancé being killed in World War II, to my father's flight from their marriage, to her being a single, working mother in the 1940's and 50's. She took the same approach to the macular degeneration in her eyes. She would seek to use that extraordinary will power and focus, training it on the healing of her eyes.

It would be a difficult journey for her, calling into question everything that she held dear: relying on herself, counting on God to continue to assist her in those places where she could not carry herself, and finding a way to make a way of out of no way. Losing her sight would mean a shift from the independence that she had experienced most of her life, becoming dependent on others to care for her and to drive her around. She found herself slogging through this dangerous place, without making any progress. She called out to God in lament and in anger, in one of her journal entries: "Lord, I am confused! I am hanging on the hem of your garment, begging for a miracle! I read in a book this morning that maybe you figured that I didn't need it, if you had not answered my prayer. Since it is happening to me, that is cruel, if that is the way that it is gonna be. I can't handle that thought. Lord, you know how afraid I am, but also I may not have believed yet that you could do this. That may be part of my problem. My hard-head and wanting to be in control slows me down in this healing. God, you know me so well. You are inside me and a part of me. Nudge me and excite me and give me the relationship with the Holy Spirit that I need."

Her biggest immediate concern was that her driver's license was expiring on her birthday in May. She was so afraid that she could not see well enough to pass the vision test in order to get her license renewed. She talked with me on the phone about it, and we discussed three options for her. I felt that she would be able to pass the vision test, and she was buoyed by my confidence. If she did not pass it, I would work with her church in Helena to provide rides for her, and people like her good friend Mary Wetzel would take her anywhere at any time. She replied to that: "Nibs, you know that I would hate that. People do not want to fool with me, and I would be so dependent on them. I would just hate that." I replied to her: "Mother, people love you in the church, in the neighborhood, and all around you. There would be so many people who would be glad to help you. And you have certainly helped so many other people yourself." She was firm, however, that she did not want the help of others: "I just cannot do that. I cannot ask people for help. Even Mary wouldn't want to do it. I would be so helpless."

Her answer to me about being helpless went to the heart of her fear of losing her eyesight and of losing the independence that she had established in order to raise me and to survive as a single, working mom. She had done it this way for almost fifty years, and now she was staring in the face of a difficult change. I offered her a third alternative on that phone call. "Mother, you could always come over to live with us. We could be your eyes over here, and so many people at Oakhurst love you—we would have no trouble finding drivers for you." She was strong in her reply: "Nibs, I am not moving over there. You've got David and Susan still to raise, and I would just be in the way. You don't have room for me." David and Susan were eleven and eight years old at that time, but Caroline and I had talked about it and were willing to take her on, if she needed us. I was also well aware of the tensions between Mother and David and Caroline, but we would work it out. I was thinking of all this, as I replied to her on the phone: "Mother, we'd be glad to do it. We've talked about moving to another house anyway, and we could just find one that would accommodate you into it. We'll wait and see what happens at the driving test, but don't get too worried. We will work it out."

God must have been listening to her prayers, because in May, 1991, she had this journal entry: "THANK YOU!!! THANK YOU, GOD, GUARDIAN ANGEL, THE UNIVERSE!!! I have my NEW driver's license! So, for four years I am safe!!!! Thank you, Father! I called Olive, and we rejoiced together. Have the strangest feeling about being a healer! Is that the way I will spend the rest of my life? I do hope so! Father, help me heal myself so I can help heal others. Or maybe I will be healed helping others. Good things have happened today!"

During this time of Mother's writings and ramblings in her soul, I was beginning to discover how much I liked writing. I also discovered that I was a good writer, and I began to write articles for *Journal for Preachers*, *Presbyterian Outlook*, *Hospitality*, and even an article for the Southern Christian Leadership Conference. Our kids told me that I should write a novel about the "untold" stories of Oakhurst, sort of a tell-all without revealing names. They had seen and heard a lot of things that only minister's children are privy to, and they were amazed at what they observed on the inner workings of the church. Such a novel was not possible for a couple of reasons. First, I could not break confidences, although such a narrative was intriguing, especially when I was having a bad church day. Second, thus far I am no good at being a novelist. I simply do not have the imaginative power to develop characters well, and in my few attempts at writing a novel, the characters have become mouthpieces for my sermonic points, rather than fully developed characters. I thus have great admiration for good novelists. I was in the midst of developing my first book, and it was a non-fiction work centered on the continuing power of racism in American culture.

This journey of new phases of our lives in our self-discovery—my writing and Mother's journey into the psychic realm as she sought to find herself—would soon be rudely and destructively interrupted as she and I faced the biggest crisis of our lives together. It happened on Highway 61 in Mississippi, on one of the roads of the Great Migration for African-Americans heading north from the white South in the earlier parts of the twentieth century.

16

Highway 61 Revisited

US HIGHWAY 61 RUNS over 1700 miles from New Orleans to Duluth, Minnesota, which is the home territory for Bob Dylan. He entitled one of his early albums "Highway 61 Revisited" in honor of his relationship to it, and in honor of its being known as the "Blues Highway." It is said that famous blues guitarist Robert Johnson made his deal with the devil at the Mississippi crossroads of Highway 49 and Highway 61, a crossroads that is near my hometown of Helena. Many Black people left the oppression of the South in the Great Migration using Highway 61 as one of the primary routes for escape to the North. Many of them landed in Chicago via Highway 61, and they brought their blues roots with them. It was also the route that Mother's brother Bud and his family used when they moved from Memphis to Chicago, and when Mother and I took the long bus ride up to Chicago to see them, the route was Highway 61.

After the bridge to span the Mississippi River at Helena was completed in 1961, Highway 61 became a primary road for people from Helena to use to go to Memphis, which was about fifty miles away. Indeed, when Caroline and the kids and I went to visit Mother in Helena, we would finish up the trip on Highway 61 in Mississippi before coming to the "Robert Johnson Crossroads" at Highway 49, then taking Highway 49 to cross the Mississippi River bridge to head into Helena. In this part of Mississippi, Highway 61 was a well-traveled two-lane road, flat and long and dangerous because of the number of cars and high speeds of many of those cars. The state of Mississippi passed a law permitting casino gambling in the state, but permitting them only on bodies of water so that the "land" of Mississippi could remain pure. The Mississippi River became a location of some of those casinos, and the first one on the River opened in 1992 near Tunica, about thirty miles from Helena.

Early in December of 1993, I had my weekly phone call with Mother, and she told me that she would be riding with Mary and Bob Wetzel to a mall on the southside of Memphis to do some Christmas shopping there. I was not certain when they were going up to Memphis, but I soon would find out that it was Friday, December 3, as I recorded in my journal: "At 11:08 PM, the phone rang, and I said to Caroline: 'It sounds like a church alarm call.' I wish that it had been a church alarm, because it was a call of a much more alarming nature. It was Sue Hudson from Mother's church in Helena, and she said: 'Nibs, this is Sue Hudson. I want to make sure that you have heard from people from Arkansas.' My heart skipped a beat, and I replied: 'No, Sue, I haven't heard anything—what's going on?" She told me that Mother and the Wetzels had been in a terrible auto accident on Highway 61, and that they all were seriously injured. She indicated that they had all been taken to Elvis Presley Trauma Center in Memphis. It was stunning news. I called the Presley Trauma unit and found out that Mother had two broken legs and a broken hip. I made reservations to fly into Memphis the next morning. I got a call from someone at the Trauma Center at 2 AM to tell me that they had taken Mother to surgery to operate on her hip and that the surgery would last three-to-four hours. I went on to bed at 2:30 AM, got up at 4:30 AM and flew out to Memphis at 8:30 AM." During those two hours of a fitful sleep, I was wondering and wrestling: "Was this it? Was this the time that I had dreaded all my life? Was this the time when Mother would die and leave me?"

This would be our longest journey together. The phone call that I had received from Sue Hudson was one that I had been thinking about all of my adult life. As an only child, I knew that when the crisis for Mother came, it would be on me. I felt both the burden of that obligation but also the joy of having the opportunity to be there for Mother, as she had been there for me all my life. Fittingly for my life history, my main question for myself would be: "Am I up to this task? Will I be a good son?" I wanted so much to be up to the task of taking care of Mother. I knew that we would now be switching roles: she had taken such good care of me when I was a child and a boy. In many ways, I would now become the parent to her, and it was a scary transition indeed.

I met the Wetzel children at the Memphis airport, and we went to the hospital together. They let us into the ICU unit where Mother and Mary and Bob Wetzel were, and the staff told us that they looked pretty bad. Mother had a huge respirator down her throat and was unconscious, recovering from the surgery. I felt weak when I saw her, and then the emergency room physician came to tell me that she only had a 50–50 chance of survival. Upon hearing that, I broke out into a cold sweat and felt faint and sat down. Mother was 74 years old, and it seemed to me that this was it, the end. A great ICU nurse named Julie came to me when the doctor left and said that the odds of Mother's survival were much greater than the doctor had said. "I've been around this ICU a lot," she said, "and I'd say your mother's chances are more like 80–20. So, don't lose hope—we'll take good care of her." What an angel sent to me at that moment!

This began a two week stretch in which I stayed close to Mother, arranging for her care and beginning to trade places with her in our relationship. I was now the caregiver and the provider, and she was the recipient. On Sunday, she regained consciousness, and they took the respirator out. She squeezed my hand and said, "I love you." I told her that I loved her and that we would get her through this. She was shocked at her predicament, and she asked about Mary and Bob Wetzel. I told her that they had both been seriously injured, but their chances of recovery were good too. She began to wonder when she would get back home. I told her that we would take it one day at a time. "But, Nibs," she said, "who will take care of the cat and get the mail and pay the bills?" I told her: "Mother, we are working on that. The Sellers have brought your car up for me to use, and Sue Sellers will take care of the cat and will get your mail and save it for me. I'm already on your checking account, so I will be paying the bills. You worry about starting to heal—we'll take care of the rest." She moaned: "Oh, Nibs, I can't believe that this happened to me. Why did it have to happen to me? What happened to me? I don't remember."

I had gotten the narrative from the Wetzels and from her minister, and I replied: "As far as I can piece it together, Bob was driving you and Mary back from your Christmas shopping trip in Memphis. It was dark and raining, and y'all were on Highway 61. All of a sudden, a man who was drunk and who had been to the casino crossed the center line and ran headlong into your car. You were sitting in the back seat, and apparently the impact was so great that your seat belt snapped, and you slid up under the driver's seat. The police said that if your seat belt had not snapped, you would have been cut in two." She gave a look of recognition and replied:

"What happened to the other driver?" I shook my head and said, "As often happens in these drunk driver cases, he was not hurt—only bruises." She then went back into "Mother" mode: "But, where will you stay? You can't afford to stay in the hotel all this time." I replied: "Now, I told you not to worry about that kind of stuff—besides, Jean has offered to let me stay with her in Byhalia, and actually Brown and Kaye [my cousin and his wife from Helena] live near here, and I'll be staying with them."

The week got much rougher, if possible. They did surgery on her other broken leg and had to put her in traction. Fortunately, neither of us knew that she would remain in traction for seven weeks—if she had known that, she would have refused to do the surgery. The strong, independent single woman, able to take on the world most of her life, was now reduced to having her legs "chained up," as she called it. She could feed herself, but soon her strong and stubborn will kicked in, and it worked both for her and against her. She was enraged because she felt trapped in the traction (and she literally was), and she could do nothing for herself except feed herself. She began to resist any efforts to assist her, and finally one of the nurses told her that she would have to start trying to heal, or she would never make it home again.

That motivated her for a little while, and I began to feel better about her recovery. I was still at Brown and Kaye's home, and I had been gone from my home for ten days. While I was talking on the phone with cousin Jean about Mother's predicament and whether or not I could get Mother back to Atlanta any time soon, the emergency telephone operator broke in and said that there was an urgent call for me. I trembled as the operator connected me with the emergency—surely Mother had taken a much worse turn. The emergency call, however, turned out to be Caroline telling me that the daughter of one of Oakhurst's elders had died suddenly, and that I needed to call the elder. I did that, and they had a strong desire for me to do the funeral early the next week. "Wow," I said to myself after I had hung up, "this is both terrible news and good news." Terrible in that Angela had died. Good in that I would have a reason to return to Atlanta. I hated to leave Mother, but there was nothing that I could really do, and I was exhausted. Jean, Brown and Kaye, and Helena neighbors and friends all said that they would be checking on her.

I gave Mother the bad news, that I was returning to Atlanta for a few days. She was sad and disappointed, but she said that she knew that I had to go back to work. I told her that we could move her over to Atlanta with us as soon as possible, but she said, "No, Nibs, I don't want to bother you all. You are so busy." I told her, "But it will be easier on me if you are closer to us." She hmphed and said "I want to stay here where friends and neighbors are—you all don't have time for me anyway." Since she would not be able to be moved for a long time, I let that one go for the time being. I told her that I would leave on Monday, do the funeral on Tuesday, then return on Thursday for the weekend, that Caroline would preach in my absence.

She seemed satisfied with that, but we had one more big bridge to cross. Her strong will kicked went to work in the wrong direction, and she started refusing to eat, saying that nothing tasted good. At that time, hospital food was notoriously bad, so I had sympathy for her, but I urged her to eat. Her new internist told me and her that she would need to start eating, or they would consider putting a feeding tube in her nose so that she could build up her strength. At this point, I had medical power of attorney, so on the day that I left to fly back to Atlanta, I approved the feeding tube for Mother if she did not start eating.

The next day, the feeding tube was put in, and when I got back home to Atlanta, I got a call from the nurses' station, saying that Mother kept pulling the feeding tube out of her nose. I was impressed with her iron will to be able to do that, but I called her to tell her to leave the feeding tube in, so that she could regain her strength and begin to heal. She said that she would cooperate. I led the funeral at Oakhurst, and given my emotional state, it was powerful and moving on so many levels. Towards the end of that day, I got a call from Mother's doctor, telling me that Mother was continuing to tear the feeding tube out of her nose. I was surprised at that—wow, it was painful to do something like that! The doctor was surprised, too, but he let me know that I had two choices: take the tube out and let her starve, or tie her arms down, so that she could not pull the tube out. Wow! I had to make a hard, hard decision! I asked the doctor: "What do you think her chances are of making it through this?" I could almost hear him shaking his head, as he replied: "Well, she obviously has a strong will. So if we can just get some nutrition into her, I think that she has a good chance." I reluctantly replied, "Okay, tie her arms down and tell her that I approved it."

I flew back to Memphis the next day. I had left Mother's car at Brown and Kaye's home, and they brought it to the airport and left it for me to use—such a great gift! I got the car and drove to the hospital, and Mother was infuriated with me—legs in traction, arms tied down, and a feeding tube in her nose. No warm greeting when I arrived in her hospital room. Rather: "Nibs, do you see that I am a prisoner here? I can't believe that you told them to tie my arms down! Did you really approve that? Why would you do that?" I wanted to smile, but I knew better—if only I could help her find a way to use her will for healing rather than to her detriment. I told her: "Mother, I did it to save your life. Everything I've done for you over these last three weeks is to save your life and help you get back home. You do want to do that, don't you?" She sighed and said: "Nibs, I don't really know right now. I know that I can't go on in prison like this." I made an offer to her: "Okay, Mother, let's try this. I'll be here several days, and I will personally feed you the meals that you get. If you agree to try that, I'll tell them to take the ropes off your arms and the feeding tube out. What do you say?" She sighed again and said, "All right, Nibs, I will try it, but I don't know if it will do any good. And I tell you this. If I ever get out of here, I'm going to tie you down and put a feeding tube in your nose and see how you like it." "Okay, Mother" I said, "if that's what it takes to get you out of here, that is a deal." By the end of the day, her arms were freed, and the feeding tube came out.

That day began a long process of healing for her. I was back with her, which pleased her, even though she knew that I would not be able to stay as long as she wanted. She began to eat, and she began to cooperate with the hospital staff. She began to use her strong will for her own healing, instead of just shutting down in her anger, which certainly was deep and certainly was warranted. She persisted in moving towards healing, and it began to happen. On one of my next visits to see her, she had to use the bedpan while I was there, so I got it for her. She used it and needed to be cleaned up. She said: "Nibs, call the nurse to come clean me up." I told her, "Mother, I'll be glad to do it—the nurses are pretty busy at the beginning of their shifts." She replied: "Nibs, no I don't want you to have to do that—you don't need to see me this way." I came back: "Mother, you changed my diapers all the time—now, I'm just repaying the favor." "That's true," she said, and to my surprise, she let me wipe her bottom and clean her up.

We eventually got her to a situation where she could enter a rehab center after forty-five days in the hospital. I tried to talk her into getting into a rehab center near us in Atlanta, but she was still in traction, and she wanted to be near her home in Helena, where she hoped to return. Cousin Jean also tried to talk her into coming to the Atlanta area, but she was adamantly against it. We got her into a rehab center in Southaven, a suburb of Memphis in Mississippi. It was near Brown's house and much closer to Jean in Byhalia, and it was only about fifty miles from Helena, taking the dreaded Highway 61.

This began a pattern of my returning to visit with her every ten days to two weeks, and I would stay at Brown's and Kaye's nearby, visit with Mother, go down to Helena to check her house, get the mail, and pay her bills. It was an exhausting time for all of us, and I am grateful to Caroline and our children, to family and friends who sustained us. The elders at Oakhurst collected donations to provide funds for my travels back and forth to see and to take care of Mother. Others helped also, as I note in a journal entry from January 24, 1994:

> I am waiting in a Valujet plane waiting to take off for Memphis. Mother was moved to rehab a week ago, where she will be able to get out of traction for a few hours each day. She may be able to get out it entirely in ten days or so. She was pretty depressed about having to continue to be in traction after forty-one days, but she has come a long way. It is odd to go back and forth between these two worlds—not only geographical space but psychic space as well. Old connections, long in disarray, are being re-established. I've been staying with Brown and Kaye, and they have been so gracious and hospitable. Lyda Kitchens sent me a huge check this week to assist in my care for Mother.

Finally, after seven weeks in traction, Mother was able to come out of that confinement and to begin to strengthen her leg muscles and begin to learn to walk again. She could do occupational and physical therapy, and she also was required to do group therapy to talk about her feelings about the car wreck and her long confinement in the hospital. On one of my visits to her in the rehab center, I met with the social worker, who told me that they might have to release Mother because she refused to go to group therapy. Such an early release would mean that she would have to go into a nursing home or come to Atlanta near us. I went into Mother's room and told her the situation. I asked her why she would not go to group therapy. She replied: "I tried it, but it's just a bunch of old people talking about their feelings." "What is the problem with that, Mother? You're old and injured too." She snapped back: "I don't want to talk about my feelings, Nibs—it's just a bunch of psycho mumbo-jumbo." I came back: "Mother, I spend a lot of my time as a pastor talking with people about their feelings, and it usually helps them." "Yeah, but I'm not one of your clients, Nibs, I'm your mother." "That's true, Mother," I replied, "but you will have to do this, or we will be in a mess. They will kick you out, and you'll have to go to a nursing home. Then you won't ever get back home. Is that what you want?" "No, Nibs, I want to go home." I concluded it for us: "Then, you'll have to go to group therapy, Mother, there is no way around it. If you don't want to talk, just say 'I'll pass.'"

Mother agreed to go to group therapy and continued to make progress, so much progress that the rehab staff began to talk about a date to discharge her to go home, with supervised care. I began to make arrangements for her to have twenty-four-hour care at her home in Helena. I knew that she would not like it, but I hoped that the reward of going home would be incentive enough to allow it—she could not go home without it. She agreed to allow nursing care in her home. Jean was uneasy about Mother going to her home in Helena because she thought that she should come to our house in Atlanta. Mother, however, was dead-set on getting back to her home. Returning to her home, to her own space had been her goal since she first made the turn toward healing in early December. I flew into Memphis at the end of that week, went to Helena to make sure that everything was set for her. I was also anxious about being a good son to Mother. Was I making the right choice to allow her to back to her house rather than come to Atlanta? She was so strong in wanting to go home, and I knew that she would be miserable in Atlanta, and thus we would be miserable too. I returned to Atlanta, and three days later, I came back to pick her up and take her to her home in Helena.

Here is my journal entry from the day (March 7, 1994) that I was picking her up and taking her home: "7:05 AM—I am up and at Brown and Kaye's in their kitchen. Today is the day. After ninety-four days, today is the day. I slept pretty well last night, but I am anxious about getting Mother home and about how she will do at home. But the motions are set, so here we go. I can feel the anxiety building as I get ready to go over to get her and make the short (geographically) but long (spiritually) journey home. So, please, God, help me on this. Help me trust You. You've brought her through these thirteen tough weeks, and I'll trust you for this next step. Actually, I think that my main anxiety rests where it usually rests—with me. Am I a good son? Have I done enough? Should I have pushed Mother more to come to Atlanta?"

I picked Mother up, and she was both ready to get home and scared of getting home at the same time. I had alerted the neighbors to get ready to help me carry her up the three steps of the front porch into the house, and they were ready when we arrived. As Bert, L.P., and I grasped her wheelchair to carry her up, she said: "I hate for you all to have to do this."

Bert replied: "Ms. Mary, you know that we are glad to do this for you. We are so glad that you are finally home!" After we got her in, Mother asked me to wheel her back to the back porch where she could look out on the back yard. As I opened the door for her to look out, she said: "O Lord, you don't know how glad I am to be back here. Nibs, I never thought that I would ever make it back here. Thank you so much for making this possible." I gave her a hug and replied: "Mother, you did most of the work. I am so proud of you for the true grit that you showed—not surprising, but still hard to do."

I had arranged for an African-American mother/daughter team to provide the twenty-four-hour care that Mother needed for a while. I thought that it would be hard to find someone, but once the word got out that I was paying a living wage for this work, I had no trouble finding good care givers. Mother especially liked the daughter, a younger woman in her forties named Stephanie Long, who brought expertise, compassion, and a sense of humor to her overnight care for Mother. The competency of the caregivers and Mother's enthusiastic reception of them made things much easier for me. I cut back my trips down there from every ten days to every three-to-four weeks. She received in-home physical therapy and advanced quickly to using a walker, then a cane, which she used off and on for the rest of her life. After about a month, she let me know that while she appreciated the twenty-four-hour care, she wanted to cut back. We stayed with Stephanie as the overnight person, and after two weeks, Mother would be on her own. I called her the first night that she was by herself, and I said to her: "Mother, I am uneasy about this. Are you sure that you don't want to keep Stephanie a little bit longer?" She was adamant, though: "Nibs, I know that I can do this. I am ready. After all, I have not had any solitude for a long time. I have not been by myself for five months, so I am definitely ready."

It turned out fine. She re-learned to drive, with the provision that she would not drive out of town. Even though one of her hips had survived the car wreck intact, the other hip soon had arthritis set up in it, and she would have to endure another surgery for hip replacement, with a stint in the same rehab unit. Then she would have knee replacement surgery, with rehab again—both of these surgeries in the next two years after she had come home. For both of these, I would do the traveling back and forth to get her through the surgeries, using the same wonderful support network that had developed from the original accident.

Mother gradually returned to normal life. She would make trips over to see us once a year, and we would continue our twice annual visits to her. She was no longer driving over to see us, but now was flying. I would fly over to get her at Helena and take her to the Memphis airport, where she would set off all kinds of alarms in the metal detectors because she had so many steel rods in her legs. At first, she was miffed by this development, not wanting to call attention to herself. After a while, it became a joke, and she began to tell the security people at the airport about her "special" condition.

Mother had made a remarkable recovery from this terrible auto accident and from the long hospitalization and convalescent period. As I write this, I am now the age that she was—seventy-four plus—when she was in the car wreck. I cannot even begin to imagine how I would react if I had to endure something like Mother did at this age. Her recovery was testimony to the fortitude and determination that she had displayed all of her life. Her recovery and her dependency on others also softened her attitude towards others. She had always been gentle with me, but most of the time that generosity did not extend very far in terms of her attitudes towards others. Previous to this accident and its aftermath, when I would come to visit her, she would always have negative things to say about many of her closest allies. After this shock, she began to be a bit more generous towards others and less judgmental.

After her death, I did not find any of her journals that were written after the car wreck. I don't know if she did anymore journaling after that, but I am assuming that she did not. Since I did not know that the journals existed until after her death, I was never able to ask her about it. I know that her belief in God remained strong, and indeed, she saw God as the one who had pulled her through this awful time. In this period of extreme suffering and confinement, she found out that she was loved, that people would step up for her, that people would take care of her, that she was no longer that snoring little girl, who was rejected and abandoned by everyone—by her mother's death, by her father's death, by her husband's betrayal and flight, by her brother's death. I believe that she discovered that she was truly loved.

Though I found no journals from this period, I did receive a letter from her that indicated that I had passed the test as a "good son." Here is that note, written in early 1995, about a year after she had returned home: "Morning! Thank goodness for a son named Nibs! It's wonderful to be able to turn lots of problems over to you and see you handle them so well!

Thank you so much. I hope David and Susan take such care of you when you need it. Love you dearly, Mother."

17

Going Home

In April, 1995, my first book, *While We Run This Race*, was published. In the same month an article on Oakhurst Church and on Caroline's and my leadership appeared in *Time Magazine*.[1] Mother was delighted in both of these events, and she was even more joyful when several of the Helena churches, including her own First Presbyterian, invited me to Helena to speak about the book and Oakhurst. She was thrilled when a front page article ran on the events in the local paper, and she called me to say: "Nibs, they are all excited about your coming to Helena to speak. I'm so glad to have you back to do this. And there is a front-page article about you in the daily *World* [her euphemism for the then-daily Helena newspaper, *The Helena World*]. They've got your photo on the front page too! I'm so proud of you!" I replied, Yes, Mother, I'm glad to be coming back to do this. Thanks for making it happen." Mother had initiated the process by talking with her pastor at First Presbyterian.

The local paper did run a story on the events, and it was entitled "Presbyterians to Hear Reverend Gibson Stroupe," and it began like this: "The Reverend Gibson Stroupe of Decatur, Georgia, a Helena native, will be the guest minister at the First Presbyterian Church in Helena this Sunday. Reverend Stroupe, known as 'Nibs' to his Helena friends, is pastor of the Oakhurst Presbyterian Church in Decatur and is the son of Mrs. Mary Elizabeth Stroupe of Helena. He and the members of Oakhurst

1. Christopher John Farley, "The Gospel of Diversity."

Presbyterian were the subjects of a full-page article in a recent edition of *Time* magazine. That's unusual enough—to be pastor of a church which rates an entire page in one of America's foremost news magazines—but Stroupe's leadership and the church's uniqueness is what merited the coverage. You see, according to *Time*, Oakhurst is 'that rarest of institutions: half-black, half-white, and entirely harmonious.'"

That last phrase was liberal, white wishful thinking—Oakhurst was hardly "entirely harmonious," but we were trying. We made many mistakes, but we learned a lot along the way. Caroline and I would later write a book for our denomination on the Oakhurst story.[2] For these days in May, 1995, however, I was so glad to be able to make Mother proud in such a public way, preaching at the church that had nurtured me and continued to do so for her, and to have our town recognize that. Mother's bank, which had loaned her and Bud the money to buy her house, had the *Helena World* article laminated for her and for me—I still have it hanging in my home office.

Mother and our son David also had begun a kind of reconciliation. In doing the research for this memoir, I talked with David about his memory of those trying days. He indicated, as I thought, that Mother never apologized to him, but that she did cease making her hurtful comments to him and about him in his presence. He also noted his own agency in this process: "I began to perceive that the space in Grandma's house was small and that she probably felt invaded by us sometimes. So I learned to go out on the screen porch by myself at her house and play with my Game Boy, and I tried to hold it down when I was inside the house. I also decided to study what Grandma liked and to make myself knowledgeable and inquisitive on that. I asked her about the furniture that she was always finding and re-doing. I also got into science, since she was such a fan of rocks and geodes. I learned about those, and we could talk about them. So I felt that things got a lot better, as I worked on these kinds of things. As a present for the last Christmas she was alive, she gave me the Stephen Jay Gould Book *I Have Landed* and wrote in the opening page: "I hope all of your plans work out as you wish." I still have that book in my office. So even if she never felt comfortable saying such things to us, I know she cared for Susan and me and wanted us to have a great life."

Even though there was some reconciliation with Mother, she did pay a price for her judgmental and harsh attitude towards David. Although

---

2. Nibs Stroupe and Caroline Leach, *O Lord, Hold Our Hands*.

Mother and Susan got along well, both David and Susan told me that it was like walking on eggshells when they were in Mother's home after Mother's difficult engagements with David. They both were very careful around her. That tentative approach came at the cost of their intimacy with Mother—they could never feel like they could be themselves around her, their Grandma and my beloved Mother. Although Mother never mentioned this dynamic to me, I know that she felt it. I got confirmation of that tension and lost intimacy after she died. After Mother's death, I had a conversation with Debbie Reece, who helped to take care of Mother at the end. Debbie told me: "You know, Nibs, I asked Ms. Mary if she had any regrets about her life. She said that she really did not have any regrets. She had raised you, and you had turned out so well. She was so proud of you! Then, she paused a bit, and said: 'I wish that I had gotten to know my grandchildren better—I loved them, and they loved me, but we never got very close.'"

As the years went on, Mother was still in recovery from her horrible car accident, but she also made it a point to come to our home for David's and Susan's high school graduations. On both occasions, she was driven from Helena to the outskirts of Atlanta by her church friend and former customer Lyda Kitchens, who had friends in the suburbs of Atlanta. Lyda was a just a bit younger than Mother, but she loved long-distance driving. Lyda did not want to drive in "big city" traffic, so I would meet them on the west side of Atlanta and drive Mother in from there. Lyda had always been gracious to our family—it was the same Lyda Kitchens who gave me a ride on that rainy, cold day when I was in the second grade, the same Lyda Kitchens who had given me such a generous donation for traveling after Mother's car wreck. Lyda joined the circle of Mother's neighbors, Sue and LP Sellers, and Bert and Ann Lewis, who all checked up on Mother and kept me posted on anything that they thought that I needed to know.

Mother and I would certainly need all of that circle of friends and more in the last years of her life. In early April of 2003, I had gone over to Helena to take care of her during her "trigger-finger" outpatient surgery in Memphis. That went well, but our most difficult journey began with a phone call from neighbor Sue Sellers in mid-June of that year. Sue called me to tell me that Mother had lost a lot of weight in the last month, and that Mother was having trouble breathing. I immediately called Mother to check on her, and she agreed that she was having trouble, and that she would love for me to come over and check on her. She had recently switched to Dr. Johnny Paine as her primary care doctor in Helena, and that was a great blessing for me—he had been the boy who lived across the street from us and with whom I had played a lot. I called him to talk about Mother, and he told me that I needed to come see her. He had done an X-ray of her lungs and had seen a mass there that he hoped was pneumonia. He had given her antibiotics for it, but it had not responded. He was afraid that it was cancer, and he recommended that I take her to a pulmonologist in Clarksdale, Mississippi, across the River.

I made an appointment for her with the pulmonologist for Friday and flew into Memphis on Wednesday, rented a car, and drove down to Helena. Here is part of my journal entry for that day: "I am at Mother's, and she is not in good shape. She has agreed to go back to Atlanta with me on Saturday, and I am thinking that it may be permanent. I haven't told her that yet, but I am guessing that she knows it already. She told me today that she remembered how tired her father got with his lung cancer, and she felt the same way. She is scared. She told me that if it was cancer, she would not take any treatment for it—she had lived long enough. It may yet be pneumonia, but the signs point to cancer. I'll call Johnny Paine tomorrow to get her scans and stuff for the pulmonologist in Clarksdale for our appointment on Friday. I called Azzie Preston in Decatur tonight, and she will try to set up an appointment for Mother to see someone in the Dekalb Medical system next week. So I believe that this is the beginning."

We saw the pulmonologist that Friday, and although he would not confirm that Mother had lung cancer, he indicated that she had pneumonia, emphysema, and two masses in her lungs. He suggested further testing and was glad to hear that she was going back to Atlanta with me. We had many adventures getting her back to Atlanta, centering mainly on getting her a portable oxygen tank to use on the plane trip to Atlanta. The tanks were clunkers back then, but we lugged it onto the plane and stored it in the overhead bin, in case Mother needed it. Being the woman of strong will, she did not use it on the flight to Atlanta!

Our Oakhurst elder Azzie Preston had gotten her an appointment with a top lung specialist at Dekalb, Dr. Stubbs, on Monday. Here is my journal entry for that process: "We got bad news today from Dr. Stubbs, or at least I got bad news. He took me into another room by myself to tell me that it almost certainly was cancer and that it was extensive. He told me that if it were his mother, he would advise against doing treatment for the cancer. Mother will have a biopsy on Wednesday, so we will go from there, but it looks pretty bad right now. Many people have helped me so far—Caroline and Susan getting Mother's room set up, Mother's neighbors in Helena, Azzie getting Mother the doctor's appointment. Caroline said tonight that Mother indicated that she couldn't believe that this was happening to her, that she had not been sick long and had never been really sick in her life. I hate to see her stripped of her dignity in this process, but I am committed to seeing her through this process, whatever is on the other side."

The biopsy results came in on Thursday, and it was lung cancer. Through Azzie's help again, we got an appointment with Dr. Szabo, an oncologist, on Friday. Soon after I told Mother the bad news, I asked her: "I am so sorry to hear this news, but we will get you through it. We're going to see the cancer treatment guy on Friday, and he will ask about treatment. I know that you said that you do not want treatment for it, and I will leave that decision up to you. I'd like for you to try the treatment, but that is your decision." She surprised me when she replied: "Nibs, I have been thinking about this, and I think that I would like to try treatment, if the doctor recommends it. If not, I'll just go back home to die." I stepped in and said: "Mother, I'm glad that you want to try the treatment! If he doesn't recommend it, then we will keep you here for the dying. We want you near us." She came back strongly: "We'll cross that bridge when we get to it. But I'm going back home one way or another—after treatment, during treatment, or no treatment."

Even as cancer and pneumonia and emphysema gripped her lungs, her strong will continued to work—she was determined to get back home. The oncologist Dr. Szabo gave us the bad news on Friday. Mother had small cell lung cancer, which was incurable. He noted, however, that chemotherapy would shrink the masses in her lungs, and that it would improve her quality of life for the next year or eighteen months. Without chemotherapy, Mother would have two-to-three months. The one qualification was whether or not the cancer had spread to her brain and/or bones. An MRI and a bone scan the next week determined that the cancer had not spread, and that was some good news. The oncologist was young and gentle and compassionate with her, and Mother liked him. She decided to try chemotherapy, and it was scheduled for July 11.

In the meantime, there had been developments in our family. Our son David and his girlfriend Erin had given birth to their first child, Emma, in February of that year in Houston, and we had gone over to see her. Once Mother's cancer was diagnosed, they decided to fly over to

Atlanta so that Mother could meet her great-granddaughter and also to celebrate Caroline's birthday over the July 4 weekend. Caroline's mother had died suddenly in Chattanooga in 2000, and that was a big loss for us all. On the weekend of David's and Erin's and Emma's arrival to see Mother, Caroline's brother brought her dad Herman down from Chattanooga to meet Emma and to see Mother for perhaps the last time. We still have a lovely photo now in our dining room of each of the great-grandparents holding Emma for the first time.

It was a chaotic but moving weekend with all the extra family members. Mother's head must have been spinning over the process of the previous ten days. It had been quite a time—from my arrival in Helena on Wednesday to our visit with the pulmonologist in Clarksdale on Friday, to the flight to Atlanta on Saturday, to the lung specialist's bad news on Monday, to the biopsy on Wednesday, to the meeting with the oncologist on Friday, to the bone scan and MRI the next Monday, to the arrival of family, including Mother's great-granddaughter, to preparation for chemotherapy and extended stay at our house. I am so grateful to Caroline for all of her great hospitality and love for Mother in this trying time. My head and heart were spinning also, but as in the terrible auto accident of 1993, I would cope by taking one day at a time. I was seeking to do the best that I could, juggling Mother's lung cancer and treatment and her new residence in our home, with my work at the church, with taking care of Mother's home in Helena, and with various community ministries in which the church was involved.

Mother began chemotherapy for her lung cancer on July 11, and it did not go well. It made her weak and nauseous. It also made her much grumpier towards everyone. Caroline and I and Susan (who was home from Macalester College for the summer) did our best to make her more comfortable, but it was an untenable situation. Away from her beloved home in Helena, under attack from lung cancer, invaded by toxic chemotherapy—all these put Mother in a trying time. She took it out on Caroline and Susan for the most part, but she would not eat or drink anything, for fear of vomiting it back up. I remembered her vomiting after trying a cigarette many years ago, and I knew that we were in for a difficult journey. She fainted on one occasion from dehydration, and that at least helped to focus her on drinking water.

She continued chemotherapy every two weeks, but she also constantly insisted that she wanted to go home. An opportunity for doing this presented itself in that David and Erin were getting married in late

August in Houston, and they wanted Caroline and me to preside at the ceremony. I told Mother that we would pay a sitter to come and stay with her at our house while we were gone over the weekend of the wedding. She responded: "Nibs, I'm not going to stay here with a total stranger in a place that is not my home." I replied: "I don't think that you are strong enough to make the trip to Houston with us, so we'll have to do this. We don't have a choice on this." "Yes, you do," was her quick reply, "you can take me back home, leave me there, and I'll be fine until you come back to get me. That is an off week for chemo, anyway, and the neighbors will help me, if I need it." It would be a tremendous logistical problem for us, but I decided to try to do it. We could take her over to Helena, then go to Houston, then pick her up on the way back. "Okay, Mother, we'll try it, but you have to promise me that you will not drive or do anything else like that at home." She spoke up: "I promise, Nibs, and I won't do anything stupid." I came back: "But, Mother, let's get someone to stay with you in your house while you are there." She replied just as strongly: "Nibs, I just want to be myself in my house in Helena. There are just too many people around me here. I love you all, but I just need some time to myself to absorb all this."

Caroline and I were worn out at that point, so we agreed to work it out so that Mother could be at home for a few days. We went through a lot of craziness in order to get Mother to her house for that weekend, and here is how I noted it in my journal: "I'm sitting here in Mother's kitchen—we made it over here after a tiring drive yesterday. I will leave Mother on her own Friday-Sunday while we go to Houston for the wedding. It has been and will continue to be a wild sequence. Caroline and I drove Mother here yesterday from Atlanta after renting a car. Then I took Caroline up to Memphis today where she flew back to Atlanta, then she and Susan will fly to Houston on Thursday, then I'll drive to Memphis, leave the car there, then fly to Houston, rent a car there, then fly back here on Sunday while Caroline and Susan are flying back to Atlanta, then I'll drive Mother back to Atlanta on Tuesday."

A bit before I was getting ready to drive to Memphis in order to fly to Houston, Mother's longtime friend Mary Wetzel drove up to Mother's house. The year before all of this happened, Mary and her husband Bob had moved to a senior living center in Blytheville, about ninety miles from Helena. They had tried to get Mother to move there with them, but she had refused to leave her home. Seeing Mary drive up on this day in the midst of Mother's travail, I thought to myself: "Oh, no, here's Mary, and I'll have to stay and visit for a while—I may be late for the plane." Instead, Mary brought great news: she had heard about our situation with leaving Mother by herself for the weekend, and she had come to stay with Mother, unbeknownst to me or Mother. I knew that Mother would have resentment about this, but Mary said that she would not take "No" for an answer. From my point of view, it was a Godsend, and to my surprise, Mother did not put up much resistance. I could fly to Houston and participate in the wedding and festivities, without constantly worrying about Mother's safety while staying by herself.

We made it to Houston for a fine wedding and celebration, and I drove Mother back to Atlanta for her next round of chemotherapy. This began a pattern of her doing several rounds of chemotherapy, then me bringing her home for a week or so in between. She gradually began to tolerate the chemotherapy and began to get stronger. In the meantime, her eyesight had begun to weaken even more, and on one of the trips to Helena, I took her to the ophthalmologist to have her eyes checked. Mother reminded me that her driver's license had expired while she was with us in Atlanta, and she indicated that she was going to ask the doctor to give her a special permit to drive. She could do this because in Arkansas at that time, older people could get a restricted driver's license if their ophthalmologist approved it. I told her that I did not think that it was a good idea for her to drive, but she was adamant about asking the doctor about it.

We visited the ophthalmologist, and as he was finishing up her eye tests, I was sitting behind her. She asked him: "Dr. B, do you think you would be able to write me a letter to get my driver's license? I really do need to start driving again, and my health is improving. I would just drive to the familiar places in town. What do you think?" He looked at me, and I shook my head "No," and he told her: "Well, Ms. Stroupe, your eyes are not yet improved enough for me to do that. But they might be better on your next visit. Let's check them again next time and see where we are." Mother was disappointed, but I was so glad to have been with her and to have been able to give input on her driving, especially since she did not see me give the disapproval signal to the doctor. I knew, and I think that he knew, that Mother would not be back for another eye test. As we drove back to her house, Mother said: "Well, I guess that you are satisfied that he wouldn't write me the letter." I replied: "Mother, it's not a matter of satisfaction—it's a matter of being safe. I am sad that you can't drive at this point, but there are plenty of people in Helena who will take you wherever you want to go." She slowly shook her head and replied, "Yeah, but I hate to ask them. I hate being so dependent on people. You wait and see—it will be your turn one of these years—let's see how you like it." I agreed, saying, "I'm with you on this, Mother, I'm sure that my turn will come, but for now, it is what it is. I'll be glad to call people for you, if you'd like." She said, "No, Nibs, I'll do it, but I'll hate it." "Well, Mother, I know that there is no bright side to this situation, but just be glad that you have friends who are eager to give you rides, when you are back here in Helena." Being the Calvinist that I am, however, I gave her car key to the neighbor and took the spare key back with us to Atlanta. She would never drive her car again, a situation which I knew she hated.

18

Final Days

On one of the days during that same trip back to Helena, Mother was grumpy all day. She told me that I was hovering over her, and we had been haggling all morning. When I asked her what was wrong, she said that her pastor told her that he would call her and pick her up for the annual church fish fry late that afternoon. I had heard the call, and I replied that I had heard him say that the fish fry was tonight, not that he would pick her up. I told her that I would be glad to take her, but she angrily replied: "They don't want me there anyway, so I'm not going." "Mother, they do want you there—that's why he called you." I finally cajoled her into going, and she had a fine time. Everyone was glad to see her, and they told her that they had missed seeing her, and that they were praying for her.

We brought Mother back to our house that fall for three more rounds of chemotherapy. She tolerated those better and gradually began to feel better. As she began to feel better, she began to want to go home, or at least to want something to do at our house. We let her do a few chores, like washing dishes. She was famous for her chocolate chip cookies, which she began to make and to send to Susan and David. Her cookies tasted so good because she always put bacon grease in them!

We went back to see her oncologist in late October, and he was pleasantly surprised at how much the tumors in her lungs had shrunk. I recorded my thoughts in my journal: "I am beginning to think that Mother's pluck and drive will enable her to survive a lot longer than the doctor had originally predicted (six-to-eight months). She is in better shape than when I got her in June. His prediction then was Christmas-February, which still may be the case, but she'll have to crash sometime soon in order for that to happen."

Mother once again pressed vigorously to go home, and the oncologist agreed that after a few more rounds of chemotherapy, she could go home for Thanksgiving and even stay for Christmas, which was music to her ears. I talked with Debbie Sellers Reece, daughter of Mother's neighbor Sue Sellers, about watching over Mother. Debbie had been a nurse before a terrible heart attack earlier in the year, and she was recuperating next door at Sue's house. Debbie could now drive, and she agreed to watch over Mother and to drive her where she needed to go. I insisted on paying her, but she replied: "Nibs, I love Ms. Mary Elizabeth, and I would do anything for her, so no pay is needed or wanted—I won't take it. And, if Ms. Mary ever gets to the point of failing, you know that she wants to be at home, and I will stay with her. None of us wants her in a nursing home to die." I reluctantly but gratefully agreed, and I indicated that we would revisit the agreement later. I flew to Memphis with Mother and then drove her down to Helena on the day before Thanksgiving, and she remained in her home through her beloved Christmas holidays. David and Erin and granddaughter Emma joined Caroline and Susan and me at Mother's small house for part of the holiday.

I went back to Memphis in early January to get Mother and bring her back for more rounds of chemotherapy, and she tolerated those well, but she insisted once again on coming back to Helena. I brought her back to Helena in mid-February, but she had given me a scare on the previous Sunday when she fainted in worship while I was preaching. It frightened me, and I went down into the congregation to see about her, but Caroline told me to go ahead and finish leading worship, that she would tend to her. We had several nurses in the congregation who helped Caroline get Mother out of the sanctuary. Mother was confused when she woke up in the narthex, so Caroline called for an ambulance, which took her to the hospital. They ran all kinds of tests on her, but could not find any causes for the loss of consciousness other than dehydration. When she agreed to drink more water, we agreed to allow her to return to her home in Helena, which was her top priority. I left her in Debbie's oversight and returned to Atlanta.

On February 29, 2004, the final step of Mother's journey began. I got a call from Debbie right after worship that Sunday, and she told me that Mother had fallen at her home and broken her hip. The emergency services in Helena had taken her to Methodist Hospital in Memphis, the same hospital where I was born. I flew down to Memphis to be with her while they did surgery to repair her hip, and she made it through that. She was frail, but soon after the surgery, she went back to the same rehab center in Southaven, Mississippi, where she had gone after the car wreck in 1993. I flew back and forth from Atlanta several times to check on her.

She had made a remarkable recovery in rehab in 1993, but this time she dug in her heels and would not cooperate at all. I tried to coax her, then cajole her into trying to do the therapy, but she refused all kinds. Since she was refusing, it meant that she couldn't stay in the rehab center. The neighbor Debbie Reece kept me apprised of the situation when I was back in Atlanta, and I told Debbie that if Mother didn't cooperate, I would need to bring her to our house or put her in a nursing home. Debbie replied: "No, Nibs, Ms. Mary just wants to go home, and I will be glad to stay with her at her home, if you will allow that. You know that she will be grumpy and miserable if she is not at home." We both knew that the end was near for Mother, and I thanked Debbie for her offer and told her, "I won't be able to pay you much, but I'll do what I can. I know that you are not in the best physical shape, so let's plan to hire some women to come and assist you in staying with her." Debbie responded: "Nibs, I don't want any money from you—just pay what you can, when you can. And yes, we'll need to hire some people to help with Ms. Mary. I know some sitters that I can talk with." I thanked her and said, "Well, let's agree to this—after Mother dies, you can stay as long as you want in the house." Debbie agreed to that, and we developed that plan.

That night I had a dream about Mother, and here is what I wrote in my journal: "I dreamed about Mother early this morning. She was with us here in the living room in our house, and she looked healthy. In the dream, however, I knew that she was sick in rehab in Southaven. I couldn't figure out how she could in two places at once, in such varying degrees of health. Then Mother and I were in her bedroom in Helena, and her face changed to be like a very sick person's face. I hugged her and cried out: 'I don't want you to die—don't go yet.' She did not reply—indeed, her facial expression was similar to the one she had when she had fainted at church."

On March 26, an ambulance brought Mother from rehab to her home, where Debbie and I were waiting for her. She told us: "I'm so glad to be home. Thank you for doing this. I don't know how much longer I can go on, but when I go, I want to go right here." We indicated that we were glad that we could work it out for Mother to be able to stay at her home of fifty-seven years. Debbie and I both thought that it would only be a month or so before Mother died. Mother was no longer receiving chemotherapy, so we knew that the cancer would begin to spread. Once again, Mother proved to have a stronger will than any of us thought. She lasted seven more months, and we ended up bringing in sitters around the clock, because Debbie's health was still precarious after her heart attack.

I continued to go back and forth every two weeks or so, to visit Mother, to relieve Debbie, and to pay Mother's bills. It was a grind, but I was grateful to be able to keep Mother in her home. Mother did not like having all the sitters in her home—she told me she just wanted to be by herself. Because she was not able to get herself out of bed or walk, it was not possible for her to stay by herself, and I knew that the lack of solitude was probably the worst punishment of all for her. On my last trip to see her in October, she was growing increasingly confused, but she still was lucid some of the time. I had begun to miss the sharp-witted and sometimes sharp-tongued woman who was my Mother. We had definitely changed roles now—I was the parent, and she was the child.

On this visit, as I prepared to leave to go back to Atlanta, Mother was sitting in her chair in the living room, and she told me: "Nibs, you are pretty amazing. How did you do it?" I replied: "Well, I have a great Mother, and I give thanks for that." She chuckled and said: "No, I meant how did you do this? How did you set up two realities?" I thought of my earlier dream when Mother had been in two places and had been healthy in one of those places. "What do you mean, Mother?" She stated: "I mean, how did you set up two of my houses?" "But, Mother, you are in your house now—I don't understand what you are asking me," was my reply. She came back: "I mean that you have set up two houses—this is not my real house. How did you get me here?" I said to her: "Mother, this is your house—what are you asking me?" "I mean," she said, "that this is not my house—if it were my house, no one else would be in it. It can't be my house, even though it looks like my house." I said gently but firmly: "Mother, this is your house. You have to have assistance here because you can't walk." She had the last word, however: "Well, it's not my house, I can just tell you that."

I flew back to Atlanta, and late the next evening, Debbie called me to tell me that Mother was having a very difficult time, being nauseated and needing some words of comfort. I told her to put Mother on the phone, and I said: "Mother, how are you doing? Debbie says that you are not doing well." She replied, "Nibs, I am just so tired, so tired, so tired of it all. I don't know what to do. I just want someone to take over." I swallowed hard, and told her: "Mother, I am glad to help you. You can just let go. You do not have to hold on. It is okay to let go, and you know that I love you." She said to me, "Oh, Nibs, you know that I love you. I am so proud of you. You have taken such great care of me." I responded: "Mother, just rest, just let go. I will be over to see you soon. Thank you so much for all that you have done for me." I asked her to put Debbie back on the phone, and I asked Debbie to keep me posted on Mother's condition. Debbie called me back thirty minutes later, a little bit before midnight: "Nibs, Ms. Mary just died. She just wanted to hear your voice one more time, and you gave her permission to let go." We both cried together. Although I had been anticipating this for many months, it was hard to believe. This woman of such an iron will, such a great and powerful presence in my life—she had now passed into the next level. It is only now, after almost seventeen years, that I am really able to say that my mother has passed from this realm. Such a presence for me. She died in the same bedroom where I began this memoir, with her own sense, I am sure, of being trapped and unable to move. But at least she was at home.

I called David and Susan to tell them. We had been making plans to meet in Houston that weekend for a mini reunion with David and family, but we all changed our plans to meet now in Helena to say good-bye to Mother and to Grandma. The next few days after her death are sort of a blur to me. We had her funeral at her church, First Presbyterian in Helena, and I gave the eulogy at her funeral, which she had asked me to do. Included in the bulletin for the funeral service for Mother were these words from Dorothy L. Sayers, which her pastor had chosen and which I thought were so appropriate for Mother's life and approach:

> This is it. This is what we have always feared-
> The moment of surrender, the helpless moment
> When there is nothing to do but let go. . .
> "into Thy Hands"—into another's hand
> No matter whose: the enemy's hand, death's hand
> God's. . .The one moment not to be evaded
> Which says, "You must," the moment not of choice
> When we must choose to do the thing we must
> And will to let our own will go. Let go.
> It is no use now clinging to the controls,

Let someone else take over. Take, then, take. . .
There, that is done. . .into Thy hand, O God.[1]

We then drove over to Byhalia, Mississippi, where her body was buried with the ancestors in Byhalia Cemetery. After we had gotten back to Atlanta, I wrote this narrative in my journal on November 7: "I'm sitting in our dining room with brilliant sunshine coming in on a cool but pretty fall afternoon. This time last week we were pulling up to the Byhalia cemetery, fifty minutes late for Mother's burial because I got lost, using cousin Jean's directions for a shortcut through Hernando. As I told the kids while we were driving to the cemetery, Mother was undoubtedly laughing at me because she told me never to do what Jean said. But, they had waited, and the burial went well. Caroline and I returned to the cemetery on Wednesday before we returned to Atlanta. We saw Mother's grave next to Bud and Flossie. We also found Gran's and BB's and Hart's and Granddaddy's graves, all in the same area as Mother's. I'm so glad that Mother's is snuggled in there too. It's still hard to believe that she is gone. I've cried, and I continue to cry, though the sadness has not penetrated deep inside me yet. She was such a presence in my life, indeed the main presence. I'm glad that I developed to celebrate her presence rather than being dominated by my father's absence. Perhaps that is one of the reasons that I'm not devastated at Mother's death. I had already given thanks for all her gifts to me, and I was able to repay her a little bit. I was able to carry her through, all the way to the end, keeping her at home, providing great care for her (thank God for Debbie) and having her pass so peacefully."

In my searching through all of my letters and papers from Mother after her death, I found a letter from her to me, written a couple of years before she was diagnosed with the lung cancer that killed her. It is precious to me, and I'll leave this memoir with her words to me, as I have started crying as I type them: "Morning! I wanted to tell you how much I have enjoyed being your Mother! Thanks for loving me in spite of my faults and being bossy and all that stuff. Your love, concern, and actually caring how I am, and what you can do to help me have made this a great journey! THANKS!!!! Love you, Mother."

---

1. Dorothy L. Sayers, *Four Sacred Plays*, 347.

Epilogue

I KEPT MY WORD to Debbie Reece, and she remained in Mother's house for over thirteen years, until Debbie died suddenly in February, 2018. She paid me what rent she could during that time. She tried to scrape up the funds to buy the house, but even by Helena's depressed price level, she could not afford to do it. None of that was a troublesome issue to me—she had taken such good care of Mother and enabled her to stay in her beloved home until the end. There was no question in my mind that Debbie would stay in Mother's house as long as she wanted to.

After Debbie's death, we drove to Helena to get the house ready to sell. We had come back one more time to clean it out and to claim some of Mother's furniture and belongings, because we had a buyer in hand. By the time that we finished that day, the house was barren, and for the first time (and last time) I would see it that way, stripped of furniture and people. I thanked Mother and the house for giving me such great shelter and nourishment over many, many years, and as we closed and locked the door, I waved good-bye to the house that had been so important to Mother for almost sixty years. I thought of Mother one more time and remembered a poem that I had discovered in her journals. It is the only poem of hers that I ever remember seeing, and it is a fitting closing to her life and to this memoir, written in 1991:

> When I put out to sea and
> Cross to the Other side,
> Sing no sad songs for me!
> Let glory reign.
> The sunrises and the sunsets
> Will be a part of me,
> I'll run and play with

Comets and stars through eternity—
So, throw your caps in the air
And let breezes clear your eyes,
And, I'll watch and love
And take care of you,
Singing praises to God
All the time.

—Mary Stroupe

Bibliography

Berryhill, Elizabeth. *Cup of Trembling: A Play in Two Acts.* Seabury, 1958.

Cobb, James C. *The Most Southern Place on Earth: The Mississippi Delta and the Roots of Regional Identity.* Oxford: Oxford University Press, 1994.

Duster, Alfreda, ed. *Crusade for Justice: The Autobiography of Ida B. Wells.* Negro American Biographies and Autobiographies. Chicago: University of Chicago Press, 1970.

Farley, Christopher John. "The Gospel of Diversity." *Time Magazine*, April 24, 1995.

Finley, Randy. "Crossing the White Line: SNCC in Three Delta Towns, 1963–1967." The Arkansas Historical Quarterly 65 no. 2 (Summer 2006): 117–37.

Friedersdorf, Conor. "Doubting MLK During a Strike in Memphis." *The Atlantic*, January 13, 2018.

Gould, Stephen Jay. *I Have Landed: The End of a Beginning in Natural History.* Cambridge: Harvard University Pres, 2011.

Meeks, Catherine and Nibs Stroupe. *Passionate for Justice: Ida B. Wells as Prophet for Our Time.* New York: Church Publishing, 2019.

Obama, Barack. *Dreams of my Father: A Story of Race and Inheritance.* New York: Crown, 2007.

Paton, Alan. *Cry, the Beloved Country.* New York: Scribners, 1948.

Sayers, Dorothy L. *Four Sacred Plays.* London: Victor Gollancz Ltd, 1948.

Sloan, James M. *The Great Question Answered: Or, Is Slavery a Sin in Itself (Per Se?) Answered According to the Teaching of the Scriptures.* Classic Reprint. London: Forgotten Books, 2019.

Smittle, Stephanie. "Helltown born and raised: A Q&A with Bankroll Freddie." *Arkansas Times*, April 22, 2021.

Stroupe, Nibs. *While We Run This Race: Confronting the Power of Racism in a Southern Church.* Maryknoll: Orbis, 1995.

Stroupe, Nibs and Caroline Leach. *O Lord Hold Our Hands: How a Church Thrives in a Multicultural World.* Louisville: Westminster John Knox, 2002.

www.ingramcontent.com/pod-product-compliance
Lightning Source LLC
Chambersburg PA
CBHW060818190426
43197CB00038B/2015